State Supreme Courts

Contributions in Legal Studies
Series Editor: *Paul L. Murphy*

State Supreme Courts

POLICYMAKERS IN THE FEDERAL SYSTEM

EDITED BY Mary Cornelia Porter
AND G. Alan Tarr

CONTRIBUTIONS IN LEGAL STUDIES, NUMBER 24

Greenwood Press
WESTPORT, CONNECTICUT
LONDON, ENGLAND

Acknowledgment

"State Supreme Courts and the Legacy of the Warren Court: Some Old Inquiries for a New Situation" by Mary Cornelia Porter and "The New York Court of Appeals and the U.S. Supreme Court, 1960–1976" by Daniel C. Kramer and Robert Riga © *Publius: The Journal of Federalism* 8, no. 4 (Fall 1978) are hereby reprinted by permission of *Publius*.

Library of Congress Cataloging in Publication Data
Main entry under title:

State supreme courts.

(Contributions in legal studies, ISSN 0147-1074;
no. 24)
Bibliography: p.
Includes index.
1. Courts of last resort—United States—States.
I. Porter, Mary Cornelia.   II. Tarr, G. Alan (George
Alan)   III. Series.
KF8736.S8   347.73'36   81-13431
ISBN 0-313-22942-2   347.30735   AACR2

Library of Congress Catalog Card Number: 81-13431
ISBN: 0-313-22942-2
ISSN: 0147-1074

First published in 1982

Greenwood Press
A division of Congressional Information Service, Inc.
88 Post Road West
Westport, Connecticut 06881

Printed in the United States of America

10 9 8 7 6 5 4 3 2 1

Blow me!!.

Contents

vi   *Contents*

Figures

Tables

MARY CORNELIA PORTER AND G. ALAN TARR

Introduction

The composite work of the courts in the fifty states probably has greater
significance (than that of the U.S. Supreme Court) in measuring how well
America attains the ideal of equal justice for all. The state courts of all
levels must annually hand down literally millions of decisions which
determine the vital issues of life, liberty and property.[1]

Justice William Brennan

In 1971 the California Supreme Court, "exploding a legal bombshell,"
invalidated the state's system for financing public education. The effects
of *Serrano* v. *Priest* were profound and wide ranging. California not only
equalized the resources available to all school districts, but used the
opportunity to consider complementary structural and organizational
reforms as well. In some states, supreme courts sustained similar challenges to excessive reliance on the property tax to finance education. In
others, the threat of lawsuits compelled legislatures to reconsider school
finance schemes. Despite the U.S. Supreme Court's ruling that the Equal
Protection Clause of the Constitution does not command equalization of
interdistrict per-pupil expenditures, state supreme courts have, relying on
state constitutional provisions, mandated equal educational opportunity
for all children, whatever the wealth of their districts.[2]

Despite its stunning impact on educational and fiscal policies throughout
the states, *Serrano* is hardly unique—state supreme court rulings have
historically had significant effects within the states and upon the nation as
a whole. Since they render the final decisions in most litigation that pro-
ceeds beyond courts of the first instance and intermediate courts of appeal,
state supreme courts have been responsible for structuring state legal
environments. Their decisions, apart from their immediate effects, con-

---

An earlier version of this introduction was presented as a paper at the 1980 Annual Meeting
of the American Political Science Association, Washington, D.C., August 28–31, 1980.

stitute precedent that influences decisions of subordinate courts—and of courts in other states as well. State supreme courts not only enforce societal norms, but develop innovative policies in public and private law. Only rarely, as when California voters amended their constitution to legitimize the judicially invalidated dealth penalty, is activist policymaking challenged. Finally, as justices of the U.S. Supreme Court have acknowledged, state decisions often provide the bases for their own rulings.[3]

If anything, the opportunities for state supreme court policymaking are even greater today, for the Burger Court's "new federalism" has allowed, indeed has enthusiastically encouraged, state high courts to expand their policymaking roles. A handful of these courts have responded by interpreting their state constitutions as generously as—and in some instances even more generously than—the Warren Court construed the federal document. Other courts have followed their leads. In addition, the continuing judicialization of policy questions has propelled state supreme courts into novel areas. The famous *Quinlan* "right-to-die" case in New Jersey, *Serrano,* and the Alaska Supreme Court's ban on plea bargaining illustrate the important policy questions decided by state supreme courts.[4]

This introduction establishes the context and classifies the varieties of judicial policymaking. We speculate—as do the contributors—about factors that precipitate, facilitate, and otherwise have bearing on state supreme court activism. We argue—supported by the essays in this book—that judicial policymaking at the highest state level plays a significant part in shaping vertical and horizontal federal relationships. We and the essayists hope that this book makes a contribution to the body of research on state high courts, and that it provides fresh perspectives on and frameworks of analysis for the continued study of these institutions.

THE POLICYMAKING CONTEXT[5]

STRUCTURES

There is no typical state court system. Some states, such as Virginia and Idaho, have unified and simplified their court systems by reducing the number and types of courts and establishing clear jurisdictional boundaries among them—as recommended by the American Bar Association's Model State Judicial Article. Other states, Alabama and Colorado, for example, have responded to case pressures on their court systems in incremental fashion, creating a patchwork of special-purpose courts with overlapping jurisdictions. Thirty states have established intermediate courts of appeal (ICAs) to handle part of the heavy appellate work load; the remainder continue to vest all appellate jurisdiction in the supreme court. The structural variations even include the highest appellate courts: although most states have a single court, Texas and Oklahoma have separate supreme courts for civil and criminal appeals.

The effects of these structural variations on state supreme court policy-making are uncertain. Judicial reformers have long argued that the consolidation of state trial courts would produce greater efficiency and an impartial and uniform brand of justice and would facilitate centralized administration of the state court system by the chief justice. On the other hand, some observers have suggested that hierarchical administration of state court systems is unlikely to be effective, since chief justices typically lack the necessary resources and managerial expertise. Although some impressionistic evidence exists, the arguments of reformers rely more on exhortation than on empirical data. Research is needed that will assess the effects of court consolidation—and of court unification generally—on the operations of state court systems.[6]

Recent research indicates that the presence of ICAs does affect state court operations, for obviously the division of appellate responsibilities alleviates the work-load pressures of supreme courts. As more routine appeals are routed to the ICA, the highest court is in a position to devote time to questions that are from a policy standpoint more pressing and significant—and interesting. The institution of an ICA in North Carolina, for example, permitted the state supreme court to achieve "a position of true leadership in the legal development of the state." But whether the existence of an ICA is a necessary or sufficient condition for policy innovation by the supreme court is another matter and requires additional research.[7]

MODES OF SELECTION

State constitutions prescribe five methods for selecting state supreme court justices: partisan election, nonpartisan election, legislative appointment, gubernatorial appointment, and the Missouri Plan, which, aiming for "merit selection," provides for a combination of appointment and election. In those states that elect judges, gubernatorial appointment to fill unexpired terms is a prime means of initial accession, and—given the frequency of re-election for sitting judges—those initially appointed usually retain their judgeships.

Many reformers claim that merit selection, which guarantees the legal profession substantial influence over judicial recruitment, eliminates irrelevant political factors from consideration and thus tends to produce a qualified and independent judiciary. The proponents of merit selection have enjoyed considerable success: since 1940, when the Missouri Plan was first instituted, twelve states have adopted the system for staffing state supreme courts.

If merit selection does produce a more qualified judiciary, it might well account for differences in the quality of state supreme court policymaking. However, its virtues are not universally admitted. (Indeed, the very term *merit selection* is loaded, implying that judges selected by alternative methods are recruited without regard for merit.) Reformers' claims about the superiority of judges not beholden to "politics" are countered by evidence that judges recruited by other methods do not differ significantly in prior legal experience, the quality of their legal education, or other relevant qualifications. The claim that the Missouri Plan insulates judicial recruitment from political influences is equally dubious. Observation of the operation of the Missouri Plan reveals that it merely substitutes the "politics of bench and bar" for electoral politics or, put another way, obligates judges to elites rather than nonelites.[8]

CHARACTERISTICS OF THE JUSTICES

As is the case with public officials generally, state supreme court justices tend to be white, male, middle aged, and middle or upper-middle class. They are closely connected to the states in which they serve, for most are native sons by birth or rearing, and many attended the state law school. A significant majority have held prior public office, have had prior judicial experience, and have developed more than nominal ties to the Republican or Democratic party in the state. For most, elevation to the state supreme court represents the culmination of their political careers.

Previous political science research has focused on the effects of judicial background characteristics—either separately or in combination with institutional or environmental factors—in attempting to account for judicial policymaking and activism. Numerous studies have investigated the effects on judicial outputs of one or a combination of the following independent variables: a justice's party affiliation; patterns of party affiliation on a particular court; a justice's religious, ethnic, and regional identification; judicial career patterns; perceptions of the judicial role; the mode of judicial selection; and state and regional political cultures. Although this literature has produced interesting and suggestive data, contradictory findings among various studies and the methodological problems involved in such research caution against generalizing about the effects of background variables.[9] It should also be noted that these studies—because they must look at judicial behavior in a series of similar cases to achieve statistical significance—cannot account for particular instances of state supreme court innovation.

LEGAL CULTURE

Legal culture refers to norms and expectations that govern the legal processes and guide the behavior of participants in that process. As

Richard Richardson and Kenneth Vines put it, legal cultural norms prescribe "the insulated posture that judges are expected to maintain from pressures and interests, the litigation inputs that are admissible for decision making, and the sorts of guidelines judges should use in arriving at decisions."[10] Although considerable similarity exists among the legal cultures of the various states, state legal cultures do, nonetheless, differ, and these differences may help to explain variations in state supreme court policymaking.

Of paramount importance are attitudes held by state justices toward their proper roles and the legitimacy of policymaking—attitudes largely shaped by legal training, prior experiences and political activities, and interactions with other actors in the judicial system. In other words, justices tend to reflect their states' political and, in particular, legal cultures, and students of judicial behavior have observed that although justices in the fifty states may disagree about the meaning of and/or necessity for "judicial legislation," a fair degree of consensus exists about the judicial role on particular courts. The New Jersey Supreme Court's conscious and proud adherence to the activist tradition established by the great legal reformer Chief Justice Arthur Vanderbilt is illustrative of the closeness between legal culture and the concept of judicial role, whereas the passivity of the Rhode Island and Virginia courts is said to reflect the basic conservatism of those states.[11]

Equally indicative of a state's legal culture—and especially of its officials' and citizens' acceptance, or at least tolerance, of judicial policymaking—is the inclusion in state constitutions of guarantees such as the right to privacy, to clean air and pure water, and to be free from gender-based discrimination. Construing documents that reflect such lively topical issues virtually requires state supreme courts, whatever their inclinations, to engage in broad policymaking.[12] Constitutional or statutory provisions that permit advisory opinions, facilitate class action and taxpayers' suits, and grant generous rule-making powers to supreme courts expand the range of issues that confront the courts. By establishing an ICA and giving the high court discretionary control over its docket, the state relieves it of trivial petitions and case-load pressures and allows it to devote more attention to broad policy questions.[13]

Finally, although reaction to state supreme court policymaking might be supposed to be reflective of a state's legal culture, public opinion is an invalid indicator. Some instances of judicial activism elicit no public response whatsoever—unsurprising given the low visibility of, and public indifference to, state supreme courts. This does suggest that the courts have the leeway to indulge in all manner of policymaking. As illustrated by the aftermaths of major policy initiatives by the California Supreme Court, it cannot be assumed that the response, when it occurs, reflects consistent public attitudes toward judicial activism. Following *People* v. *Anderson,* which held that capital punishment violated the state constitution, voters adopted a constitutional amendment that overrode the decision. Yet *Serrano* I and II, equally salient instances of judicial policymaking, were calmly accepted.[14] Given the infrequency and unpredictability of public reaction, it is unlikely that justices regard it as providing cues about appropriate judicial behavior, which returns attention to the concept of judicial role and the factors that contribute to its shaping.

VARIETIES OF POLICYMAKING[15]

The form, content, type, and effect of state supreme court policymaking is as richly varied as the politics of the fifty states. The most prominent examples of this policymaking closely resemble the sort of activity associated with the U.S. Supreme Court. Yet other instances—for example, the use of the inherent powers doctrine to compel adequate funding for the courts—have no parallel in the federal court system.[16] Some state supreme court policymaking—for example, noncompliance with U.S. Supreme Court decisions—exceeds the bounds of legitimate judicial activity. Other instances involve nothing more than the traditional operations of common law courts. Despite this diversity, it is possible to distinguish six major categories of state supreme court policymaking.

MAJOR CATEGORIES OF STATE SUPREME COURT POLICYMAKING

Innovative Policymaking. Although in some sense all policymaking entails innovation, as used here *innovative policymaking* refers to policymaking (a) that either overturns an existing state policy or fills a gap in state policy; (b) in which the initiative comes from within the state supreme court, rather than being mandated by either federal authorities or other branches of state government; and (c) that imposes specific policies. Most frequently, constitutional interpretation supplies the basis for such policymaking. State supreme courts have, for example, used state constitutions to strike down regulations affecting individual privacy rights—criminal abortion laws, sodomy statutes, and laws forbidding the private use of marijuana. They have also pioneered policy in areas ignored by state executives and legislatures, such as passive euthanasia and gender discrimination. They have extended protection to politically ineffective groups by delineating the rights of religious and tribal minorities, the mentally ill, the "poor," homosexuals, tenants, and juveniles. They have used economic due process arguments to invalidate fair-trade laws and other forms of economic regulations, contending that the measures in question were passed in response to the demands of special-interest groups and, resulting in higher consumer prices, did not serve the general public.[17]

Agenda-Setting Policymaking. State supreme courts engage in *agenda setting* when their decisions—by upsetting long-standing policies, practices, or traditions without enunciating alternative policies—force state political authorities to find alternative means of pursuing their policy objectives. State supreme courts have in recent years proved receptive to policy-oriented litigation aimed at forcing political authorities to reform public policies. For example, rulings invalidating school finance schemes, zoning and land-use regulations, and plea bargaining have all forced state authorities to reconsider important state policies.

Richard Lehne observed that

the designation of agenda items does influence the tone and direction of public policies, but it does not determine their content. . . . even when new programs are enacted, neither their general orientations nor their detailed provisions are foreordained.[18]

The effects of agenda-setting policymaking are twofold. On the one hand, such policymaking reorders the policymaking priorities of the political branches and affects the distribution of political power by focusing attention on unacceptable inequities in existing policy. On the other hand, rather than usurping the policymaking responsibilities of the political branches, agenda setting gives legislatures and executives substantial latitude in devising new—and at times fresh and imaginative—approaches to pressing problems.[19]

Complementary Policymaking. Rulings that either aid state legislative goals or relieve state legislatures of the onus of taking politically awkward stands constitute *complementary policymaking*. State supreme court activism of this sort has been both prevalent and diverse. For example, state high courts have invalidated requirements for extraordinary majorities to approve the issuance of municipal bonds, a type of public debt restriction imposed to combat nineteenth-century abuses and now considered counterproductive. They have also struck down, or severely modified, the application of automobile guest statutes, which legislatures concede are outmoded, but have failed to repeal.[20]

It is, however, in the common law of torts that state supreme courts have made their greatest contribution to state policy. For some time they have been engaged in eliminating the tort immunities of governmental bodies and charitable corporations. Stepping into legislative lacunae, they have developed doctrines of product liability and comparative negligence that provide greater protection for consumers. Long before the U.S. Supreme Court extended constitutional protection, they defined a legally protected right of privacy. By providing for recovery for prenatal damages, they have in effect made decisions about when ''life'' begins. Calling upon the ancient doctrine of public trust, they have equalized rights to access to shores and beaches.

Common law policymaking of this sort is as widely accepted as it is widespread. In part, this may be due to the incremental manner in which policy is fashioned; in part because such lawmaking falls within the traditional purview of the courts; and in part because, as one commentator suggested, courts can accurately assess public needs:

> The test for propriety of any judicial change in the law is the society's readiness for and probable approval of change. Theoretically this is about the same as the test for legislative change in the law. Yet it requires a more delicate testing of, or guessing at public attitudes, since legislators through their political contacts have readier means of measuring social pressures than judges have. . . . Nevertheless, judges can be and quite often are . . . more aware of major surges in social attitudes . . . with respect to problems that regularly come before the courts and do not come before legislatures.[21]

Elaborative Policymaking. The term *elaborative policymaking* refers to state high court extension of precedent enunciated by the U.S. Supreme Court. Examples include state supreme court rulings in areas as diverse as the rights of defendants, the right to privacy, and the equal protection of the laws. Since state supreme courts have considerable leeway in responding to the Court's initiatives, the decision to give broad effect to a Supreme Court ruling constitutes a policy choice of substantial importance.[22]

Restrictive Policymaking. The term *restrictive policymaking* refers to state high court limitation and/or evasion of policies developed, by the U.S. Supreme Court, usually to protect state policies from invalidation. As such, it constitutes the converse of elaborative policymaking. Thus in the aftermath of the Supreme Court's *Escobedo* ruling, many state supreme courts either distinguished cases at hand on factual grounds or gave an unduly narrow interpretation of the Court's decision. State supreme court noncompliance in the religion and criminal justice areas also fall into this category.[23]

Institutional Policymaking. The term *institutional policymaking* describes judicial activity, some of it nondecisional, directed toward preserving the autonomy and integrity of the courts and the judicial process. It takes the form of lobbying individual legislators to support particular bills and/or goals, developing the inherent-powers doctrine to ensure adequate funding for the courts, disciplining members of the bench and bar, and exercising the rule-making authority of the courts. Because such policymaking promotes concerns of the judicial branch, and is not directed to the wider polity, it is—from the judicial perspective—particularly unobjectionable. Even the most conservative and passive justices find activism in the pursuit of institutional goals entirely appropriate.[24]

STATE SUPREME COURT POLICYMAKING IN A NATION OF STATES

American federalism is best understood as a political process rather than a structural arrangement. The three levels of government interact and share functions and cooperate and influence one another in countless ways. The vertical relationships between the central government and the states has been described as "chaotic marble cake federalism," in which political actors have available "multiple cracks" through which they may influence governmental policy. In addition, the states participate in a lively form of horizontal federalism, each learning and borrowing from the experience of other states.[25] Within these contexts, the patterns of reciprocal influence between state supreme courts and the U.S. Supreme Court indicate that the state courts play a role, albeit one different from that of the Supreme Court, in the development of vertical federalism. The patterns of communication and interaction among state supreme courts reflect the operation of a horizontal federalism that significantly affects subnational policymaking.

VERTICAL FEDERALISM

State supreme court participation in the vertical processes of federalism is demonstrated by their development of federal constitutional law in five distinguishable, but not completely unrelated, ways:

First, since state as well as federal courts are obliged to enforce the U.S. Constitution, and since such a miniscule percentage of the constitutional rulings of state supreme courts are reviewed by the highest federal tribunal, state supreme courts make both a qualitatively and quantitatively impressive contribution to the corpus of federal constitutional law.

Second, state high courts directly influence the fashioning of federal constitutional law by lighting the way for the U.S. Supreme Court. Indeed, the Supreme Court may postpone tackling certain issues until it has a body of cases upon which to draw. Justice William Brennan, a member of the New Jersey Supreme Court before his elevation to the U.S. Supreme Court, acknowledged that his own opinions in

such important and controversial areas as reapportionment, obscenity, the first amendment's guarantee of religion, the rights of criminal suspects and the application to the states of the fifth amendment's privilege against self-incrimination have drawn much from trail-blazing state court opinion.[26]

Less directly, state justices formulate or, more accurately, engender constitutional law through their responses to U.S. Supreme Court rulings. Numerous impact studies have documented lower court compliance with and defiance of various forms of limiting, distinguishing, evading, and generally eroding high court rulings. The Supreme Court in turn responds to the responses. To cite one example, state high court reaction to the ambiguities of *Escobedo* v. *Illinois* convinced the Court that it needed to clarify its rulings about the rights of suspects in police custody. The result was the far more detailed *Miranda* mandate.

Paradoxically, state supreme court erosion of federal judicial mandates may actually facilitate the task of the Supreme Court by providing it with the leeway to make unpopular decisions. As one observer noted:

> If the state high courts diligently applied the spirit, as well as the letter of Supreme Court criminal decisions, probably most of the guilty would go free. As a result the critics of the law and order faction of the society would, no doubt, increase. Thus, the narrowing of these decisions may serve to remove pressure from the Court, allowing it greater freedom than public opinion otherwise would.[27]

In this sense state supreme courts perform a mediating function between federal constitutional commands and prevailing practices in the state.

Finally, by making their own uses of Supreme Court decisions, state supreme courts serve as repositories of constitutional law. One effect of *Murdock* v. *Memphis,* in which the Supreme Court held it was precluded from reviewing state court constructions of state law, is that state high courts, relying on state constitutional provisions similar to those in the federal Constitution, have the option of picking and choosing among applicable Supreme Court interpretations of "due process of law," "the free exercise of religion," "unreasonable searches and seizures," and so on. Employing this technique, some courts, ignoring the Burger Court's "counterrevolution," have acted as keepers of the Warren Court's flame, especially in criminal justice cases. (As demonstrated by the survival of economic due process in the states, this practice of lodging the rejected Supreme Court doctrines in state constitutions and law is not new.)[28] In this respect state supreme courts may well be regarded as trustees for discarded constitutional doctrine that the Supreme Court may again deem to be serviceable for the nation as a whole.

In sum, the interactions between state supreme courts and the U.S. Supreme Court are considerably more complex and less hierarchical than an examination of their legal relationships might suggest. In fact, as they respond to each others' initiatives, the high courts of the states and the nation produce a "hybrid" state-federal constitutional law. Contributors to this book have ingeniously described the relationship as

> analogous to that prevailing between the coach of a professional football team and its quarterback. The quarterback will in most cases follow the coach's game plan. However, this may well be the fruit of the quarterback's suggestions. Moreover, he may, on the odd occasion, call for a plunge where the coach has ordered a pass, a sweep where the coach would prefer an off-tackle slant or even try a play he has thought up on the spot.[29]

HORIZONTAL FEDERALISM

Although discussions of federalism typically focus on interactions between state and national governments, interactions among the American states are an equally important component of the federal relationships and contribute to policy development throughout the states. Jack Walker discovered regional patterns of information flow and emulation, with particular states consistently providing policy leadership. Virginia Gray, on the other hand, maintained that diffusion patterns vary by issue-area and degree of federal involvement, with different states giving policy direction in one or the other areas.[30] Whatever their differences, both studies underscore the influence that a state may exert on policymaking in sister states.

Similarly, state supreme court decisions also have consequences beyond a state's borders. Indeed, one may suspect that horizontal federalism is particularly important in judicial policymaking. State supreme courts are likely to confront demands for policy innovations similar to those in other states. Since in comparison with legislatures or administrative agencies courts have limited control over their agendas, they cannot easily ignore challenges to current practices. Moreover, the proliferation of groups using litigation to achieve policy reforms virtually ensures that battles won on one front will be refought on others. The activities of the "Serranoists" in the school finance cases exemplify a more general phenomenon.[31] Yet even in the absence of organizational sponsorship, the success of reformist arguments in one state supreme court is likely to spur litigation raising similar claims in several others.

In addition, the process of judicial decision is conducive to sympathetic consideration of policy innovation by sister courts. Aware of judges' precedent-orientation, counsel typically inform state supreme courts of how other courts have resolved similar problems. Although these decisions do not constitute authoritative precedents, the frequency of intercourt citations suggests that they may nonetheless prove persuasive. The persuasiveness of innovative decisions by other courts may be enhanced if judicial policymaking occurred in the process of interpreting a constitutional provision similar to that under consideration. Thus "after California's decision that 'cruel or unusual' was intended to be broader than 'cruel and unusual,' every state having a 'cruel or unusual' provision [became] susceptible to the argument that their provisions should be interpreted as California's was." However, even in the absence of similar constitutional provisions, sister state precedents are important. "Simply from a psychological perspective, a state court may be expected to resist being the first into an area just as it will want to avoid being the last."[32] Furthermore, such precedent may provide justification and encouragement for boldness on the part of less adventurous courts. Finally, given the work-load constraints that affect state supreme court decision making, the precedents furnish solutions that obviate the need for *de novo* policy development.

CONTINUITY AND CHANGE IN STATE SUPREME COURT POLICYMAKING

Some conclusions may be drawn about trends in state supreme court policymaking. Most obvious are the changes, both long and short term, in the issues that come before the courts. The American tendency to judicialize policy questions and the increasing tendency of individuals and organizations to pursue social and economic reform through litigation have virtually ensured that courts, whether or not they welcome it, would be confronted with important and novel policy issues. The "new judicial federalism" so eagerly espoused by the Burger Court and the timely rediscovery of state constitutions have encouraged litigants to base claims on state, rather than federal, constitutions and to bank on expansive interpretations of state, rather than narrow construction of (perhaps similarly worded) federal, guarantees of individual rights.

Long-term developments have facilitated assumption of this leadership role. By creating ICAs and giving judges greater control over their dockets, states have made it possible for their highest courts to focus on important policy issues, and state supreme courts have seized these opportunities. A study of selected state supreme court dockets over a one hundred-year period documents a shift from commercial to noncommercial cases and concludes that

[state supreme court] judges have come to view their role less conservatively. They seem to be less concerned with the stabilization and protection of property rights, more concerned with the individual and the downtrodden, and more willing to consider rulings that promote social change.[33]

This concern for the rights of "the individual and the downtrodden" is most certainly and clearly reflected in civil liberties decisions. For decades it was the U.S. Supreme Court that, by incorporating provisions of the Bill of Rights, extended protection against state infringements of individual liberties. Today it is state supreme courts, using long-neglected provisions of state constitutions, that are fashioning the most generous guarantees for civil rights. Equally significant, although less heralded, decisions at common law have also expanded the protections accorded disadvantaged groups and individuals.

Recognition of these accomplishments, however, should not obscure the degree of continuity in state supreme court policymaking. State supreme courts have always been active policymakers, particularly in the development of complementary and institutional policy. Their contributions to American federalism—vertical and horizontal—are not new, but newly discovered. Their influence on public policy within and beyond the borders of their own states will not only continue, but, as a result of new directions pursued by the U.S. Supreme Court, will undoubtedly increase.

NOTES

1. William J. Brennan, Jr., "State Supreme Court Judge Versus United States Supreme Court Justice: A Change in Function and Perspective," *University of Florida Law Review* 19 (1966): 225–37.

2. Paul L. Trachtenberg, "Reforming School Finance Through State Constitutions: Robinson v. Cahill Points the Way," *Rutgers Law Review* 27 (1974): 365–463; Serrano v. Priest I, 487 P.2d 1241 (Cal. 1971); Id., 557 P.2d 929 (Cal. 1976); *Education Finance Center, Education Commission of the States, School Finance in the States* (1978); Norman C. Thomas, "Equalizing Educational Opportunity Through School Finance Reform: A Review Assessment," *University of Cincinnati Law Review* 48 (1979): 225–319; San Antonio Independent School District v. Rodriguez, 411 U.S. 1 (1973).

3. People v. Anderson, 493 P.2d 880 (Cal. 1972), *cert. denied*, 405 U.S. 958 (1972); William J. Brennan, Jr., "Some Aspects of Federalism," *New York University Law Review* 39 (1964): 945–61.

4. Williams v. Florida, 399 U.S. 78, 133 (1970); Oregon v. Hass, 420 U.S. 714, 719 (1975); Warren E. Burger, "The Interdependence of Our Freedoms," *Akron Law Review* 9 (1976): 403–10. For literature on the new judicial federalism, *see* William J. Brennan, Jr., "State Constitutions and the Protection of Individual Rights," *Harvard Law Review* 90 (1977): 489–504; A. E. Dick Howard, "State Courts and Constitutional Rights in the Day of the Burger Court," *Virginia Law Review* 62 (1976): 874–944; Robert D. Brussack, "Of Laboratories and Liberties: State Court Protection of Political and Civil Rights," *Georgia Law Review* 10 (1976): 533–64; "Project Report: Toward an Activist Role for State Bills of Rights," *Harvard Civil Rights-Civil Liberties Law Review* 8 (1973): 271–350; Donald E. Wilkes, Jr., "The New Federalism in Criminal Procedure: State Court Evasion of the Burger Court," *Kentucky Law Journal* 62 (1974): 421–51; id., "More on the New Federalism in Criminal Procedure," *Kentucky Law Journal* 63 (1975): 874–94; id., "The New Federalism in Criminal Procedure Revisited," *Kentucky Law Journal* 64 (1976): 729–52; Kenneth L. Karst, "Serrano v. Priest: A State Court's Responsibilities and Opportunities in the Development of Federal Constitutional Law," *California Law Review* 60 (1972): 720–56; *In re* Quinlan, 355 A.2d 647 (N.J. 1976); Serrano v. Priest I and II, *supra* note 2; State v. Buckalew, 561 P.2d 289 (Alaska 1977); Peter J. Galie, "State Constitutional Guarantees and Protection of Defendants' Rights: The Case of New York, 1960–1978," *Buffalo Law Review* 28 (1979): 157–94. For a dissenting note on state supreme courts as guardians of civil liberties, *see* Burt Neuborne, "The Myth of Parity," *Harvard Law Review* 90 (1977): 1105–31.

5. This section is based, in part, on Henry R. Glick and Kenneth N. Vines, *State Court Systems* (Englewood Cliffs, N.J.: Prentice-Hall, 1973); Herbert Jacob and Kenneth N. Vines, "State Courts and Public Policy," in *Politics in the American States: A Comparative Analysis*, ed. Herbert Jacob and Kenneth N. Vines (Boston: Little, Brown & Co., 1971), pp. 242–68; Bradley C. Canon and Dean Jaros, "State Supreme Courts—Some Comparative Data," *State Government* 42 (1969): 260–64.

6. The literature on court unification is summarized in Larry Berkson and Susan Carbon, *Court Unification: History, Politics, and Implementation* (Washington, D.C.: U.S. Govern-

ment Printing Office, 1978). For further discussion, *see* G. Alan Tarr, "The Effects of Court Unification on Court Performance," *Judicature* 64 (1981): 356–68.

7. Robert A. Kagan et al., "The Business of State Supreme Courts, 1870–1970," *Stanford Law Review* 30 (1977): 121–56; "Note: Courting Reversal: The Supervisory Role of State Supreme Courts," *Yale Law Journal* 87 (1978): 1191–1214; Daryl Fair, "State Intermediate Appellate Courts: An Introduction," *Western Political Quarterly* 24 (1971): 415–24; Roger D. Groot, "The Effects of an Intermediate Appellate Court on the Supreme Court Work Product: The North Carolina Experience," *Wake Forest Law Review* 7 (1971): 548–72.

8. James Herndon, "Appointment as a Means of Initial Accession to Elective State Courts of the Last Resort," *North Dakota Law Review* 38 (1962): 60–73; Richard A. Watson and Rondal G. Downing, *The Politics of the Bench and the Bar: Judicial Selection Under the Missouri Nonpartisan Court Plan* (New York: John Wiley and Sons, 1969); Bradley C. Canon, "The Impact of Formal Selection Processes on the Characteristics of Judges— Reconsidered," *Law and Society Review* 13 (1972): 579–93. For a cogent argument in favor of popular election of judges, *see* Philip L. Dubois, *From Ballot to Bench: Judicial Elections and the Quest for Accountability* (Austin: University of Texas Press, 1980); Henry R. Glick, "The Promise and Performance of the Missouri Plan: Judicial Selection in the Fifty States," *University of Miami Law Review* 32 (1978): 509–41; Victor Eugene Flango and Craig R. Ducat, "What Difference Does Method of Judicial Selection Make: Selection Procedures in State Courts of Last Resort," *Justice System Journal* 5 (1979): 25–44; Burton M. Atkins and Henry R. Glick, "Formal Judicial Recruitment and State Supreme Court Decisions," *American Politics Quarterly* 2 (1974): 427–49.

9. Robert A. Heiberg, "Social Backgrounds of the Minnesota Supreme Court Justices: 1858–1968," *Minnesota Law Review* 53 (1969): 901–37; John W. Patterson and Gregory T. Rathjen, "Background Diversity and State Supreme Court Dissent Behavior," *Polity* 9 (1976): 610–22; Francis H. Heller, "The Justices of the Kansas Supreme Court, 1861–1975: A Collective Portrait," *University of Kansas Law Review* 24 (1975–76): 521–35; Walter A. Borowiec, "Pathways to the Top: The Political Careers of State Supreme Court Justices," *North Carolina Central Law Review* 7 (1976): 280–85; Glick and Vines, *State Court Systems*, pp. 47–51; Bradley C. Canon, "Characteristics and Career Patterns of State Supreme Court Justices," *State Government* 45 (1972): 34–41; Jerry K. Beatty, "Decision-Making on the Iowa Supreme Court—1965–1969," *Drake Law Review* 19 (1970): 342–67; Dean Jaros and Bradley C. Canon, "Dissent on State Supreme Courts: The Differential Significance of Characteristics of Judges," *Midwest Journal of Political Science* 15 (1971): 322–46; Malcolm C. Moos, "Judicial Elections and Partisan Endorsement of Judicial Candidates in Minnesota," *American Political Science Review* 35 (1941): 69–75; Stuart S. Nagel, "Ethnic Affiliations and Judicial Propensities," *Journal of Politics* 24 (1962): 92–110; id., "Political Party Affiliation and Judges' Decisions," *American Political Science Review* 55 (1961): 843–50; S. Sidney Ulmer, "The Political Party Variable in the Michigan Supreme Court," *Journal of Public Law* 11 (1962): 352–62; Malcolm M. Feely, "Another Look at the 'Party Variable' in Judicial Decision-Making: An Analysis of the Michigan Supreme Court," *Polity* 4 (1971): 91–104; Jamie B. W. Stecher, "Democratic and Republican Justice: Judicial Decision-Making on Five State Supreme Courts," *Columbia Journal of Law and Social Problems* 13 (1977): 137–81; John T. Wold, "Political Orientations, Social Backgrounds, and Role Perceptions of State Supreme Court Judges," *Western Political Quarterly* 27 (1974): 239–48; Wold, "Political Orientations"; Karst, "Serrano v. Priest."

10. Richard Richardson and Kenneth N. Vines, *The Politics of Federal Courts: Lower Courts in the United States* (Boston: Little, Brown & Co., 1970), pp. 8–9.

11. Henry Robert Glick, *Supreme Courts in State Politics: An Investigation of the Judicial Role* (New York: Basic Books, 1971); Theodore L. Becker, "A Survey of Hawaiian Judges: The Effect on Decisions of Judicial Role Variations," *American Political Science Review* 60 (1966): 677–80; Edward N. Beiser, "The Rhode Island Supreme Court: A Well-Integrated

Political System," *Law and Society Review* 8 (1973): 167–86. *But see* Robert J. Sickels, "The Illusion of Judicial Consensus: Zoning Decisions in the Maryland Court of Appeals," *American Political Science Review* 59 (1965): 100–104; Wold, "Political Orientations"; Karst, "Serrano v. Priest."

12. Charles R. Adrian, "Trends in State Constitutions," *Harvard Journal on Legislation* 5 (1968): 311–41; William F. Swindler, "State Constitutions of the 20th Century," *Nebraska Law Review* 50 (1971): 577–99; "Note: Stepping into the Breach: Basing Defendants' Rights on State Rather than Federal Law," *American Criminal Law Review* 15 (1978): 339–81; Lawrence M. Newman, "Rediscovering the California Declaration of Rights," *Hastings Law Journal* 26 (1974): 481–511; Gerald B. Cope, Jr., "Toward a Right of Privacy as a Matter of State Constitutional Law," *Florida State University Law Review* 5 (1977): 633–745; George F. Butterworth, "People v. Triggs: A New Concept of Personal Privacy in Search and Seizure Law," *Hastings Law Journal* 25 (1974): 575–601; Gerald Solk, "Privacy in Alaska: Milestone or Malaise?" *Texas Southern University Law Review* 4 (1976): 50–65; Erb v. Iowa St. Bd. of Public Instruction, 216 N.W.2d 339 (Iowa 1974)—a teacher could not be found morally unfit due to an adulterous act; A. E. Dick Howard, "State Constitutions and the Environment," *Virginia Law Review* 58 (1972): 193–229; Lujuana Wolfe Treadwell and Nancy Wallace Page, "Equal Rights Provisions: The Experience Under State Constitutions," *California Law Review* 65 (1977): 1086–1112.

13. "Taxpayers' Suits: A Survey and Summary," *Yale Law Journal* 69 (1960): 895–924; William M. Goodman and Thom Greenfield Seaton, "Ripe for Decision: Internal Workings and Current Concerns of the California Supreme Court," *California Law Review* 62 (1974): 309–64; Ronan E. Degnan, "The Supreme Court of California, 1970–1971: Adequacy of Representation in Class Actions," *California Law Review* 60 (1972): 705–19; James P. Harvey, "Michigan Constitutional Law—Power of the Supreme Court to Modify Substantive Law by Rule-Making Authority," *Wayne Law Review* 20 (1973–74): 233–38; literature cited *supra* note 7.

14. Jack Ladinsky and Allan Silver, "Popular Democracy and Judicial Independence: Electorate and Elite Reactions to Two Wisconsin Supreme Court Elections," *Wisconsin Law Review* (1976): 128–69; Mulkey v. Reitman, 413 P.2d 825 (Cal. 1966), *affirmed,* 387 U.S. 369 (1967); People v. Anderson, *supra* note 3; Serrano v. Priest I and II, *supra* note 2.

15. For another typology of judicial policymaing, *see* Glick and Vines, *State Court Systems,* 93–102.

16. Carl Baar, "Judicial Activism in State Courts: The Inherent-Powers Doctrine," pp. 129–151, this volume.

17. *See* literature cited *supra* note 4. *See also* "Camping on Adequate State Grounds: California Ensures the Reality of Constitutional Ideals," *Southwestern University Law Review* 9 (1977): 1157–1210. On the rights of religious minorities concerning the use of peyote, *see* People v. Woody, 394 P.2d 813 (Cal. 1964); Arizona V. Whittingham, 504 P.2d 950 (Ariz. 1973), *cert. denied,* 417 U.S. 946 (1974). On sodomy and "deviant" sexual practices, *see* State v. Pilcher, 242 N.W.2d 348 (Iowa 1976); State v. Saunders, 381 A.2d 333 (N.J. 1977). On abortion, *see* People v. Barksdale, 503 P.2d 275 (Cal. 1972); State v. Barquet, 262 So.2d 431 (Fla. 1972). On marijuana, *see* Ravin v. State, 537 P.2d 494 (Alaska 1975); People v. Sinclair, 194 N.W.2d 878 (Mich. 1972). On sexual privacy between consenting adults, *see* State v. Callaway, 542 P.2d 1147 (Ariz. 1975); Commonwealth v. Balthazar, 318 N.E.2d 478 (Mass. 1974); *cf.* with Doe v. Commonwealth, 425 U.S. 901 (1976), which let Virginia's antisodomy statute stand. On euthanasia, *see In re* Quinlan, *supra* note 4. On sex discrimination, *see* Sail'er Inn v. Kirby, 485 P.2d 529 (Cal. 1971). On the mentally ill, *see* Roberts v. Superior Court, 508 P.2d 309 (Cal. 1973). On tenants' rights, *see* Jack Springs, Inc. v. Little, 280 N.E.2d 208 (Ill. 1972); Boston Housing Authority v. Hemingway, 293 N.E.2d 831 (Mass. 1973). On juveniles, *see* Johnson v. Joint School District #60, 508 P.2d 547 (Idaho 1973). On substantive due process, *see* Monrad G. Paulsen, "The Persistence of

Substantive Due Process in the States," *Minnesota Law Review* 34 (1950): 91–118; id., "'Natural Rights'—A Constitutional Doctrine in Indiana," *Indiana Law Journal* 25 (1950): 123–47; John A. C. Hetherington, "State Economic Regulation and Substantive Due Process of Law," *Northwestern University Law Review* 53 (1958): 226–51; "Counterrevolution in State Constitutional Law," *Stanford Law Review* 15 (1963): 309–29.

18. Richard Lehne, *The Quest for Justice: The Politics of School Finance Reform* (New York: Longman, 1978), pp. 200–201.

19. On school finance, *see* Serrano v. Priest I and II and literature cited *supra* note 2. The seminal New Jersey school finance case is Robinson v. Cahill, 303 A.2d 273 (N.J. 1973). In Robinson II, 339 A.2d 193 (N.J. 1975), the court, having lost patience with legislative foot dragging, enjoined further educational expenditures throughout the state until its original order to equalize expenditures was obeyed. The U.S. Supreme Court denied certiorari in Robinson, 414 U.S. 976 (1973). On zoning and land use, *see* Southern Burlington County N.A.A.C.P. v. Township of Mt. Laurel, 336 A.2d 713 (N.J. 1971), *cert. denied,* 423 U.S. 808 (1975); Harold A. McDougall, "The Judicial Struggle Against Exclusionary Zoning: The New Jersey Paradigm," *Harvard Civil Rights-Civil Liberties Law Review* 14 (1979): 625–54; Jay C. Shaffer and Kenneth E. Meiser, "Exclusionary Use of the Planned Unit Development: Standards for Judicial Scrutiny," *Harvard Civil Rights-Civil Liberties Law Review* 8 (1973): 384–418. For a critical view of judicial activism in this area, *see* Robert P. Inman and Daniel L. Rubinfeld, "The Judicial Pursuit of Local Fiscal Equity," *Harvard Law Review* 92 (1979): 1662–1750. For the Robinson saga, *see* Lehne, *Quest for Justice.*

20. "Judicial Activism and Municipal Bonds: Killing Two-Thirds With One Stone," *Virginia Law Review* 56 (1970): 295–333. Auto guest statutes were sustained by the U.S. Supreme Court in 1929; Silver v. Silver, 280 U.S. 117. For some state cases that invalidated on common law or equal-protection grounds, *see* Brown v. Merlo, 506 P.2d 212 (Cal. 1973); Henry v. Bauder, 518 P.2d 362 (Kan. 1974); Johnson v. Hassett, 217 N.W.2d 771 (N.D. 1974); McConville v. State Fair Automobile Insurance Co., 113 N.W.2d 14 (Wis. 1972). California statutes regulating public employee bargaining rights neither deny nor grant the right to strike, thus imposing the task of sanctioning or forbidding strikes on a "reluctant" judiciary; Laura V. Best, "Strikes by Public Employees: The Consequences of Legislative Inattention," *Santa Clara Law Review* 20 (1980): 945–69.

21. Leflar, "Appellate Judicial Innovation," p. 341. For a general, and seminal, discussion, *see* Karl Nickerson Llewellyn, *The Common Law Tradition: Deciding Appeals* (Boston: Little, Brown & Co., 1960). For a strong defense of judicial activism, *see* Robert A. Leflar, "Appellate Judicial Innovation," *Oklahoma Law Review* 27 (1974): 321–45. On governmental bodies, *see* Henry T. Zale, "Judicial Abrogation of Governmental and Sovereign Immunity: A National Trend with a Pennsylvania Perspective," *Dickinson Law Review* 78 (1973): 365–400. On charitable corporations, *see* Bradley C. Canon and Dean Jaros, "The Impact of Changes in Judicial Doctrines: The Abrogation of Charitable Immunity," *Law & Society Review* 13 (1979): 969–86. On privacy, *see* Samuel D. Warren and Louis D. Brandeis, "The Right to Privacy," *Harvard Law Review* 4 (1890): 193–220. On the beginning of "life," *see* Mone v. Greyhound Lines, Inc., 331 N.E.2d 916 (Mass. 1975). On public trust, *see* Borough of Neptune City v. Borough of Avon-by-the-Sea, 294 A.2d 47 (N.J. 1972); Joseph L. Sax, "The Public Trust Doctrine in Natural Resource Law: Effective Judicial Intervention," *Michigan Law Review* 68 (1970): 471–566.

22. "Indigent Prisoner Defendants' Rights in Civil Litigation: Payne v. Superior Court," *Harvard Law Review* 90 (1977): 1029–40; "Constitutional Law—Petty Offender's Right to Demand Trial by Jury: Petty Offenders Have Peers in Alaska—Baker v. City of Fairbanks," *Washington Law Review* 46 (1970–71): 827–36; Andrew M. Roman, "Commonwealth v. Richman: A State's Extension of Procedural Rights Beyond Supreme Court Requirements," *Duquesne Law Review* 13 (1975): 577–98; George R. Moore, "Expanding Criminal Proce-

dural Rights Under State Constitutions," *Washington and Lee Law Review* 33 (1976): 909–33; literature cited *supra* notes 4, 12, and 17.

23. Escobedo v. Illinois, 378 U.S. 478 (1964); Bradley C. Canon, "Organizational Contumacy in the Transmission of Judicial Policies: The Mapp, Escobedo, Miranda, and Gault Cases," *Villanova Law Review* 20 (1974): 50–79; G. Alan Tarr, *Judicial Impact and State Supreme Courts* (Lexington, Mass.: Lexington Books, 1977).

24. Henry R. Glick, "Policy Making and State Supreme Courts: The Judiciary as an Interest Group," *Law & Society Review* 5 (1970): 271–91; James Duke Cameron, "The Place for Judicial Activism on the Part of a State's Highest Court," *Hastings Constitutional Law Quarterly* 4 (1977): 279–93.

25. Morton Grodzins, "Centralization and Decentralization in the American Federal System," in *A Nation of States: Essays on the American Federal System,* ed. Robert A. Goldwin (Chicago: Rand McNally and Co., 1963), pp. 9–15; Jack L. Walker, "Diffusion of Innovations Among the American States," *American Political Science Review* 63 (1969): 880–99.

26. Brennan, "Some Aspects of Federalism," p. 947.

27. "Judicial Federalism: The Rights of the Accused in New Jersey," *Rutgers Law Review* 23 (1969): 530–68, 567; Escobedo v. Illinois and literature cited *supra* note 22; Miranda v. Arizona, 384 U.S. 436 (1966).

28. Murdock v. Memphis, 20 Wall. 590 (1875); references and literature cited *supra* notes 4, 12, 17, and 21.

29. Ronald J. Greene, "Hybrid State Law in the Federal Courts," *Harvard Law Review* 83 (1969): 289–326; Daniel C. Kramer and Robert Riga, "The New York Court of Appeals and the U.S. Supreme Court, 1960–1976," p. 175, this volume.

30. Walker, "Diffusion of Innovations"; Virginia Gray, "Innovation in the States: A Diffusion Study," *American Political Science Review* 67 (1973): 1174–85. For an application of Walker's theory to judicial decision making, *see* Bradley C. Canon and Lawrence Baum, "Patterns of Adoption of Tort Law Innovations: An Application of Diffusion Theory to Judicial Doctrines," *American Political Science Review* 75 (1981): 975–87.

31. Gerald C. Lubenow, "The Action Lawyers," *Saturday Review,* August 26, 1972, pp. 36–42. *See also* literature cited *supra* note 2.

32. "Project Report," pp. 318, 317. People v. Anderson, *supra* note 3.

33. Kagan et al., "The Business of State Supreme Courts," p. 155.

PART I.

CONSTITUTIONAL POLICYMAKING

1.

MARY CORNELIA PORTER

State Supreme Courts and the Legacy of the Warren Court: Some Old Inquiries for a New Situation

THE WARREN COURT, THE BURGER COURT, AND STATE SUPREME COURT ACTIVISM

Since the advent of the Burger Court, Justice William Brennan, among others, has noted and applauded the increasing tendency of those presenting civil libertarian claims to rely less on U.S. Supreme Court interpretation of the federal Constitution and more on state court readings of state constitutions. In much the same farewell-to-the-Warren-Court spirit, legal commentators have reviewed and indicated ways that state courts have, and might, base rulings on state constitutions. Scholarly interest has been revived in the one hundred-year-old principle that the Supreme Court will not review state supreme court decisions based upon an "independent" and "adequate" state ground. The Burger Court's restriction on access to federal courts has led one federal judge to predict that state courts will assume increasing responsibility for defending federal rights. Techniques that state courts might employ to adjudicate federal claims have been canvassed.[1]

The Burger Court's fashioning of a "new federalism," characterized by deference to state and local governments in areas as diverse as criminal justice, education, apportionment, censorship, welfare assistance, inter-

I thank my former student, Carol Spielman, for her research assistance and Professor Henry J. Abraham for inspiring an earlier version of this chapter presented on his panel "Judging and Legislating, Activism and Restraint: The External Quest for a Viable Line" (Annual Meeting of the American Political Science Association, Washington, D.C., September 1–4, 1977).

3

state commerce, and labor-management relations, has served to encourage state court libertarian activism.[2] The criminal justice rulings are illustrative. Here the Court, following the position of Justice John Marshall Harlan, has urged state legislatures and courts to develop principles that are fair and appropriate to a variety of local situations. State courts may not interpret the federal Constitution more narrowly or broadly than does the Supreme Court, but "a state is free *as a matter of its own law* to impose greater restrictions on police activity than those the Court holds to be necessary upon federal constitutional standards."[3]

The court also appears more than willing to refuse appeals over which, it could be argued, it has jurisdiction. In a search-and-seizure case, for example, the Court had to remand to determine whether the California Supreme Court had rested its (obviously sloppily worded) decision on the state or federal Constitution or both. Despite the plea of the state's attorney that the Court establish guidelines for such cases, the Court meekly accepted the state court's certification that its decision was based on both constitutions and denied certiorari.[4]

Despite his differences with the majority, Justice Brennan found some solace in the "new federalism," which

need not be a mean-spirited doctrine that serves only to limit the scope of human liberty. Rather, [federalism] must necessarily be furthered significantly when state courts thrust themselves into a position of prominence to protect the people of our nation from governmental intrusions on their freedoms.[5]

As Warren Court activism generated much discussion about the proper functions of the Court and the quality of its work, the new "prominence" of state supreme courts has similarly drawn attention to their policymaking roles as "protectors" of the nation's "freedoms" and to the caliber of their decisions as well. This study, focusing on the high courts of California, Michigan, New Jersey, and Alaska and drawing on criteria established by Archibald Cox and Hans Linde, evaluates state court activism in terms of success in drawing a "viable line between judging and legislating."

The four courts are recognized as innovative, well administered, and standing at the apex of "modern" and "simple" judicial systems. They represent, outside the South and Southwest, a geographical distribution. The California Court, considered to be the most prestigious in the nation, has a history of civil rights activism. The New Jersey court system, where the scholarly and idealistic tradition of the great reformer, Justice Arthur Vanderbilt, still dominates, operates in what might be termed a unique judicial culture. The Michigan Court, intensely "political," has received considerable attention from political scientists. The Alaska Court writes on a relatively clean slate and interprets a constitution that reflects expansionist Supreme Court interpretation of the Bill of Rights as well as the cherished individualism of the nation's last frontier.[6]

JUDICIAL ACTIVISM AND SELF-RESTRAINT

THE UNITED STATES SUPREME COURT

Judicial activism and *self-restraint* are terms that elude precise definition. They may have a political connotation, referring to judicial attitudes toward elected bodies and officials; the federal relationships; public opinion; and the extent to which the Court exercises its constitutional, statutory, self-defined, and practicable ("John Marshall has made his decision, now let him enforce it") authority. They may have reference to the art and science of judging—modes of constitutional and statutory construction; the uses of precedent, history, and the decisions of other courts; inclinations concerning the acceptance of "controversial" (however defined) cases; employment of techniques such as the remand to avoid making hard-and-fast decisions; the timing of the issuance of final orders; the nature of the Court's commands; and the skills of argument and rhetoric.

The designation *judicial self-restraint* is, however, as Charles Black pointed out with some acerbity, loaded, conjuring up a vision of a recklessly shooting-from-the hip versus a perspicaciously prudent Court.

Perhaps it is not so marvelous that this slogan should have enjoyed the vogue it has. Its phrasing, though pithy, is a work of art. . . . "Judicial timidity" or "judicial buck-passing" would have less appeal. . . . [T]he concept of "restraint" sits with particular appropriateness next to the concept "judicial."[7]

Black made a point. Judicial activism is seldom defended on its own terms; the words *self-restraint* establish the ground rules for the debate over the desirable role and modus operandi of the Court. The well-known reasons for this need not be repeated here. Among the most widely agreed upon canons of judicial self-restraint are the following: Justices should not be guided by their policy preferences. They should "defer" to other branches of government and the states. The Court should give such impeccably argued, cogent, and intellectually persuasive reasons for what it does that disagreement with a decision may be matched by respect for the supporting opinion (many activists would agree here)—for the very essence of judicial statesmanship is judicial craftsmanship.

STATE COURT ACTIVISM: SOME DEFINITIONS

High state court *activism* may be defined in somewhat the same ways as is Supreme Court activism. Differences also exist. The first way to identify state court activism is in terms of the relationships between the highest state and federal courts and, for purposes here, the Burger Court. The four courts under discussion have put considerable distance between themselves and the Supreme Court—and make no bones about it. The California Court rejected the first modification of *Miranda* v. *Arizona,* declaring that whatever the Supreme Court might have to say "was not persuasive authority in any state prosecution in California." The New Jersey Court, without the question being presented at the trial or inter- mediate appellate levels, invited a defendant's counsel to argue that the state guarantee against unreasonable searches and seizures, although iden- tical in wording to the Fourth Amendment, establishes stricter standards for consensual searches. Then in accordance with (its own) argument, it asserted its "right to construe [the] state constitution in accordance with what we conceive to be its plain meaning." The Michigan Court, while giving "due consideration" to rulings that restricted the right to counsel at pretrial line-ups, nonetheless found that the Court had not established adequate protections. Basing its decision on its "constitutional power to establish rules of evidence," the court held, "independent of any federal constitutional mandate," that Michigan defendants were entitled to legal assistance. The Alaska Court found completely "unpersuasive" the rea- soning behind a Burger Court self-incrimination ruling.

We need not stand idly and passively by waiting for constitutional direction from the highest court of the land. . . . We are not bound to follow blindly a federal constitutional principle if we are convinced that the result is based on unsound logic.[8]

Instances of Supreme Court rulings that state courts have overextended federal constitutional guarantees "present," wrote one commentator, "the anomolous spectacle of the highest federal court taking a dimmer view of federal rights than state courts." If "rights broader than the Burger Court's" are to be granted, "then more liberally oriented state courts must act evasively."[9]

So they have acted, not in the more usual way of seeking a route to escape the Court's mandate, but to avoid its jurisdiction. Evasion within this context occurs when a state court makes it abundantly clear that its decision rests on state grounds no matter what the Court has said. In *People* v. *Anderson,* for example, the California Court invalidated capital punishment on the ground that it violated the state ban against the impo- sition of cruel or unusual punishment. The state's attorney general, peti- tioning for Supreme Court review, angrily denounced this effort "to defeat the jurisdiction of [the] Court . . . by purporting to decide the issue on the basis of an identical provision in the state constitution."[10]

Evasion may also be detected when a state court makes the point of explaining that state and federal claims, despite their similar wording, have separate and distinct meanings. Concerned that California courts have not always made this clear, the high court has become more succinct about the dual basis of its rulings.

Although for the sake of convenience we often refer to both constitutions, our decision today is based upon our reading of applicable Fourth Amendment law and our own determination of the proper construction of the California Constitution.[11]

Evasion may also be prospective. The California high court, picking up clues that the Supreme Court might rule otherwise, held that the state constitution and state public policy prohibit de facto school segregation and mandate the presence of counsel at probationary hearings.[12]

A second characteristic of activist state courts is their tendency to build on foundations established by the Supreme Court, to anticipate and stimulate liberal Court rulings, and to provide leadership for courts in sister states. The California Court, faithfully following the Warren Court's "two-tiered" equal-protection analysis (laws adversely affecting "fundamental rights" of "suspect classes" will be "strictly" scrutinized and, absent the justification of a "compelling" state interest, invalidated), has determined that the right to an education is "fundamental," and that poverty and sex are "suspect" classifications. This is further than the Supreme Court is willing to go. Before the Supreme Court did so, the California Court ruled against antimiscegenation and death penalty statutes and invalidated the prohibition against abortion.[13]

Invalidating convictions stemming from clandestine police surveillance of public restrooms and the confiscation of bank records, the California Court developed the doctrine of the right to a "reasonable expectation of privacy." The New Jersey Court said that the right to privacy, under extraordinary circumstances, includes the right to die.[14]

The New Jersey Court in *Southern Burlington County N.A.A.C.P.* v. *Township of Mt. Laurel* ruled that municipalities may not employ zoning regulations to fence out low-income families. The California Court threw, albeit temporarily, that state's (and by extension all) affirmative action program(s) into doubt. Following *Serrano* v. *Priest,* the momentous California decision that invalidated the state's method of financing public schools, similar suits were instituted throughout the nation.[15]

A third characteristic of activist state courts is their propensity to make policy, not "interstitially" as Justice Oliver Wendell Holmes might say, but openly, boldly, and creatively. The California and New Jersey courts have been closely involved in state education and tax policies. *Serrano* v.

Priest I and II and *Robinson* v. *Cahill* I through VII are examples. *Serrano* mandated the legislature to pay for schools in a way that would not make the quality of a child's education "a function of the wealth of his parents and neighbors," that is, reliance on the property tax could no longer be as great. *Serrano* II, handed down five years later, rejected the legislature's new plan and has reportedly been the cause of proposals that would radically reorganize the state's entire school system. *Robinson* I held that the state's school finance scheme violated the New Jersey constitutional command for the creation of a "thorough and efficient" educational system. *Robinson* VII enjoined further educational expenditures until the court's order had been obeyed. In *Mt. Laurel,* the New Jersey Court blamed the state's tax structure, which substantially finances municipal and educational services from local property taxes, for the adoption of zoning regulations beneficial to the tax rate.[16] By holding that zoning regulations must serve regional needs by permitting a wide range of housing choice, and that the state must bear the major burden for financing education (the state's share, before *Robinson,* was 28 percent; on the average, states contribute 40 percent), the New Jersey Court has done all but rewrite the state tax code.

The Michigan and Alaska courts have taken giant steps that could lead toward the decriminalization of marijuana, not only because of rulings that the right to privacy protects the use of the drug in the home, but because of judicial determination that the drug is not harmful. The New Jersey Court, by authorizing the removal of life-support equipment from Karen Quinlan, not only made state policy, but established precedent whose universal importance may as yet be only dimly understood.[17]

Finally, activist state courts exude a self-confidence that can only be described as pride of place. In New Jersey judicial reform was the cornerstone of the movement for constitutional revision, successfully culminated in 1947. The high court justices frankly claim, within the limitations imposed by their concept of the judicial role, a policymaking function and have been especially creative in using the common law to effect social change. One justice revealed the court's activist strategy:

The quality of judicial writing is one of encouraging the legislature, setting activities in motion which will have secondary consequences to lead the senators and assemblymen to act. *This is the essence of democracy.* We can encourage the legislature to pass laws or taxes without directing them to do that. This is the wonder of our system, and besides *it works to accomplish judicial objectives.* (Emphasis added.)

Another frankly admitted that "no thicket [is] too political for us."[18]

Off-the-bench writing is illustrative of this sort of judicial *Weltanschauung*. From the perspective of the California high court's tradition of defending minority rights in the face of "public outcry and indignation," Chief Justice Donald Wright, making the case as strongly as an American judge ever has, gave this "cogent" justification for an activist jurisprudence that has few compunctions about "violat[ing] majority sentiment":

[I]n our system only the judiciary can guarantee that "general values" will endure and that the rights of all, including those of impotent minorities, will be protected as the Constitution requires. Compared to legislatures, judges are less influenced by the elective process and are generally more insulated from transitory public whim. Additionally, a reviewing court is confronted with the equities and realities in a way uncommon in either the legislative or elective branches of government. . . . Finally, and most importantly, a court *must* consider a law every time a litigant interposes a constitutional challenge. However much we may wish to ignore such a challenge, we cannot do so and remain faithful to our oath. A court cannot wait until the public pressure which instigated passage of a particular law has subsided. . . .[19]

CRITERIA FOR EVALUATING STATE SUPREME COURT ACTIVISM

The criteria for judging state supreme courts cannot be exactly those that are applied to the Supreme Court. First, state court activism is fairly common and generally accepted for a number of reasons. Continued or continuous tenure involves some measure of public approval. Procedures for the removal of judges are flexible compared with those provided for in the federal Constitution. With a few exceptions, state supreme courts have a low visibility. In some states unpopular decisions may be overruled by popular referenda; in others by legislatively initiated constitutional change. A number of state legislatures and/or state constitutions, by providing for intermediate appellate courts, by granting discretionary control over the docket, and by permitting advisory opinions, have tacitly encouraged judicial policymaking.

Second, state supreme courts have considerably more leeway than their federal counterpart. They are not constrained by considerations of federalism. The reach of their decisions is limited, and they have not felt compelled, in the interests of prudence, to avoid "political questions" or to refrain from passing judgment on the necessity for, or wisdom of, economic regulatory regulation. Their decisions may be based on the common law, state or federal statutes, and on state and federal constitutional grounds, either separately or in combination. They hear the kinds of cases that seldom reach federal courts; as pertains to workman's compensation and products liability, state courts have, one study noted, become increasingly "concerned with the individual and the downtrodden" and are becoming "more willing to consider rulings that promote social change."[20]

Finally, state courts may dare to tread where the Supreme Court does not. For instance, it might be considered improper for the Supreme Court and yet entirely proper for a state court to hold that a school finance law violates the Equal Protection Clause of the federal Constitution. The state court, presumably more knowledgeable about local conditions, is in the better position to make informed judgments affecting ways that state and local governments raise revenue, allocate resources, and provide services. State supreme courts, in sum, are free in the classical Brandesian sense to "experiment."[21]

But within this framework it is possible to assess state court activism in more-or-less traditional terms, and justices of activist courts, scholars who make it their business to critique state court opinions, and those who would welcome the development of a corpus of state constitutional law have suggested, in a very general way, at least three standards that should be followed by activist courts. The courts should be sensitive to political realities, should show an awareness of the judicial function, and should explain themselves well; that is, decisions should be principled. Such standards are, of course, applied to the Supreme Court—the differences are of degree, not kind. It should be emphasized that what follows does not constitute a comprehensive assessment of the four courts under discussion. The examples are just that—examples.

POLITICAL SENSITIVITY: CALIFORNIA AND NEW JERSEY

A court need not "follow the election returns," but it should not ignore them either. The price of *Miranda,* it has been said, was the "Safe Streets Act." The same sort of worry arises about the backlash effects of activist state court rulings, especially in California where the public may easily dispose of unpopular legislative and judicial decisions. "If the court gets the reputation," one commentator warned,

fairly or unfairly, of being "soft" on criminals, it could subject itself to repeated attacks by petition-carriers. And if the people overrule the court too often, it would be harmful to the judicial branch of government.[22]

In much the same vein, a result-oriented court would do well not to give the impression of scrambling around for reasons to justify a decision. Reasons should not be tailored for particular outcomes; rather outcomes should flow from precedent and well-established principles—a point made by California justices arguing against the majority's abrupt post-*Harris* abandonment of the federal, and (to them) opportunistic embrace of the state constitution.

The majority's approach makes it abundantly clear that the vigor with which the newly discovered separate and independent state constitutional interpretations are asserted ebbs and flows depending on the approval or rejection by that majority of a particular constitutional interpretation, which in a given case, emanates from . . . the Supreme Court.[23]

The California Court's handling of *People* v. *Anderson* provides an all-too-vivid illustration of the difficulties created by a political court. To begin with, the court rejected Anderson's earlier claim that capital punishment violated the Eighth and Fourteenth Amendments. "The fixing of penalties," said the court in the classical language of judicial self-restraint, "is a legislative function." Another case, in which the court had reached the same conclusion,[24] awaited disposition by the Supreme Court, and no executions were planned pending its ruling. Suddenly the court reopened *Anderson* and appointed new counsel who was ordered to argue that the death penalty violated the state constitutional ban against cruel and unusual punishment—an argument the court hastily accepted just six weeks later.

The precipitateness of the ruling and the court's fortuitous discovery of (minor) differences in otherwise similar state and constitutional provisions were widely attributed to the court's (mistaken) assumption that the Burger Court would sustain the death penalty. The sudden switch to the state ground, vociferously brought to the public's attention by then Governor Ronald Reagan, had more than a little to do with the ensuing popular referendum that, by a vote of almost two to one, reinstated capital punishment.

Anderson, from the advantageous perspective of hindsight, was ironic and tragic. Had the court waited a few months longer, it would have had the opportunity, later taken, to invalidate the death penalty on the basis of *Furman* v. *Georgia.*[25] As it was, the court's action looked like a trick played on the people, the legislature, and the Supreme Court, with the result that the citizens of California presented the spectacle of themselves trooping to the polls to enshrine the death penalty in their constitution.

Second, a court that feels impelled to direct a legislature in the paths of righteousness should act with the greatest forbearance. A legislature faced with a difficult mandate such as a *Serrano* or *Robinson* should be permitted considerable time and space in which to maneuver. The *Serrano* court laid down only the broadest of guidelines and did not rule on the subject for five years. After three years, five intervening rulings, and endless legislative-executive-judicial negotiations, the *Robinson* court refused any longer to "stay its hand out of appropriate respect for other Branches of government." The final order was a last-ditch response to legislative intransigence.

This court, as the designated last resort guarantor of the constitution's command, possesses and must use power equal to its responsibility. Sometimes, unavoidably incident thereto and in response to a constitutional mandate the court must act, often in a sense to encroach on areas otherwise reserved to other Branches of government. . . . [T]here comes a time when no alternative remains. That time is now.[26]

While the storm over *Robinson* raged, the court handed down *Mt. Laurel*. Anxious to avoid a second confrontation, the court tactfully vacated that part of the trial court's judgment that ordered the town to submit a new zoning plan: "It is the local function and responsibility . . . to decide on details. . . . The municipality should first have full opportunity to act without judicial supervision."[27]

THE JUDICIAL FUNCTION: CALIFORNIA, ALASKA, AND MICHIGAN

The second standard for judging activist courts pertains to how well they perform the judicial function, and what is referred to here is a variant of the old familiar theme that the Supreme Court's primary responsibility is to act as a "republican schoolmaster," to conduct an ongoing seminar on the meaning of democracy. The idea has been usefully modified and sharpened by Archibald Cox.

The Court's opinions may sometimes be the voice of the spirit, reminding us of our better selves. In such cases . . . it quickens moral education. But while the opinions of the Court can help us shape our national understanding of ourselves, the roots of its decision must already be in the nation. The aspirations voiced by the Court must be those the community is willing not only to avow but in the end to live by. For the power of great constitutional decisions rests with the accuracy of the Court's perceptions of this kind of common will. . . .[28]

Assuming that we do share a "common will," it must be expressed in our constitutions. Where else? It is here that Hans Linde's thesis, combining with the Court-as-educator view, furnishes a yardstick for taking a measure of activist state courts. Drawing upon the historic role of state courts, Linde contended that critics of Supreme Court activism are way off the mark.

Throughout the states it is taken for granted that large areas of law-making are left to the courts. . . . The accepted dominance of courts in state laws extends to their own "anti-majoritarian" role in review of their coordinate political branches in state and local government. Yet neither judges nor critics seemed concerned that state courts should fear for their own survival.[29]

Students of the Court, Linde charged, have remained so "consistently occupied with the judicial process" that they have treated "constitutional law as a consequence of judicial review, rather than vice versa." Constitutional law is not about what "judges should do," but what "government should do." The Court's task is to "elucidate the Constitution in terms that could, if heeded, make judicial intervention unnecessary." The meaning of the Constitution is to be found in its past. That is not to say that judges must be "strict constructionists," but simply "constructionists," "understanding judicial review as . . . construing the living meaning of past political decisions."

Elaborating on this concept of the judicial function, Linde maintained that state courts are obliged to engage in the same sort of rigorous constitutional construction. This is necessary because when the wording of state and federal guarantees is substantially the same, and when the Supreme Court rejects a state court's broad construction of a federal right, then, by implication, the Court has also ruled that the state constitution, unless its meaning was previously illuminated, does not guarantee the claimed right. The "effect," Linde warned, "is to delegate the interpretation of those state guarantees to a shifting majority of the United States Supreme Court."

More importantly, state constitutions are qualitatively different from the federal counterpart even when the wording may be the same.

Freedom of religion might be understood differently in New Jersey or Delaware than in Massachusetts or South Carolina. A punishment common in puritan Massachusetts might be regarded as highly unusual and cruel in aristocratic Virginia.[30]

Recent changes in state constitutions, adopted either by citizen referenda or constitutional conventions, indicate specific concerns for protections that are broader than those granted by (Supreme Court interpretation of) the federal Constitution. The 1963 Michigan constitution, for example, guarantees "freedom of expression" for "all persons" on "all subjects." A delegate to the Constitutional Convention explained that it was the intent of the constitution's framers not only to "reaffirm traditional guarantees, but to enlarge the orbit of protected communication."[31]

To develop a corpus of alternative constitutional law—essential to reflect the nation's diversity and to assure that our rights and liberties receive protection from more than one (not always reliable) source— Linde urged state judges to understand, develop, and explain their own constitutions in the light of the "original understanding" of their framers and in comparison with Supreme Court interpretation of the federal Constitution. If reliance on the state ground is to be more than a gimmick, dusted off and used when times are "bad" and returned to storage when times are "good," careful and respectful explication of state constitutions is in order.[32] This, for high state courts, is the essence of the judicial function.

During the Warren Court era and the first years of the Burger Court, state courts, especially the California high court, tended to make slap-dash references to the state ground—something thrown in for good measure. In *Serrano* I the state ground was relegated to a footnote. In *Serrano* II, in which the court had to reckon with the Supreme Court's *San Antonio Independent School District* v. *Rodriguez*[33] decision sustaining a school finance system against an Equal Protection challenge, there was no choice but to explain that although two-tiered equal-protection analysis was not serviceable for Fourteenth Amendment purposes, it could still be applied to the state's equal-protection guarantee. For support the court cited criminal justice rulings resting on state constitutional grounds, including one from the Alaska high court—hardly the sort of thing Linde had in mind.

If a state court undertakes to evolve an independent jurisdiction under the state constitution, it must give as much attention and respect to the different constitutional sources and to striving for some continuity and consistency in their use as we ask of the United States Supreme Court justices. . . . This will not be accomplished by searching ad hoc for some plausible premise in the state constitution only when the federal precedents will not support the desired result nor by collecting citations from other state courts, deciding "constitutional law" without identifying or analyzing their constitutional authority, if any.[34]

Anderson, although questionable in other respects, is more satisfactory. The court, drawing on historical accounts and documents, recognized a difference between the ban against "cruel or" and "cruel and" unusual punishments. "The delegates to the constitutional convention of 1849 . . . were aware of the disjunctive form and . . . its use was purposive."[35] It was up to the state courts to honor that choice and to keep the meaning of those words alive.

Anderson broke new ground, and although the court discussed the textual similarities of the two constitutions, it was not faced with the problem of reconciling its opinion with one of the Supreme Court. The more common situation is that state courts have some obligation to explain why they do not follow the latest, and thereby the most authoritative, interpretation of the federal Constitution; for the most part they fail to give good, if any, reasons for deciding that state standards are higher than the unacceptable federal standards. This was particularly awkward for the California Court, which relied heavily on Warren Court criminal justice rulings. The Alaska Court, in *Baker* v. *Fairbanks,*[36] provides an exception—and a model.

Here the court held, *Duncan* v. *Louisiana*[37] to the contrary, that petty as well as serious offenders must be provided with a jury trial. The court could, of course, have simply cited the state constitution and let it go at that. What is exemplary about *Baker* is that the court went beyond references to "the intention and spirit" of its constitution and the "kind of life and ordered liberty'' that is an Alaskan's proud heritage and painstakingly explained its differences with the Supreme Court. Agreeing with the *Duncan* rationale that convenience and expediency might well dictate drawing a line between the rights of serious and petty offenders, the court argued that the Constitution, in guaranteeing the right to trial by jury, makes no such distinctions; nor, in the right to counsel cases, had the Supreme Court made such distinctions. Since the Constitution itself nowhere authorizes withholding rights on the basis of expediency, no exceptions can be made.[38]

Contrast this with the California Court's refusal in *People* v. *Brisendine* to follow the Supreme Court's holdings that the Fourth Amendment allows searches and seizures during a routine custodial investigation. The court apparently thought that it was under no obligation to explain why the state's standards were higher and did no more than to ''reaffirm''

a basic principle of federalism—that the nation as a whole is composed of distinct geographical and political entities bound together by a fundamental federal law but nonetheless responsible for safeguarding the rights of their citizens.[39]

The Michigan Court's ''dialogue'' with the Supreme Court, falling between *Baker* and *Brisendine,* is instructive. In *People* v. *Bloss* the court reversed the conviction of an owner of an adult bookstore on First Amendment grounds. On appeal, the Supreme Court, citing *Miller* v. *California,* remanded. Three years later the Michigan Court sustained its earlier decision on the grounds that the act complained of had taken place before the establishment of the *Miller* standards, and because the court could not construe statutes regarding the dissemination of obscene materials ''without further legislative expression.'' The court then cryptically cited the newly adopted constitutional guarantee of ''freedom of expression'' on ''all subjects.''[40] It may be surmised that the very brief opinion was a warning to the legislature that the criminal obscenity law might not withstand scrutiny under the state constitution, and thus the failure to construe the constitution is understandable. The point, however, is not that the court deferred to the legislature in the approved self-restraining manner, but that it has a golden opportunity to develop a ''Michigan constitutional law'' concerning obscenity in particular and freedom of expression in general, ''thereby sidestepping the vagaries and ever changing legal crosswinds associated with federal decisions interpreting the First Amendment to the United States Constitution.''[41] Linde would approve.

JUDICIAL CRAFTSMANSHIP

''Judicial legislation,'' as noted earlier, is more ''acceptable'' at the high state than at the federal level, which is not to say that state courts have no obligation to justify their policymaking decisions in "principled" terms. What constitutes a principled Supreme Court decision is open to debate, but certainly what Cox had to say about craftsmanship on the nation's highest Court may apply to state courts as well.

The ability to rationalize a constitutional judgment honestly in terms of principles referrable to legal precedent and other accepted sources of law is, by the lawyer's tradition, an essential major ingredient of the Court's power to command acceptance and support. In the case of judicial rulings the power of legitimacy is thought to depend largely upon the realization that the major influence in a decision is not personal fiat, but principles which bind the judges as well as the litigants, and which apply uniformly to all men not only today but yesterday and tomorrow.[42]

In Relation to the Supreme Court: Alaska. One test of judicial crafts-manship for high state courts lies in the skill with which they handle Supreme Court precedents with which they do not agree. In this respect *Baker* marks an outstanding success, *Brisendine* is an ordinary failure, and *Bloss* presents the full potential. The Alaska Court is conscious of and conscientious about its responsibility to explain its independence of and differences with the highest Court in the land. In another case that court canvassed conflicting federal appellate decisions concerning compulsory hairstyles for school children, noted the lack of direction from the Supreme Court, and rested its decision to invalidate such regulations on the basis of the "liberty guaranteed by the state constitution." The court cited its habit of relying on the state constitution, again emphasizing the point that it has never felt obliged "to interpret [its] constitution in the same manner the Supreme Court . . . has construed parallel provisions of the federal constitution."[43]

"Principles which apply uniformly . . . today, yesterday and tomorrow": New Jersey. The *Quinlan* decision, undoubtedly one of the most activist handed down by any court in the nation, was roundly condemned by the state's attorney general who accused the court of usurping the legislature's authority to decide if brain death constitutes legal death. The court's confident claim to the contrary, it is the legislature, he contended, that is in the best position to speak for the "moral judgment" of the community.[44]

His claim may be true enough, but—and this is the crux of the matter, as it is so often when courts "legislate"—the legislature had failed to come to grips with the increasingly pressing and awesome moral, legal, and economic problems raised by medicine's capacity to maintain non-sapient life. A first step had to be taken, and it so happened that it was taken by a court. The state's decision not to appeal must be attributed, at least in part, to a sense of relief that the court had been willing to tread where others had not dared.

If this were "all" the court had done, the decision might be defended on purely humanitarian grounds. But as A. E. Dick Howard reminded us, courts are not "knights errant."[45] *Quinlan,* to stand the test of time, must provide a principle for future cases. The court enunciated that principle in terms that are comprehensible to legislators, the medical and legal professions, and patients and their families.

Karen Quinlan's case, the court said, was not analogous to situations in which courts have ordered relatively simple procedures, such as blood transfusions, for patients whose chances for recovery were good. There the state's interest in maintaining life was compelling. In the present instance the state's interest weakens "and the individual's right to privacy grows as the degree of bodily invasion increases and the prognosis dims. Ultimately there comes a point at which the individual's rights overcome the state's interest."[46] It is said that "hard cases make bad law"; not so for *Quinlan.*

CONCLUSIONS

The advent of the Burger Court and the refusal of some high state courts to accept its minimal standards for the protection of the rights of the accused has dramatically increased scholarly interest in state court libertarian activism and interpretation of state constitutions. This interest, in turn, now goes beyond exploring the possibilities presented by activist court rulings on state constitutions and extends to posing inquiries about the quality of the decisions themselves.

Some inquiries are similar to those raised about activist supreme courts and for much the same reasons. Howard put it this way:

There are some genuine concerns . . . that a state judge should mull before mounting an activist horse. . . . Fuzzy though the bounds between legislative and judicial acts may be, the spirit of our system (not to mention the texts of our constitutions) tells us that the roles of judges and legislatures are not the same. There are some questions that, because they require a legislative weighing of interests and facts, judges are not well equipped to answer. Even without attempting to define what is inherently "judicial" and what is inherently "legislative," it is certainly important to ask what judges do well and what they do badly.[47]

This view, however, overlooks the fact, mentioned earlier, that a considerable difference exists between state and federal court oversight of state governmental activities. For example, a directive from the Supreme Court to redistrict or to bus children to achieve racial balance in schools or a federal judge's assumption of responsibility to operate schools or prisons give rise to cries of "judicial legislation." A *Serrano* or a *Mt. Laurel,* on the other hand, may result in a productive judicial-legislative

dialogue. The statement also ignores a fact of political life. State representatives are subject to formidable constituent and interest-group pressures.
The rash of challenges to state school finance systems following *Serrano*
and *Robinson,* and the subsequent reform measures enacted, is evidence
enough of the need for prodding by courts (absent some other institution)
to remind legislators, especially those from wealthy districts, of their
obligation to provide equal educational opportunity. I would change Howard's formulation to suggest that we ask not what state judges can do
"well" and "badly," but how well state judges go about the business of
making public policy.

For "legislate" they will. Many state courts are in the midst of political
thickets in ways federal courts seldom are, and as Linde pointed out, this
has never worried anyone very much. It is the promise and influence of
the Warren Court and the trends established by the Burger Court that have
changed matters. During the Warren Court era controversial libertarian
rulings could be blamed on far-away Washington, and libertarian courts
simply claimed that they were following directives from the highest bench.
Now an activist libertarian court, which wishes to continue in the spirit of
the Warren Court, must not only respectfully differ with the Supreme
Court, but is in the position of taking the heat itself. State courts are now
on the firing line. For those who applaud the development of state constitutional law protective of civil rights and liberties—and Chief Justice
Warren Burger as well as Justice Brennan may be counted in their number[48]—the concern is that activist courts remain effective and avoid antag-
onizing both legislatures and the public. Activist courts must adhere to
standards for decision making—standards that are variants on some of the
canons of judicial self-restraint. The search for a viable line between
judging and legislating, as concerns state courts, directs us not so much to
evaluating *what* state courts do as to evaluating *how* they do it. If this
sample of rulings from a few activist courts is at all representative, they
are "legislating" rather well and, thanks to the Burger Court, are getting
better at it all the time.

NOTES

1. Murdock v. Memphis, 20 Wall. 590 (1875); William J. Brennan, Jr., "State Constitutions
and the Protection of Individual Rights," *Harvard Law Review* 90 (1977): 489–504; A. E.
Dick Howard, "State Courts and Constitutional Rights in the Day of the Burger Court,"
Virginia Law Review 62 (1976): 874–944; "Of Laboratories and Liberties: State Court
Protection of Political and Civil Rights," *Georgia Law Review* 10 (1976): 533–64; "The New
Federalism: Toward a Principled Interpretation of the State Constitution," *Stanford Law
Review* 29 (1977): 297–321; "Project Report: Toward an Activist Role for State Bills of
Rights," *Harvard Civil Rights-Civil Liberties Law Review* 8 (1973): 271–350; Donald E.
Wilkes, Jr., "The New Federalism in Criminal Procedures: State Court Evasion of the

Burger Court," *Kentucky Law Journal* 62 (1974): 421–51; id., "More on the New Federalism," *Kentucky Law Journal* 63 (1975): 874–94; Younger v. Harris, 401 U.S. 37 (1971); Philip Tone, "The Federal Constitution in State Courts: The Increasing Responsibilities of State Judges," *The Judge's Journal* 16 (1977): 2; "Protecting Fundamental Rights in State Courts: Fitting a State Peg to a Federal Hole," *Harvard Civil Rights-Civil Liberties Law Review* 12 (1977): 63–111; Kenneth L. Karst, "Serrano v. Priest: A State Court's Responsibilities and Opportunities in the Development of Federal Constitutional Law," *California Law Review* 60 (1972): 720–56.

2. The phrase is widely employed. *See* literature cited *supra* note 1. On criminal justice, *see* Gustafson v. Florida, 414 U.S. 260 (1973). On education, *see* Milliken v. Bradley, 418 U.S. 717 (1974). On apportionment, *see* Mahan v. Howell, 410 U.S. 315 (1973). On censorship, *see* Miller v. California, 413 U.S. 15 (1973). On welfare, *see* Jefferson v. Hackney, 406 U.S. 535 (1973). On interstate commerce, *see* Hughes v. Alexandria Scrap Corp., 426 U.S. 794 (1976). On labor-management, *see* National League of Cities v. Usery, 426 U.S. 833 (1976).

3. *See, e.g.,* Harlan's concurrence in Williams v. Florida, 399 U.S. 78, 133 (1970). *See also* Oregon v. Hass, 420 U.S. 714, 719 (1975).

4. People v. Krivda, 426 P.2d 1262 (Cal. 1971), *cert. denied,* 412 U.S. 919 (1973); Petitioner's Brief for Certiorari, id. at 7, 10–11.

5. *See* Brennan, "State Constitutions," p. 53.

6. For a general discussion, *see,* Henry R. Glick and Kenneth N. Vines, *State Court Systems* (Englewood Cliffs, N.J.: Prentice-Hall, 1973). *See also* Ravin v. State, 537 P.2d 494 (Alaska 1975), esp. 501.

7. Charles L. Black, Jr., *The People and the Court* (New York: Macmillan, 1960), pp. 88–89.

8. Harris v. New York, 410 U.S. 22 (1971), *modified,* Miranda v. Arizona, 384 U.S. 436 (1966). People v. Disbrow, 545 P.2d 272, 280 (Cal. 1976), followed Miranda. State v. Johnson, 346 A.2d 66, 68 n.2 (N.J. 1975), rejected Schenckloth v. Bustamonte, 412 U.S. 218 (1973). People v. Jackson, 217 N.W. 2d 22, 27–28 (Mich. 1974), rejected Kirby v. Illinois, 406 U.S. 682 (1972). Scott v. State, 519 P.2d 774, 783–85 (Alaska 1974), rejected Williams v. Florida, *supra* note 3.

9. California v. Byers, 402 U.S. 424 (1971); California v. Green 399 U.S. 149 (1970); Michigan v. Bloss, 413 U.S. 909 (1973); Michigan v. Payne, 412 U.S. 47 (1973); Wilkes, "The New Federalism," pp. 433–34.

10. People v. Anderson, 483 P.2d 880 (Cal. 1972), *cert. denied,* 405 U.S. 958 (1972); Petitioner's Brief for Certiorari, id. at 11.

11. People v. Triggs, 506 P.2d 232, 237 n.5 (Cal. 1973).

12. On segregation, *see* Milliken v. Bradley, *supra* note 2; Crawford v. Board of Education, 551 P.2d 28 (Cal. 1976). On probation, *see* Morrissey v. Brewer, 408 U.S. 471 (1972); People v. Vickers, 503 P.2d 1313 (Cal. 1972). *See also* "Civil Rights in the Burger Court Era," *Akron Law Review* 10 (1976): 360, 363.

13. On poverty, *see* Serrano v. Priest I, 487 P.2d 1241 (Cal. 1971); San Antonio Independent School District v. Rodriguez, 411 U.S. 1 (1973). On sex, *see* Sail'er Inn v. Kirby, 485 P.2d 529 (Cal. 1971); Frontiero v. Richardson, 411 U.S. 677 (1973). On antimiscegenation, *see* Loving v. Virginia, 388 U.S. 1 (1967); Perez v. Lippold, 198 P.2d 17 (Cal. 1948). On death penalty, *see* Furman v. Georgia 408 U.S. 238 (1972); People v. Anderson, *supra* note 10. On abortion, *see* Roe v. Wade, 410 U.S. 113 (1973); Doe v. Bolton, 410 U.S. 179 (1973); People v. Barksdale, 503 P.2d 275 (Cal. 1972).

14. People v. Triggs, *supra* note 11; "People v. Triggs, A New Concept of Privacy in Search and Seizure Law," *Hastings Law Journal* 25 (1974): 575–601; *In re* Quinlan, 355 A.2d 647 (N.J. 1976).

15. Southern Burlington County N.A.A.C.P. v. Township of Mt. Laurel, 336 A.2d 713 (N.J. 1971); Bakke v. Regents of the University of California, 533 P.2d 1152 (Cal. 1976). The U.S. Supreme Court, while upholding the principle of affirmative action, held that Bakke should be admitted to the medical school at Davis; 438 U.S. 265 (1978).

16. Serrano v. Priest I, *supra* note 13, at 1244; Robinson v. Cahill I, 303 A.2d 273 (N.J. 1973); id. VII, 339 A.2d 193 (N.J. 1975); Serrano v. Priest II, 557 P.2d 929 (Cal. 1976); *New York Times*, February, 2, 1977, p. 1, col. 1; Southern Burlington County N.A.A.C.P. v. Township of Mt. Laurel, *supra* note 15.

17. Ravin v. State, *supra* note 6; People v. Sinclair, 194 N.W. 2d 878 (Mich. 1972); *In re* Quinlan, *supra* note 14.

18. "Project Report," pp. 307–12; quoted in Richard Lehne, *The Quest for Justice: The Politics of School Finance Reform* (New York: Longman, 1978), pp. 53, 43. This work provides a superb analysis of the Robinson case and its aftermath.

19. Donald R. Wright, "The Role of the Judiciary: From Marbury to Anderson," *California Law Review* 60 (1972): 1267.

20. *See generally* Herbert Jacob and Kenneth N. Vines, "State Courts and Public Policy," in *Politics in the American States,* ed. Herbert Jacob and Kenneth N. Vines (Boston: Little, Brown & Co., 1976), pp. 242–68; John A. C. Hetherington, "State Economic Regulation and Substantive Due Process of Law," *Northwestern University Law Review* 53 (1958): 226–51; Hans A. Linde, "Judges, Critics and the Realist Tradition," *Yale Law Journal* 82 (1972): 227–55; Howard, "State Courts"; Robert A. Kagan et al., "The Business of State Supreme Courts, 1870–1970," *Stanford Law Review* 30 (1977): 121–56, 155.

21. San Antonio Independent School District v. Rodriguez, *supra* note 13; Serrano v. Priest I, *supra* note 13. "It is one of the happy incidents of the federal system that a single courageous state may . . . serve as a laboratory, and try novel social and economic experiments without risk to the country," Justice Brandeis dissenting in New State Ice Co. v. Liebmann, 285 U.S. 262, 311 (1932).

22. Miranda v. Arizona, *supra* note 8; Omnibus Crime Control and Safe Streets Act, 18 U.S.C., sec. 921 (1968); Ronald Blubaugh, "The Mosk Doctrine," *The California Journal* (May 1976): 154.

23. Harris v. New York, *supra* note 8; People v. Disbrow, *supra* note 8, at 284–85. For further criticism, *see* George Deukmejian and Clifford K. Thompson, Jr., "All Sail and No Anchor—Judicial Review Under the California Constitution," *Hastings Constitutional Law Quarterly* 6 (Summer 1979): 975–1010; Ronald K. L. Collins and Robert C. Welsh, "The California Constitution Turns into a Political Ploy," *Los Angeles Times,* July 17, 1980, pt. 2, p. 7. For one justice's defense of the California high court's interpretation of the state constitution, *see* Ronald K. L. Collins and Robert C. Welsh, "An Interview with Stanley Mosk," *The Western Law Journal* (March-April 1981): 1–9.

24. People v. Anderson, *supra* note 10; *In re* Anderson, 447 P.2d 117, 130 (Cal. 1968); People v. Aikens, 450 P.2d 258 (Cal. 1969), *cert. denied,* 403 U.S. 952 (1971); discussion based on Edward L. Barrett, Jr., "Anderson and the Judicial Function," *Southern California Law Review* 45 (1972): 739–49.

25. Rockewell v. Superior Court, 556 P.2d 1101 (Cal. 1977); Furman v. Georgia, *supra* note 13.

26. Robinson v. Cahill VII, *supra* note 16, at 204.

27. Southern Burlington County N.A.A.C.P. v. Township of Mt. Laurel, *supra* note 15, at 734.

28. Ralph Lerner, "The Supreme Court as Republican Schoolmaster," *The Supreme Court Review 1967*: 127–80; Eugene Rostow, "The Democratic Character of Judicial Review," *Harvard Law Review* 66 (1959): 193–209; Archibald Cox, *The Role of the Supreme Court in American Government* (New York: Oxford University Press, 1976), pp. 117–18.

29. Linde, "Judges, Critics," p. 248.

30. Ibid., pp. 251–54; Hans A. Linde, "Book Review," *Oregon Law Review* 52 (1973): 330, 333. Howard made a similar point, "State Courts," pp. 933–44.

31. Art. 1, sec. 5; Harold Norris, "A 'Freedom of Expression' in the New Constitution," *Detroit Lawyer* 31 (1963): 190–91.

32. Linde, "Book Review."

33. Serrano v. Priest I, *supra* note 13, at 1249 n.11; Serrano v. Priest II, *supra* note 16, at 947–52; San Antonio Independent School District v. Rodriguez, *supra* note 13.

34. Hans A. Linde, "Without 'Due Process': Unconstitutional Law in Oregon," *Oregon Law Review* 49 (1970): 146.

35. Chief Justice Wright's view of the decision in "The Role of the Judiciary," p. 1272; People v. Anderson, *supra* note 10.

36. Baker v. City of Fairbanks, 471 P.2d 386 (Alaska 1970).

37. Duncan v. Louisiana, 391 U.S. 145 (1968).

38. Baker v. City of Fairbanks, *supra* note 36, at 401–2; "Constitutional Law—Petty Offender's Right to Demand Trial by Jury: Petty Offenders Have Peers in Alaska—Baker v. City of Fairbanks," *Washington Law Review* 46 (1971): 827–36.

39. People v. Brisendine, 531 P.2d 1099, 1113–14 (Cal. 1975); Gustafson v. Florida, *supra* note 2. For a discussion, *see* Wilkes, "The New Federalism," pp. 311–14.

40. People v. Bloss, 201 N.W. 2d 806 (Mich. 1972); id., 228 N.W. 2d 384 (Mich. 1975); Miller v. California, *supra* note 2; Michigan v. Bloss, *supra* note 9.

41. John M. Burkoff and Victor J. Adamo, "Obscenity Under the Michigan Constitution: Protected Expression?" *Michigan State Bar Journal* 54 (1975): 964.

42. Cox, *Role of the Supreme Court.*

43. Breese v. Smith, 501 P.2d 159, 167 (Ala. 1972); Karr v. Schmidt, 401 U.S. 1201 (1971).

44. *In re* Quinlan, *supra* note 14, at 665; William F. Hyland and David S. Baume, "In Re Quinlan: A Synthesis of Law and Medical Technology," *Rutgers-Camden Law Journal* 8 (1976): 37–64.

45. Howard, "State Courts," pp. 941–42.

46. *In re* Quinlan, *supra* note 14, at 664.

47. Howard, "State Courts," p. 941.

48. Warren E. Burger, "The Interdependence of Our Freedoms," *Akron Law Review* 9 (1976): 403, 404.

2.

STANLEY H. FRIEDELBAUM

Independent State Grounds: Contemporary Invitations to Judicial Activism

Since the early years of the Burger Court, there has been a renewed interest in the prospects for the state court creativity. Considerable attention has been directed to the provisions of state bills of rights, whether linguistically distinct from or identical to federal counterparts. A number of states have fashioned a collection of "new" rights limited, in most instances, to qualified redefinitions of privacy and personal autonomy. Although the pace and scope of doctrinal advances do not always suggest the opening of a major era of libertarian activism, neither does the inventory of guarantees devised so far merely point to a succession of transient precedents.

Apart from this recent flurry of decisions, the work of the state courts remains more closely linked to the patterns of the past. It is in the conventional case law that the doctrine of independent state grounds has found recurring expression. Before the nationalization of the federal Bill of Rights, litigants were obliged to seek state rather than federal avenues of redress. The topical range has been broad, extending from familiar guarantees of personal liberties to less conspicuous safeguards affecting civil rights, economic enterprise, and property relationships.

The essential duality of the American adjudicatory process is a basic feature of the political system. The U.S. Supreme Court is precluded from reviewing state judgments unless federal questions are involved. But the mere infusion of a federal issue will not prompt scrutiny by the Court if "independent" and "adequate" state grounds are found to exist. By judicial definition, the determination in any case turns on the sufficiency of the state-law foundation on which the decision has been premised, the extent to which the nonfederal question may be viewed as independent, and the degree to which the state-related issue or issues are capable of being maintained without "fair or substantial support" in federal law.

As these principles have been developed and applied, it is clear that state courts are free to accept or to reject federal standards as long as the constitutional source is essentially state derived. Yet the state grounds set forth must be of sufficient cogency to sustain the judgment announced without any notable dependence on the federal question. Additionally, the state grounds must not be so intertwined with the federal ground as to compromise the independence of the former. Problems of ambiguity, tied to these equivocal guidelines, often will be resolved in favor of state independence, since the justices traditionally have tried to avoid charges that they have exceeded their assigned authority.[1]

In recent years, the Supreme Court has held that the adequate state ground rule is jurisdictional. Thus when state questions are dispositive, no case or controversy exists within the meaning of Article III of the federal Constitution, and any opinion rendered will be advisory. Such a pronouncement can have no binding effect "if the same judgment would be rendered by the state court after . . . [the Supreme Court] . . . corrected its views of federal laws."[2] Viewed in this light, the adequate state ground rule serves to insulate the state decision from *any* federal review. Nevertheless, the Supremacy Clause requires that the state ground advanced not be contrary to federally guaranteed rights. Minimal protective levels, established by the U.S. Supreme Court, may be surpassed. But they cannot be diluted or eroded by defiance of federal mandates or by an adroit construction of conflicting state charter provisions.[3]

As the Burger Court has begun to take on a distinct identity, the adequate state ground rule has emerged as one of the major components underlying judicial reasoning and strategy. The chief justice and other recent appointees have affirmed the advantages of ensuring an opportunity for state discretion and creativity. Justice Lewis Powell, in a concurring opinion, once referred to the values of experimentation and "imagination unimpeded by unwarranted demands for national uniformity."[4] Subsequently, when Powell wrote for the Court in a case challenging a state's system of financing public education, he rejected pleas for federal intervention coupled with a cautionary note that the Court was not placing its "imprimatur on the status quo" or denying the need for reforms initiated by individual states.[5] Justice Harry Blackmun, in an obscenity proceeding, noted his agreement with Justice John Harlan's earlier call for standards "capable of some flexibility and resting on concepts of reasonableness."[6]

To the same end but for different reasons, the proponents of a "new" federalism have been joined, more often in dissent, by holdover representatives of the Warren Court. The Supreme Court's emphasis has shifted from an overriding reliance on federal rights and their expansion to a studied deference to the state judiciaries and their products. Justices William Brennan and Thurgood Marshall, in particular, have openly urged the states to participate spiritedly in defense of what they regard as much beleaguered liberties. When a majority sustained a warrantless station house search of an automobile contrary to a state court's reversal of the conviction on Fourth Amendment grounds, Justice Marshall counseled that "it should be clear to the court below that nothing this Court does today precludes it from reaching the result it did under applicable state law."[7] Adding to a growing list of "suggestions," Brennan pointedly reminded state judges in a prisoner rights case that a state constitutional counterpart to a federal guarantee is not always needed, since a similar result might be reached as a matter of public policy.[8] He subsequently advised attorneys that the risks of not raising state law questions in state courts were "increasingly substantial."[9] Justice Brennan responded to the majority's narrowing of reputational interests under the Fourteenth Amendment by recommending that the quest for higher standards be pursued by state judges "more sensitive than is this Court to the privacy and other interests of individuals."[10]

A sampling of recent cases points to a revitalization and often an amplification of state safeguards. Doubtless, a nationwide survey would reveal that poor performance persists alongside creative productivity. By any measure, the reach of the most dramatic of state rulings necessarily is limited. Yet on the positive side, the work of activist-oriented state courts, possessed of strong common law or public policy traditions, deserves attention. The precedents established, when indicative of judicial ingenuity, are impressive and of more than passing or parochial significance. Should shared state or local issues be involved, the decisional impact clearly will transcend state boundaries and affect the resolution of like questions throughout the country.

Recent state cases fall into three categories. The first category includes areas of traditional state concern. The judicial products reveal a variety of techniques: a choice and "interpretation" of applicable federal precedents, artifices of old-style evasion, and occasionally the assumption of a "subordinate" posture to the U.S. Supreme Court that suggests some need to shunt responsibility to the national level. In the second category, the stratagem of building on minimal federally derived guarantees represents a latter-day, although not unexpected, departure in the annals of judicial activism. Of particular interest are cases extending greater protection to the criminally accused than federal precedents now afford. A third category concerns the evolution of essentially novel rights. State appellate courts in California, New Jersey, Hawaii, and Alaska have contributed substantively and substantially to the formulation of expanding concepts of liberty and equality. However, none of these courts exhibits a wholly consistent record in promoting individual rights. By the same token, courts in other states have made significant—if more modest—contributions.

TRADITIONAL MODES, UNCERTAIN RESULTS

In the wake of the Warren Court's far-reaching decisions, evasive techniques reached new levels of expertise. Outright denials of the applicability
of the Bill of Rights to the states were rare, since a theory of selective
"incorporation" had been tacitly accepted for several decades. Nevertheless, as late as 1975, the Supreme Court of Utah, alluding to an "almost
unbelievable arrogation of power by and to the federal government,"
asserted that the first eight amendments were solely limitations on Congress and the national government.[11]

Although few state courts supported this extravagant claim, compliance
with the Federal Supreme Court's opinions has not always been literal or
exacting. State courts pick and choose among federally derived precedents, sometimes even encouraged by the Federal Court, as in the economic regulatory area.[12] In addition, state judges have placed their own
glosses on doctrines in the absence of overt signs of defiance.[13] The
controversy over prescription-drug advertising, for example, raised significant questions concerning the reach of First Amendment guarantees to
protect commercial speech. Although the Supreme Court followed a reasonably predictable road, and a Virginia case raising essentially the same
issues had been accepted for review, the New York Court of Appeals
sustained a state regulation prohibiting the advertising of discount prescription-drug prices.[14] The state court cited with approval a federal district court's conclusion that "purely commercial speech—whatever may
be the scope of that term—does not enjoy constitutional protection."[15]
Five months later, the U.S. Supreme Court decided otherwise, ruling that
a Virginia law banning prescription-drug advertising violated the First
Amendment. Justice Blackmun, who wrote for the Court, emphasized that
the "notion of unprotected 'commercial speech' [had] all but passed from
the scene" a year earlier.[16]

State courts also have considerable discretion in choosing applicable
precedents in economic regulatory cases. State judges often follow the
Supreme Court's policy of deference to legislative judgments in the economic area. Yet the application of a minimal "reasonableness" test may
give rise to a considerably more exacting appraisal of legislative motives
than occurs at the federal level.[17] New York's highest court, for example,
resorted to the due process clause of the state constitution to impose a
hearing requirement in a commercial lien case despite a contrary ruling by
the Federal Supreme Court in similar circumstances.[18] To like effect,
exclusionary zoning has been subjected to far more compelling tests of
egalitarianism than the Fourteenth Amendment exacts. A series of New
Jersey cases, beginning with the *Mt. Laurel Township* case,[19] have
attracted widespread attention in confining the reach of exclusive local
enclaves and in considering regional housing needs.

Close parallels sometimes exist between federal and state constitutional or statutory language.[20] Thus the results of a lawsuit may be made to turn not only upon the linguistic skill and "findings" of state judges but also upon the degree of insulation from or amenability to federal actions. The U.S. Supreme Court, early in December 1976, held that employers were not required to provide pregnancy-related disability benefits under Title VII of the Civil Rights Act of 1964.[21] Two weeks later New York's Court of Appeals declared that such payments were mandated by the state's Human Rights Law, the pertinent provisions of which, the court conceded, were "substantially identical" to those of the federal statute. The majority pointed out that the "determination of the Supreme Court, while instructive, is not binding on our court."[22] Contrary directions in the state's previously enacted disability-benefits law, which the court chose to label "dormant," had explicitly excluded pregnancy disability benefits from coverage.[23]

One of the most dramatic of recent contrasts between federal and state judicial outcomes, involving a critical shift in premises, arose from an assessment of the validity of the New York City Emergency Moratorium Act of 1975. The law postponed payment for three years on the principal of the city's short-term notes, offering the option of long-term securities. When the act was challenged in a federal district court, the moratorium was sustained against charges that it violated the Contract Clause of Article I, the Due Process and Equal Protection clauses of the Fourteenth Amendment, and the federal bankruptcy act. The court recognized the legislature's declaration of an emergency, and in the light of federal precedents dating from the 1930s, it found the statute to be a permissible exercise of the police power.[24] By contrast, New York's Court of Appeals, in a narrow opinion renouncing the suspension of constitutional principles even in periods of emergency, ruled that the moratorium denied "faith and credit" guaranteed by the state constitution.[25] Thus premised on independent state grounds, the court's action precluded any decision, linked to the national Constitution, that might have upheld the validity of the moratorium.

It is not difficult to detect the values that prevailed in the New York Court's treatment of the pregnancy disability controversy. Setting aside considerations of economic effect, a majority apparently was persuaded that the exclusion of coverage under an employer's income insurance plan represented clear-cut sex discrimination. Financial impact cannot dictate judicial outcome, the court stressed; "the eradication of sexual discrimination . . . will normally be expensive at least in the short run."[26] Less clear were the promptings of the state court's majority in the New York City moratorium case. Was the restoration of a measure of investor confidence in state and local obligations of such importance as to induce a draconian holding? Had not the experiences of the 1930s, and the permissive nature of Supreme Court responses in its interpretations of the Contract and Due Process clauses, established a persuasive model for one of the most publicized urban crises of the 1970s? To cushion the consequences of its potentially disruptive pronouncement, the state court postponed immediate relief to the noteholders, "which might give the city no choice except to proceed into bankruptcy."[27] Yet the enigma remained: Why, under the conditions noted, did "constitutional decency" require so drastic a remedy from a state tribunal when the federal-precedent alternative might better have served a beleaguered city's immediate interests?

The options available are not always as obvious as in the New York cases. Yet in a growing number of settings, especially those marked by the absence of persuasive precedents, the constitutional or statutory framework selected as a basis of decision may be crucial in terms of outcomes. One of these settings relates to the treatment of reverse or benign discrimination in American courts that, up to this point, have failed to produce definitive guidelines.[28] In fashioning standards, room exists for considerable discretion and even creativity. The U.S. Supreme Court had an opportunity to move toward a resolution of the divisive issues in 1974, but a majority elected not to reach the merits by invoking the doctrine of mootness. Justice Brennan, in dissent, condemned this vacillation with the observation that "few constitutional questions in recent history have stirred as much debate, and they will not disappear."[29]

The Supreme Court of California subsequently held that racial preferences in admissions to a state university's medical school were unconstitutional.[30] In doing so, it relied upon the Equal Protection Clause of the Fourteenth Amendment and familiar tests of strict scrutiny of racial classifications, compelling governmental interest, and alternative means. To hold otherwise, the majority concluded, "would call for the sacrifice of principle for the sake of dubious expediency and would represent a retreat in the struggle to assure that each man and woman shall be judged on the basis of individual merit alone."[31] It is not clear why an action premised solely on federal challenges and formulas was selected as the vehicle for a pronouncement of such moment. California's Supreme Court, renowned for its activism, has often ruled on independent state grounds to advance rights and liberties beyond the levels sanctioned by the U.S. Supreme Court. Possibly, the court deliberately chose a case linked to federally devised standards to avoid a state-insulated definitiveness otherwise pursued as a positive goal. Despite the hazards of an inquiry into judicial motives, it is at least conceivable that the state court uses independent state grounds to ensure "protected" results when such a course serves the predilections of a majority and, alternatively, moves exclusively federal grounds when it wants to shift difficult or emotionally charged issues to the U.S. Supreme Court.

The range of meanings associated with the Religion clauses of the federal and state constitutions has long been the basis of protracted debate. During the past several decades the Free Exercise and Establishment provisions of the First Amendment have come to prevail on an increasingly broad scale. The provisions exhibit implicit tensions, historic ambiguities, and, at times, conflicting interpretations derived from U.S. Supreme Court opinions. The current test relating to state aid programs under the Establishment Clause is essentially three pronged. Any assistance offered must have a secular legislative purpose, a primary effect that does not advance religion, and no proclivity to entangle the state excessively in religious affairs. The simplicity of the test criteria, despite refinements introduced from case to case, affords the Court a flexibility of responses in adapting to various factual settings. In recent cases, the test has been applied in a manner deferential to state programs, and subsidies to institutions of higher education, in particular, have been sustained with the sole proviso that the funds not be used for sectarian purposes.[32]

As noted earlier, federal standards need not bind state courts electing to rest their decisions on independent state grounds. Conveniently, the sparse language of the First Amendment can often be differentiated from the more explicit wording found in many state constitutions. Thus a textbook loan program that might have met federal standards was declared invalid by the Supreme Court of Nebraska when measured against the state constitution. The prevailing majority, without passing on Establishment Clause questions, found that the principle of separation exemplified in the state charter was more exacting than the standards enunciated by the Federal Supreme Court. The court noted that the guidelines to be followed were

whether there is a public appropriation, whether the grant is in aid of any sectarian or denominational school or college, and, perhaps, more importantly, the meaning of these two terms, if they would require any further definition, is fastened down unequivocally, fundamentally, and permanently by the statement that any educational institution which receives such aid must be exclusively owned and controlled by the state or a governmental subdivision thereof.[33]

By rejecting the notion that the student rather than the school was the actual recipient of public monies, the state court effectively eliminated the "child-benefit" theory that has traditionally served as a legitimating tool in federal litigation.[34] To like effect, the Supreme Judicial Court of Massachusetts insisted that an "anti-aid" amendment had to prevail despite countervailing values that might be promoted by nonpublic schools.[35]

That federal rulings have an important impact on state court interpretations (a part of the "interplay" in judicial federalism) was evident in a Missouri case sustaining the constitutionality of a program of tuition grants to students at public and private colleges.[36] The payments were made directly to the students to enable them to secure nonreligious educational services in institutions of their own choosing. Scattered throughout the state supreme court's opinion were references to a Maryland case in which the Federal Supreme Court had sustained the payment of state funds to private institutions of higher education, the sole caveat being that the monies not be spent for sectarian purposes.[37] When the dissenters in the Missouri case pressed the point that the state constitutional prohibitions were more restrictive than the First Amendment, the majority responded by citing federal precedents differentiating higher education from parochial elementary-secondary school cases and by rejecting state-derived "public purpose" objections with obscure allusions to societal progress and betterment coupled with the need for judicial deference to the "will of the people."[38] The state's chief justice, in dissent, rejoined that he could

not see how the granting . . . of public funds to a student can be treated as a grant to the people of the state so as to avoid being a grant to a private person and also at the same time be treated as a direct grant to the student so as to avoid being an appropriation in aid of any religious creed, church or sectarian purpose of a private college.[39]

In a subsequent ruling, the same court held that federal funds, paid to the state under a program to assist educationally deprived children attending elementary and secondary schools, were subject to prohibitions barring the use of public monies to provide textbooks or to support on-the-premises instruction in sectarian schools.[40]

Symbolic displays commemorating religious holidays and the question of Sunday sales have occasioned considerable controversy. The *Los Angeles* and *Eugene* cross cases proved to be inconclusive in establishing usable guidelines applicable to seasonal exhibitions.[41] In like manner, since the Federal Supreme Court upheld Sunday closing laws almost two decades ago, little has occurred in the state courts to replace the ambivalence that has marked this troubled area.[42] Among the recent cases, a reliance on independent state grounds has served as a basis for holdings of unconstitutionality related to arbitrary and unreasonable classifications.[43] Contrary findings, in response to similar challenges, have been premised largely on federal equal-protection standards.[44] Developmental patterns remain as equivocal now as they were in an earlier era when objections to religious representations were less frequently and exactingly advanced.

The direction of the Religion Clause decisions is consistent with the traditional pattern of independent state determinations. Despite an outward mien of disharmony and evidence of divergency from the federal norms, the ambiguity of the U.S. Supreme Court's criteria permits the doctrinal diversity exhibited. The minimum guarantees flowing from the First and Fourteenth Amendments have not been weakened. It would be extravagant to claim that the different positions assumed by the state courts contravene federal rights. Viewed in terms of acknowledged First Amendment "tensions," if the denial of publicly supplied textbooks to parochial school pupils runs contrary to free exercise, it is equally indicative of a fidelity to the purposes of the Establishment provision. A parallel argument, albeit inverted, can be made regarding judicial findings in support of state aid for those attending denominational colleges. The tendency to shield state-court decisions from federal review is not compelling in these cases; instead, the notion of a federal-state conceptual intermeshing seems relevant. Considerations of national supremacy, often prominent in litigation attendant upon the Commerce and Taxation clauses, are misplaced in relation to the First Amendment's Religion clauses. A like latitude of choice and action exists in regard to the fashioning of standards in other areas descriptive of human freedoms, but causal factors, at times, are more closely identified with any overt effort to avoid the Federal Supreme Court's criteria.

EXTENSIONS OF THE FEDERAL MODEL

The notion of enlarging upon federal safeguards is attributable to concerns articulated by members of the U.S. Supreme Court as well as to assertive state judges intent upon ensuring the autonomy and distinctiveness of their courts. Both Justices Harlan and Warren Burger have stressed that a federal posture of unobtrusiveness should prevail in measuring states' criminal procedures by national standards. Burger, among others, has emphasized the importance of permitting state experimentation and innovation, particularly in the criminal justice area. During the 1970s, it appears, assurances of a broad discretion for the states became central in the Supreme Court's disposition of criminal cases.

Parallels exist between current attitudes toward state "enlargement" and approaches to the protection of Fourteenth Amendment rights during the mid-1960s. When the state-action concept reached the outer limits of its utility in advancing civil rights, the Court, in effect, extended an invitation to Congress to move beyond judicial definitions of equal protection and due process. A majority characterized the Enforcement Clause of the Fourteenth Amendment as a "positive grant of legislative power authorizing Congress to exercise its discretion in determining whether and what legislation is needed" to secure the guarantees described.[45] Yet as in the criminal justice area today, minimum federal standards continued to apply and, in all respects, remained inviolable.

The states have explored various criteria for adopting standards higher than those of the U.S. Supreme Court. A fundamental question recurs: is more stringent protection permissible only in limited circumstances when supported by a clearly delineated and perhaps an exceptional rationale? This view, rejected in Alaska, California, Hawaii, and New Jersey, is said to assume that a state's highest court serves as the functional equivalent of an intermediate appellate tribunal. To the contrary, the Supreme Court of California has emphatically declared, "in the area of fundamental civil liberties . . . we sit as a court of last resort, subject only to the qualification that our interpretations may not restrict the guarantees accorded the national citizenry under the federal charter." The first referent is state law and the rights that have developed under it.[46] The New Jersey Supreme Court has asserted that stricter standards control "as a matter of state law and policy" without respect to final determinations in the federal sphere.[47] In this regard, the Alaska Supreme Court has taken it to be its duty to enunciate additional personal safeguards "necessary for the kind of civilized life and ordered liberty which is at the core of our constitutional heritage."[48]

The fashioning of doctrinal extensions beyond federal minima is not restricted to the criminal law area. With respect to economic regulation, the Federal Supreme Court's permissiveness, almost tantamount to abdication, has encouraged the states to select the standards to be applied. The choices open to state judges are undeniably broad; whatever may be the current direction taken by the U.S. Supreme Court, the states remain free to accept, reject, or redefine traditional tests geared to local conditions and needs. A like discretion derives from the Supreme Court's language in the 1973 obscenity cases sanctioning contemporary community standards in judging arguably pornographic materials, thereby easing the local prosecutor's evidentiary burden and spurning any design to "propose regulatory schemes for the States."[49]

Judicial efforts to ensure access to migrant labor camps located on an employer's property have also raised important questions affecting First Amendment interests. In one instance permissible restraints were measured against federal guarantees combined with "independent scrutiny" tied to relevant provisions of the state constitution.[50] In another, First Amendment and other federal claims were set aside in favor of a decision in nonconstitutional terms that a state supreme court considered "more satisfactory, because the interests of migrant workers are more expansively served . . . than they would be if they had no more freedom than these constitutional concepts could be found to mandate."[51]

The Supreme Court of California has elaborated upon federal equal-protection analysis affecting "fundamental interests." Where applicable, such analysis subjects legislative classifications to a strict scrutiny that seriously undermines the general presumption of validity attaching to governmental action. It is the state that must establish a compelling interest and the necessity of the distinctions created to advance its purpose. Apart from the Fourteenth Amendment, although not contrary to its intent, the California Court has designated fundamental interests that range beyond those that figure in federal determinations. Such interests, selected independently, include education,[52] the right of the accused to a postindictment preliminary hearing,[53] unanimous jury verdicts in criminal cases,[54] and the holding of public office.[55]

As a part of an effort to enhance the quality of public education, the California decision in *Serrano* v. *Priest* represented a major step toward the reformation of local school finance systems.[56] The court held that the state's denial of equal educational opportunity, linked to discrimination on the basis of district wealth, violated equal protection. In a subsequent ruling, the justices made explicit the decision's grounding in the state constitution and affirmed a lower court ruling requiring compliance within a specified period.[57] The New Jersey Supreme Court premised similar findings of invalidity on an obscure constitutional clause providing for the "maintenance and support of a thorough and efficient system" of public education.[58] When the legislature failed to implement a statute intended to correct past inequities, the court enjoined the expenditure of school funds until the enactment of the state's first income tax law.[59] Less dramatic, although equally compelling, actions followed in a number of states with varying results.[60]

In addition to enlarging the list of fundamental interests, the California Supreme Court has developed several categories of rights that are considered vested and that trigger an independent judgment standard of review. Such rights require a trial court, by force of the constitutional separation of powers, to use its independent judgment in evaluating disputed facts, rather than merely to sustain, in a deferential manner, the determinations of administrative agencies as long as such findings are supported by substantial evidence. Rights falling within the preferred class, thereby invoking an independent standard of review, encompass statutory retirement benefits, the right to continued unemployment compensation benefits, the right to continued welfare benefits, the right to pursue a profession or trade, and job reinstatement. To qualify as vested, a right must be one "already possessed" or "legitimately acquired." In deciding whether a right is "fundamental," courts "do not alone weigh the economic aspect of it, but the effect of it in human terms and the importance of it to the individual in the life situation."[61]

As federal equal-protection analysis has been adapted to and, at critical points, parallels the development of fundamental interests and rights, so points of confluence exist and mutually complement federal and state pronouncements in the area of criminal law. An overwhelming majority of state courts unreservedly observe and follow precedents established by the U.S. Supreme Court.[62] At times even an activist tribunal like the California Supreme Court may take advantage of minimum federal standards.[63] Yet it remains for departures from the general rule of conformity to offer glimpses of a creative judicial federalism in action.

The least variance from accepted norms can be expected to occur when judges premise their findings on a nonconstitutional foundation. Courts in New Jersey, Rhode Island, and Wisconsin have asserted a nonstatutory power to review sentences that are alleged to be excessive. In doing so, they rely on an appellate court's general supervisory control of lower tribunals.[64] A cognate source of authority takes as its predicate the exercise of supervisory authority over state criminal procedure. On this basis, trial courts in California have been required to offer reasons for the denial of bail on appeal.[65] A more expansive resort to "inherent" supervisory powers over the lower courts of California has produced an exclusionary rule barring the introduction to testimony provided at a probation revocation hearing, except for certain limited purposes, when related criminal charges are preferred in subsequent proceedings.[66] To insure a "sound" and "enlightened" administration of justice, the reasoning goes, courts need not limit their demands for procedural fairness to the "rudimentary rather than the reasonable." The plain intent of the rule is to discourage the initiation of a probation revocation action until the criminal trial has been completed.

Judicial intervention, premised directly upon applicable state constitutional provisions, has been designed to offset recent Federal Supreme Court decisions narrowing Fourth Amendment protection against "unreasonable" searches and seizures and closely related Fifth Amendment safeguards against self-incrimination. As before, minimal federal standards are acknowledged but with an emphatic reservation of authority, founded on independent state grounds, to elaborate upon individual rights beyond current interpretations of what the national Constitution provides. If the theory of selective incorporation of the federal Bill of Rights is accepted with respect to federal adjudications, there are assertions of a concomitant responsibility on the part of the states to afford a higher level of protection when "local conditions" warrant. Alaska, California, and Hawaii have assumed positions of leadership in this regard, although, from time to time other states have joined in the quest for a modification of specific Burger Court decisions. As early as 1967 Justice Hugo Black, writing for a majority in *Cooper* v. *California,* stressed the power of a state "to impose higher standards on searches and seizures than required by the Federal Constitution if it chooses to do so." Black continued:

when such state standards alone have been violated, the State is free, without review by us, to apply its own state harmless-error rule [generally a holding of principle that a trial-court error not prejudicial to the defendant's rights does not require reversal] to such errors of state law.[67]

The Federal Supreme Court's articulation of what has come to be referred to as the *Robinson-Gustafson* rule[68] precipitated cogent responses from courts in several states. Justice William Rehnquist's opinion held that a custodial arrest, based on probable cause, represented a "reasonable intrusion" and authority for a search under the Fourth Amendment. The sweeping nature of the Court's pronouncement led Justice Marshall, joined in dissent by Justices William Douglas and Brennan, to cite contrary findings drawn from the case law of the states.

Prospectively, the Supreme Court of Hawaii was among the first to express opposition to the *Robinson-Gustafson* guidelines. Despite textually parallel provisions in the state and federal Bills of Rights, the Hawaii Court diverged sharply from the federal model with repeated references to the need to preserve privacy and individual integrity.[69] To like effect, the Supreme Court of California imposed a state-derived standard permitting no more than a weapons search in a traffic violation arrest. Scrutiny was limited to a "pat-down prior to transporting the defendant in the patrol vehicle."[70] The burden of justifying a warrantless search rested with the prosecution.[71] Full body searches at the scene might not be conducted in California when individuals were arrested for public intoxication[72] and, more generally, "when the person is arrested for an offense for which he will merely be cited or released on bail."[73] The Supreme Court of Alaska also held unjustifiable a warrantless general inventory search incident to an arrest where the prisoner could satisfy the conditions necessary to secure his release and where the charges against him did not require evidence that could be hidden on his person.[74]

The U.S. Supreme Court described the requirements of a "consent search," when the subject is not in custody, as importing no more than a showing that consent was "in fact voluntarily given, and not the result of duress or coercion, express or implied."[75] A majority, speaking through Justice Potter Stewart, denied that a knowing and intelligent waiver was necessary to establish the validity of the search. If the subject's knowledge of a right to refuse consent was among the elements that needed to be weighed, the Court pointed out, the prosecution was not compelled to demonstrate such knowledge to establish voluntary consent. By contrast, Justice Marshall's dissent shifted the essential point of the inquiry to the question whether the subject knew, as a matter of meaningful choice, that he had a right to refuse consent. Thus consent was to be measured in terms of waiver and not, as the majority insisted, by reference to a test of voluntariness long associated with confessions.[76]

It was the waiver standard that the Supreme Court of New Jersey elected to adopt under the search-and-seizure provision of the state constitution.[77] Despite the fact that the state constitutional language was taken almost verbatim from the Fourth Amendment, the New Jersey court asserted a right to construe the wording "in accordance with what we conceive to be its plain meaning."[78] The result was to place the burden on the state to demonstrate knowledge of a right to refuse consent, thereby pursuing the route traveled by Justice Marshall in dissent rather than the one followed by Justice Stewart for the Court.

The degree to which the sanctity of the home can be made to serve as a bulwark against warrantless arrests has been explored in a variety of contexts. State court decisions averse to such arrests emphasize that intrusions into an individual's dwelling implicate the Fourth Amendment's protection of privacy more critically than arrests in a public place. In a 1975 Massachusetts case, the state's highest court held that the police carry the burden of demonstrating "exigent circumstances excusing the lack of a warrant" when the home is invaded.[79] The Supreme Court of California expressed substantial agreement with its Massachusetts counterpart that "in the absence of a bona fide emergency, or consent to enter, police action in seizing the individual in the home must be preceded by the judicial authorization of an arrest warrant." The majority's highly selective use of Supreme Court precedents and dicta prompted a dissenter on the California Court to remark that "deference toward the United States Supreme Court is fast becoming a shell game."[80]

Few judicially contrived restraints on law-enforcement techniques have excited as much contention as the exclusionary rule. In 1961 the Supreme Court imposed the rule as a limitation on the states.[81] The addition of the *Miranda* safeguards five years later supplemented the roster of claims on which exclusion might be based.[82] What emerged from a vast judicial literature examining the exclusionary rule was recognition of a deterrent rationale, that is, the expectation that the suppression of evidence would serve to persuade law enforcement officials of the fruitlessness of conducting unlawful searches and seizures.

In the appellate courts of the states, one of the most divisive of the Federal Supreme Court's decisions limiting the reach of the *Miranda* guarantees was *Harris* v. *New York*. A majority in *Harris* declined to bar a statement, concededly inadmissible as affirmative evidence in a criminal trial, from use for impeachment purposes.[83] The Supreme Court of Hawaii, premising its action on the self-incrimination clause of the state constitution, departed from *Harris* because of what it termed a "countervailing value of protecting the accused's privilege to freely choose whether or not to incriminate himself."[84] In similar fashion, Pennsylvania's highest court refused to follow *Harris* as a precedent.[85] By contrast, the Supreme Judicial Court of Massachusetts rejected any invitation to "adopt the reasoning of the dissenting justices in [*Harris*]."[86] The New Jersey Supreme Court initially concluded that *Harris* provided a "valuable truth-finding mechanism" and that the decision had been anticipated in the state.[87] A year later the same court was more cautious in its endorsement when, in changed circumstances, it chose to impose a "stricter standard as a matter of state law."[88]

The most intense of the debates over *Harris* occurred in the Supreme Court of California. That court had long been sensitive to the proprieties of the receipt of evidence, having adopted the exclusionary rule six years before *Mapp* v. *Ohio* "[o]ut of regard for its own dignity as an agency of justice and custodian of liberty."[89] Following the decision in *Harris,* a bare majority of the California Supreme Court accepted its rationale as the law in the state.[90] But not unexpectedly, the court adhered to *Harris* only briefly; in 1976 it overruled its previous holding. A majority took pains to reaffirm a duty to protect the rights of California's citizens on independent grounds.[91] To the contrary, a lengthy dissent deplored the implications of the majority's course with the terse notation that "they pursue this new bearing when it is very apparent that the parade is marching in the other direction."[92]

Somewhat analogous to the role of the exclusionary rule in discouraging police misconduct was an inventive application of due process principles. The Court of Appeals of New York, acting on independent state grounds, dismissed an indictment on the basis of a finding that the defendant had been enticed into violating the law. The case involved what the court referred to as an "incredible geographical shell game"—police deceit designed to lure a Pennsylvania resident across the state border in an area where the markings were unclear. In forcible language not often associated with appellate review of law-enforcement procedures, a majority condemned the tactics employed as brazen, dishonest, and improper. The court sought to allay fears that a resort to due process presaged an "unmanageable subjectivity,"[93] although the potential for judicial excesses plainly existed.

The guarantee against double jeopardy, among the last of the provisions of the Bill of Rights to be made enforceable against the states,[94] has its counterpart in most of the state constitutions. Yet the interpretations of this protection have been legion. In a contemporary setting, questions have arisen concerning the bases of foreclosing prosecutions deriving from what some courts describe as a single criminal episode and what others refer to as a series of criminal acts occurring simultaneously or sequentially. Is the state precluded from proceeding against an accused by way of multiple prosecutions premised on the division of an incident into the several separate offenses that may have been committed? Or must the charges be joined at one trial to prevent possible harassment of the defendant and to promote the ends of justice?

The United States Supreme Court examined a growing catalog of tests in *Ashe* v. *Swenson*,[95] a case involving the robbery of participants in a poker game by three or four masked men. One of the accused, having been acquitted of a charge of theft against a player, was subsequently convicted of having robbed another. Yet a jury had found reasonable doubt that he was one of the thieves at all. This meant, in effect, that the same issue was being relitigated at a new trial. As Justice Potter Stewart wrote for the majority, the state "could not present the same or different identification evidence in a second prosecution . . . in the hope that a different jury might find that evidence more convincing."[96] The Court applied the doctrine of collateral estoppel as an ingredient of the double jeopardy safeguard. Viewing the principle with "realism and rationality," Justice Stewart continued, it connotes that once an "issue of ultimate fact" has been determined "by a valid and final judgment, that issue cannot again be litigated between the same parties in any further lawsuit."[97]

In a number of state courts, Justice Brennan's concurring opinion in *Ashe* has served as the focal point of a continuing debate over the meaning of *double jeopardy*. While Brennan joined the Court's inclusion of collateral estoppel as a constitutional requirement, he proceeded to weigh the merits of two of the most discussed alternatives in double jeopardy cases— the "same-evidence" and the "same-transaction" tests. The former bars a second charge only if the evidence necessary to sustain it would have sufficed to support a conviction on the first charge. Justice Brennan was sharply critical of the "same-evidence" standard as conducive to "multiple prosecutions for an essentially unitary criminal episode." In its place he urged the adoption of the "same-transaction" test requiring the prosecution to join at a single trial all of the charges that arise from a "single criminal act, occurrence, episode, or transaction." Justice Brennan described the latter test not only as best preserving the protective design of the Double Jeopardy Clause but also as promoting "justice, economy, and convenience."[98]

The Supreme Court of Pennsylvania endorsed and applied the same-transaction test, although, in its initial opinion, the basis of the decision was ambiguous.[99] On the prosecutor's petition, the Federal Supreme Court remanded for consideration whether the judgment was based on federal or state constitutional grounds or a combination of both.[100] The state court, in turn, reaffirmed its adherence to the single-transaction test and moved to insulate its findings through references to "state law determinations" and the court's supervisory power over state criminal proceedings.[101] The prosecutor's second effort to secure Federal Supreme Court review was rejected,[102] thereby reinforcing the supposition that the justices are not prone to question the designation of a state predicate leading to a result contrary to federal precedents even when evasive intent is suspected.

New Jersey's Supreme Court, in an exhaustive reassessment of the prohibition against double jeopardy, adopted the same-transaction test but without resorting to the state constitution's counterpart provision. Instead, the court pointed out, "the just result we seek may readily be attained by our exercise of the broad administative and procedual powers vested in us."[103] Pending the submission of revised rules by a criminal practice committee, pertinent sections of the Model Penal Code were incorporated by reference, thus requiring compulsory joinder of offenses based on the same conduct or arising from the same criminal episode.[104] A unanimous court described such action as "well due."[105]

The selection of means, looking toward the effectuation of the same-transaction standard, has varied among the states. In a case before the Oregon Supreme Court, the judges found that the state constitution required the same-transaction test for multiple prosecutions. But, they noted, the test did not serve to bar multiple punishments for different offenses ascribable to the same act or episode when prosecuted at a single trial.[106] Like results have also have been achieved through judicial construction of compulsory joinder statutes. Minnesota, for example, prohibited multiple prosecutions when the offenses could be attributed to a "single behavioral incident."[107]

Despite Justice Brennan's argument in *Ashe* and the record of the courts that have adopted the same-transaction test, a majority of the states remained unpersuaded. Maryland's highest court, which considered the issue at length, found neither a state constitutional-statutory basis nor a common law right on which to premise a joinder of charges.[108] The Supreme Judicial Court of Maine described itself as "now unconvinced" concerning the wisdom of adopting the single-transaction test. However, it left open the possibility that circumstances might exist where "repeated reprosecutions or successive prosecutions would amount to fundamental unfairness and a denial of due process."[109]

The Supreme Court of Hawaii, often characterized as "liberal" in the espousal of the rights of the accused, declined to embrace the same-transaction test unqualifiedly. Instead, it expressed a preference for a variable standard dependent upon circumstances. As if to avoid inexorable rules in an area of the law that has not been free from doubt, the court questioned whether "the answer to the problem of identity of offenses in the context of the double jeopardy principle lies in the selection of any single test as providing the applicable formula." The court admitted that it had applied the same-evidence test in the past, and it refused to preclude its application at some point in the future.[110]

In the midst of protracted debates over capital punishment before the U.S. Supreme Court, a number of state courts moved, on independent grounds, to resolve the principal issues raised. The Supreme Court of California assumed a customary position of leadership when, early in 1972, it proscribed the death penalty as violative of the state constitution's "cruel or unusual punishments" provision.[111] This action set in motion a remarkable sequence of events: recurring charges of judicial impropriety by the state's attorney general; unsuccessful efforts to secure review before the Federal Supreme Court;[112] and the subsequent reversal of the California Court's decision by referendum even after the Federal Supreme Court had outlawed capital punishment as then administered.[113] In succeeding state cases involving statutes specifically designed to meet federal objections to selective or discretionary practices, only the Supreme Judicial Court of Massachusetts held that mandatory capital punishment was unconstitutional.[114] The Supreme Court of New Mexico, while acknowledging its independent role as the "ultimate" arbiter of the law of the state, went on to sustain a mandatory death sentence law as comporting with federal and state constitutional standards.[115]

Less dramatic applications of cruel and unusual punishment provisions related to recidivist offenders who had been made ineligible for parole for specified periods and to those whose terms had been found disproportionate to existing levels of culpability. The Supreme Court of California, in a sweeping review of sections of the state's health and safety code applicable to narcotics crimes, held that the preclusion of parole consideration for five years or more violated the cruel or unusual punishment clause of the state constitution as "excessively severe."[116] A year earlier, the same court had assessed the administration of the state's indeterminate sentence law with critical results tied to constitutional standards of cruel or unusual punishment.[117] Without reference to state constitutional provisions but within a like context of judicial supervision of the execution of the penal laws, the Supreme Court of New Jersey vacated restitution as a condition of probation for a defendant convicted of welfare fraud. A unanimous panel, exercising what it called a "closely guarded and sparingly used authority," determined that "the human cost of such deterrence in this instance is too great" and that the condition imposed was "clearly excessive."[118]

The scope of a cruel and unusual punishment prohibition, or its functional equivalent, is both expansive and elusive. Although the safeguard plainly transcends the boundaries of current controversy over the death sentence and the terms and conditions of its imposition, the outer parameters remain ill-defined. The Federal Supreme Court denied that corporal punishment of schoolchildren offended the Eighth Amendment even in a case involving allegedly "unreasonable" or "excessive" force.[119] In most instances, the Court's holding was not offset by contrary state rulings superseding the common law privilege of a teacher to administer "reasonable" disciplinary measures including the infliction of corporal punishment.

Within a prison disciplinary context, the rights of inmates have been examined under due process guidelines. The U.S. Supreme Court, in *Wolff*

v. *McDonnell*,[120] announced that there was "no iron curtain drawn between the Constitution and the prisoners of this country" but that, at the same time, liberty interests and the range of procedural guarantees needed to be modified to meet the requirements of a "closed, tightly controlled environment." A familiar balancing test was applied with institutional interests generally and the "potential for havoc inside the prison walls" in particular figuring heavily in the weighting process.[121]

Justice Byron White's opinion for the majority in *Wolff* established a series of guidelines for disciplinary hearings. Advance written notice of the charges was made mandatory as the basis for a marshalling of facts and the preparation of a defense. The fact finders were required to supply a written statement of the evidence relied upon and the reasons for the proposed disciplinary action. The inmate was entitled to summon witnesses and to present evidence in his behalf unless such actions jeopardized institutional safety or goals. Although a right to counsel was rejected by the Court, access to assistance by a fellow inmate or the prison staff was provided in the case of an illiterate defendant or when a complex issue arose. Finally, the decision maker was to be "sufficiently impartial to satisfy the Due Process Clause."[122]

As the Court's catalog of prisoner rights developed, the most conspicuous omission lay in the absence of confrontation and cross-examination procedures. Justice White wrote of the need "to avoid situations that may trigger deep emotions and that may scuttle the disciplinary process as a rehabilitation vehicle."[123] In response, Justice Marshall's dissent went to the essentiality of such procedures to resolve factual differences.[124] The only exception, in Marshall's view, related to the need to protect the identity of confidential informants when special safeguards were warranted.[125] To Justice Douglas, in dissent, the lack of opportunities for confrontation and cross-examination was premised on a conception of prison administration that was "outmoded and indeed anti-rehabilitation."[126]

The Supreme Court of Alaska moved significantly beyond *Wolff* on independent state grounds, noting "greater due process protection," under counterpart constitutional provisions. Although the court embraced all that *Wolff* had provided, significant additions were made: confrontation and cross-examination unless exceptional institutional conditions obtained; a right to counsel when subsequent prosecution for a felony threatened to result; expanded opportunities to call witnesses and to produce documentary evidence; and the preparation of a verbatim record of the proceedings, designed to facilitate possible administrative or judicial review, instead of the "written statement" specified by the *Wolff* Court.[127]

Among the cases cited by the Alaska high court was a prisoner rights decision handed down several months earlier by the New Jersey Supreme

Court. The basis of intervention, emphasized by the New Jersey Court, went beyond procedural due process and included "the extraconstitutional 'fairness and rightness' standard effective in New Jersey." Preferences were made not only to individual rights and justice, but also to societal interests and, curiously, to the domestic tranquility mentioned in the preamble to the national Constitution. By way of additional preliminaries, the court noted the breadth of its decisional reach and cited with approval earlier language that "there is no constitutional mandate that a court may not go beyond what is necessary to decide a case at hand."

The New Jersey Supreme Court's intrusion of natural rights concepts, its allusion to an expansive judicial authority, and the intimations of a presumptive invalidity with respect to the state's prison disciplinary procedures did not lead to a marked expansion of prisoner safeguards. An unqualified right to counsel was rejected as "wholly incompatible" with institutional needs and "unessential to protection of the inmate's rights." At the same time, the court acknowledged the dilemma of a prisoner faced with the choice between testifying in defense or extenuation of the charges levelled against him and his Fifth Amendment right to remain silent. The solution, as the judges saw it, lay in the extension of a limited "use" immunity respecting the prisoner's statements as distinguished from the broader "transactional" immunity that conferred a blanket release from possible prosecution for the offense to which the testimony related.[128]

NOVEL DEFINITIONS OF HUMAN RIGHTS

A renewed emphasis on individual rights has prompted a number of state courts to move in unconventional ways and to explore an unaccustomed terrain. Yet judicial activism, no matter how intense, must be tempered by a grounding in the constitutional or statutory substratum. State charters increasingly have come to embrace a range of guarantees associated with gender-based discrimination, personal autonomy, and zones of privacy. If the years of the Warren Court have left an indelible imprint by accelerating the pace of the nationalization of the federal Bill of Rights, the decade of the 1970s presented a positive image describing the vibrancy and variety of the states' contributions.

At the same time that controversy has raged over the proposed Equal Rights Amendment (ERA), the United States Supreme Court has persisted in declining to hold that sex is a suspect classification and has agreed only to a heightened level of judicial scrutiny.[129] A number of states, by contrast, have adopted equal rights amendments or their statutory counterparts. Thus the decisional law need not rely on judicial largess alone as a basis for invalidating sex-based classifications. By considering such classifications as suspect, courts may modify or even reverse the traditional presumption of validity by requiring a showing of a compelling state interest as a condition for sustaining a questionable law or regulation.

Whether strict scrutiny or a less exacting standard is adopted, state courts have demonstrated considerable ingenuity in treating gender-related issues. State judges are at liberty to reject canards about the "proper role" of the sexes and to substitute new rules more adequately attuned to prevailing conditions. Changes in legal and popular thought have been translated into judicial guidelines. Although the same goals arguably could be attained by way of Fourteenth Amendment equal-protection analysis, an ERA groundwork has proved to be a more cogent instrument in effecting significant shifts in recognized patterns.[130]

Statutory differences between males and females have been examined in a variety of settings. In 1974 the Supreme Court of Illinois eliminated gender-based distinctions from the state's juvenile court act, thereby making the law's "protective" features inapplicable both to men and to women over the age of seventeen.[131] The same court held unconstitutional differential age requirements establishing eligibility for marriage licenses.[132] In both cases the court cited a section of the state's bill of rights guaranteeing that equal protection "shall not be denied or abridged on account of sex" in behalf of a holding that sex was a suspect classification subject to strict judicial scrutiny.

Subsequently, the U.S. Supreme Court found that a gender-related age differential affecting the sale of "nonintoxicating" 3.2 percent beer had worked an "invidious discrimination" against males. But the Court went no further than to prescribe that the classification, to be valid, must be "substantially related to achievement of the statutory objective."[133] Justice William Rehnquist, in dissent, objected to what he characterized as the majority's application of an elevated or intermediate level of scrutiny when the more permissive "rational basis" test should have sufficed.[134] In a previous decision, the Court had set aside a Utah statute differentiating parental liability for child support on the basis of a higher age of majority for males than for females. Justice Blackmun rejected the distinction on equal-protection grounds "under any test—compelling state interest, or rational basis, or something in between."[135]

The introduction of an equal rights amendment has led state courts to revise the traditional obligations and privileges attributable to divorced or unwed parents. Maryland's highest court rejected sex as a factor in allocating responsibility for child support. In doing so, it set aside the common law rule, placing the primary liability on the father, as a "vestige of the past." Henceforth, the court declared, awards were to be made on a sexless basis and shared by both parents according to the financial resources available to each.[136] Pennsylvania's supreme court held the statutory distinction between unwed mothers and fathers "patently invalid'' in sustaining the rights of the natural father of an adopted illegitimate child.[137] By contrast, the U.S. Supreme Court unanimously sustained such a distinction against due process and equal-protection challenges. A "best-interest-of-the-child" standard prevailed amid obscure suggestions that, "whatever might be required in other situations," the interests of an unwed father were "readily distinguishable" from those of a divorced father.[138] When the Federal Court moved to modify this ruling, it did so within a limited context necessitating proof of the father's "substantial relationship" with the child and admission of paternity.[139]

State courts also have sought to establish guidelines affecting the equality of persons entering into or terminating the marital relationship. The selection or change of names have had important consequences, although often symbolic ones, in determining social standing and cognate questions of status. At common law, freedom of choice exists in the absence of fraudulent intent. The Supreme Judicial Court of Massachusetts went far toward extending the common law principle to all possible situations; it reserved decision only in the case of illegitimate children where harassment of the putative father reasonably might be expected to occur. Otherwise, a majority noted, freedom of choice must remain the rule with respect to the recording and use of names if familial privacy and especially the rights of women are to be preserved.[140] In the course of a Washington opinion, the court found "no legal impediment" to parents assigning the mother's surname to a child.[141]

The thrust of state equal rights amendments is to end or at least to minimize disparate treatment of alimony and other payments that accompany divorce. The inclination to impose differing benefits or burdens has long been premised upon gender. But in this area of the law as in support cases generally, sex has declined as a permissible factor. The Pennsylvania Supreme Court held that need and the financial resources of the parties should determine the remedies. Thus the entry of a support order may lie against the wife as readily as against the husband depending upon the economic circumstances of each.[142] Not until 1979 did the U.S. Supreme Court reject state-generated stereotypes associated with alimony obligations and explicitly decline "to use sex as a proxy for need."[143]

Common law notions of interspousal immunity have been abandoned in at least half of the states. Abrogation of the doctrine is a latter-day outgrowth of the female "emancipation acts" of the mid-nineteenth century, which acknowledged the legal identity of the married woman by recognizing her right to sue, contract, and hold and dispose of property. At the same time, the Blackstonian conception of marital unity[144] persisted to prevent personal injury suits brought by one spouse against the other. The New Jersey Supreme Court ended the rule of interspousal immunity with respect to automobile negligence torts in 1970 despite statutory language to the contrary.[145] Other courts, acting to remove the barrier, also rejected the necessity of legislative intervention.[146] They found similarly wanting public policy justifications for the doctrine that advanced the preservation of marital harmony and the avoidance of fraud and collusion as compelling reasons.[147]

Efforts to define the rights of adults to engage in private consensual sexual practices and to describe other aspects of personal autonomy have led to mixed results. The U.S. Supreme Court has made clear that a federally protected right of privacy extends only to heterosexual relations.[148] In the states, pleas set forth in a variety of "deviant" contexts have yielded more positive judicial responses, but the record is hardly notable. The dismissal of a male homosexual high school teacher was sustained by the Supreme Court of Washington on the ground that his fitness had been impaired.[149] A contrary result was reached in California under far more egregious conditions.[150] When female prostitutes pressed claims of privacy by reference to the expansive language of Alaska's constitution, the state's highest court denounced the claim that men and women had an unrestricted right to possess and control their bodies where commercial gain was involved.[151] The same court had previously espoused a broadly conceived right of privacy in the home, legalizing the personal consumption of marijuana by adults[152] despite the lack of a like immunity from prosecution in other states.

The treatment of distinctions premised upon age shows little doctrinal inventiveness. Since the Federal Supreme Court has shown no disposition to designate age as a suspect classification, a rational-basis test remains the rule in judicial appraisals of mandatory retirement schemes.[153] A succession of state precedents has been almost equally unrewarding. With the possible exception of the Supreme Court of Hawaii,[154] holdings of unconstitutionality linked to age distinctions have been rare. Classifications that differentiate the rights of the "elderly" at one end of the scale and of "immature youths" at the other end have withstood equal-protection challenges. Lowered age-of-majority criteria, despite their supposed universality in application, have not served to eliminate exclusions from jury duty or to supersede age requirements that establish eligibility for elective office.[155] At the same time, such changes in majority status have had the effect of relieving parents of financial support obligations for children previously classified as dependents.[156]

The extent of parental discretion to make determinations for legally incompetent children, and more generally the authority of guardians to do so, was considered at length in the much-publicized *Quinlan* case.[157] At issue was a plea by a father to have his daughter's noncognitive, vegetative existence ended by disconnecting the life-supporting mechanism that sustained her. In an opinion recognizing a wide-ranging right of privacy, the

Supreme Court of New Jersey authorized withdrawal of the life-support system without civil or criminal liability on the part of any participant in the process. The court declared that the patient's right of privacy, asserted in the circumstances by her father, outweighed the state's interest in the preservation of life. Yet the justices denied that a parental right of privacy, viewed as a discrete interest, might serve as a basis of relief. The father's position was identified as no more than that of a surrogate; the right preserved was one of "personality" peculiar to the individual affected.

A like result was reached by Massachusetts' highest court in the case of the terminally ill patient incapable, by reason of extreme retardation, of giving informed consent for treatment.[158] The court recognized a general right of persons to refuse medical care and, in appropriate circumstances, the subordination of state concerns to the individual's right of privacy. There was, the justices agreed, a "strong personal interest in being free from nonconsensual invasion of . . . bodily integrity." Nevertheless, the court departed from *Quinlan* in refusing to entrust the ultimate decision to a guardian or to medical specialists. The responsibility lay with the courts in resolving this "most difficult and awesome question" whether life-prolonging treatment should be withheld.

CONCLUSION

If, on balance, the record of state contributions must be described as a checkered one, it nonetheless has added a new dimension to the developing pattern of American law. The earlier propensity of state courts to follow the Federal Supreme Court's leadership almost without exception has given way to a healthy skepticism and a growing sense of independence. Some of the elements are reminiscent of the textbook federalism of yesteryear, coupled with a new-found resiliency and a penchant for experimentation. In the absence of the emphatic interventionism associated with the Warren Court, the states have moved toward the restoration of their historic roles in protecting the rights of citizens.

The introduction of novel precedents never fails to produce ferment in the shaping of the law, and creative decision making has been confined so far to relatively few states and issues. A disconcerting note, common to state and federal judicial activism alike, involves the reduced reliance on legislative initiatives and the concomitant tendency to pursue and even to exalt court-contrived solutions. In several areas not usually served by the doctrine of independent state grounds, important questions of state action have been left unanswered. Public employee rights, although predicated fundamentally on First Amendment and due process guarantees, realistically are tied to collective negotiation laws that require implementation in the state courts. Whether the result of strict statutory construction or

other strategems, these rights have been variously expanded and contracted within legislative guidelines that permit broad judicial discretion.[159]
In like manner, shield laws, intended to protect reporters and other media
representatives from revealing confidential sources of information, have
been diluted at times and made to yield to the rights of defendants in
criminal trials.[160] The reluctance of the Federal Supreme Court to intervene decisively has led to uncertainty and, in some states, to a resurgence
of judicial negativism.

From time to time, objections have arisen to an undue reliance on
independent state grounds. Result orientation—an effort to achieve pre-
determined policy objectives by an artful choice of means—has been
condemned as a basis for departures from federal norms. Equally open to
censure has been a purposeful attempt to negate a litigant's right to federal
review by way of an exclusive dependence on a state constitutional predicate. What is more, the possibility exists that the initiative procedure,
where available, may be used by an irate electorate to overturn and
embarrass overzealous judges. Thus a resort to the state charters is not
without risk both to the institutional integrity of the courts and, occasionally, to the realization of individual rights secured by the national Constitution.

Despite such misgivings, indications are that the Burger Court's attitude
will encourage a proliferation of independent rulings. The dockets of the
state courts, multiform as they are, have already exhibited persuasive
evidence of a new federalism. Although judicial excesses may and have
occurred at the state as at the federal level, the products of a number of
state tribunals remain impressive, and the precedents established are likely
to affect the resolution of kindred issues elsewhere. In the course of these
realignments, it should be noted, the Federal Supreme Court has not
shown any inclination to "abdicate" on so broad a scale as to promote a
narrow provincialism.

Doubtless, the nationalization of the Bill of Rights served as a necessary
precondition for the doctrine of independent state grounds to reach fru-
ition. The danger persists that state judges may confound or even imperil
built-in national safeguards. A resort to state constitutional language is not
a roving commission; nor is it intended as an oblique cul-de-sac to inhibit
access to federally preserved rights. Implicit in a revival of state provisions
is the assumption that minimal national standards will prevail without
substantial attenuation; that growth will take place within a collaborative
framework rather than in an atmosphere subversive of one; and that, over
the succeeding decades, human freedoms will develop incrementally
through mechanisms that emphasize a positive but suitably demarcated
role for the state courts. It is only in this context that the doctrine of
independent state grounds takes on significance as an historic weather vane

of the vitality of American federalism and as an index of the system's potential as a part of an ever-changing yet remarkably enduring institutional structure.

NOTES

1. A succinct review is found in Donald E. Wilkes, Jr., "The New Federalism in Criminal Procedure: State Court Evasion of the Burger Court," *Kentucky Law Journal* 62 (1974): 421–51. Although identified with a conceptual framework characteristic of the preceding decade, a thoughtful analysis is provided in Terrance Sandalow, "Henry v. Mississippi and the Adequate State Ground: Proposals for a Revised Doctrine," *The Supreme Court Review 1965:* 187–239.

2. Herb v. Pitcairn, 324 U.S. 117, 126 (1945).

3. A recent exposition of views appears in Oregon v. Haas, 420 U.S. 714 (1975), both in Justice Blackmun's majority opinion and in Justice Marshall's dissent.

4. Johnson v. Louisiana, 406 U.S. 356, 376 (1972).

5. San Antonio Independent School District v. Rodriguez, 411 U.S. 1, 58–59 (1973).

6. Hoyt v. Minnesota, 399 U.S. 524 (1970).

7. Texas v. White, 423 U.S. 67, 72 (1975). *See also* Michigan v. Mosley, 423 U.S. 96, 120–21 (1975), raising issues related to a purported erosion of *Miranda* safeguards.

8. Baxter v. Palmigiano, 425 U.S. 308, 339 n. 10 (1976).

9. United States v. Miller, 425 U.S. 435, 454 n. 4 (1976).

10. Paul v. Davis, 424 U.S. 693, 736 n. 18 (1976).

11. State v. Phillips, 540 P.2d 936, 939 (Utah 1975).

12. Activist-"liberal" state courts are not necessarily averse to selectivity in the application of federal precedents. *See, e.g.,* some of the unaccustomed choices made by the Supreme Court of California in striking down a municipal rent-control charter amendment, because, the court found, it deprived landlords of due process safeguards; Birkenfeld v. City of Berkeley, 550 P.2d 1001, 1027–33 (Cal. 1976). *Cf.* the treatment of rent-control ordinances and of federal precedents related to substantive due process in Hutton Park Gardens v. Town Council of West Orange, 350 A.2d 1 (N.J. 1975), and associated cases.

13. Distinguishing federal precedents, the Supreme Court of Idaho held that the due process clause of the state constitution required a waiver of filing fees for an indigent old-age assistance recipient who sought judicial review of an administrative agency's decision to terminate her benefits; Graves v. Cogswell, 552 P.2d 224 (Idaho 1976).

14. Urowsky v. Board of Regents, 342 N.E.2d 583 (N.Y. 1975).

15. Population Serv. International v. Wilson, 398 F. Supp. 321, 337 (S.D.N.Y. 1975).

16. Virginia State Bd. of Pharmacy v. Virginia Citizens Consumer Council, Inc., 425 U.S. 748, 759 (1976).

17. *See, e.g.,* Baffoni v. State Dept. of Health, 373 A.2d 184 (R.I. 1977); People v. Johnson, 369 N.E.2d 898 (Ill. 1977). *Cf.* National Hearing Aid Centers, Inc. v. Smith, 376 A.2d 456 (Me. 1977); Laufenberg v. Cosmetology Examining Bd., 274 N.W. 2d 618 (Wis. 1979).

18. Sharrock v. Dell Buick-Cadillac, Inc., 379 N.E.2d 1169 (N.Y. 1978). In Flagg Bros. v. Brooks, 436 U.S. 149 (1978), decided less than two months before *Sharrock,* a divided Federal Supreme Court had found a lack of Fourteenth Amendment state action in the application of a provision of New York's Uniform Commercial Code.

19. Southern Burlington County N.A.A.C.P. v. Township of Mt. Laurel, 336 A.2d 713, *appeal dismissed and cert. denied,* 423 U.S. 808 (1975); Oakwood at Madison, Inc. v. Township of Madison, 371 A.2d 1192 (N.J. 1977). *But see* Pascack Ass'n., Ltd. v. Mayor and Council of the Township of Washington, 379 A.2d 6 (N.J. 1977), for evidences of

doctrinal "backsliding." A sampling of opinions in other states ranges from Pennsylvania's condemnation of "tokenism" in apartment zoning—Township of Williston v. Chesterdale Farms, Inc., 341 A.2d 466 (Pa. 1975)—to the acceptance of more permissive judicial standards in New York—Berenson v. Town of New Castle, 341 N.E. 2d 236 (N.Y. 1975)—and in California—Assoc. Home Builders v. City of Livermore, 557 P.2d 473 (Cal. 1976).

20. For a discussion of the "interplay" between like articles, *see* Smith v. State, 350 A.2d 628 (Md. 1976).

21. General Electric Co. v. Gilbert, 429 U.S. 125 (1976).

22. Brooklyn Union Gas Co. v. New York State Human Rights Appeal Bd., 359 N.E.2d 393, 395 n. 1 (N.Y. 1976).

23. Id., 359 N.E.2d at 397.

24. Ropico, Inc. v. City of New York, 415 F. Supp. 577 (S.D.N.Y. 1976).

25. Flushing National Bank v. Municipal Assistance Corp. for the City of New York, 358 N.E. 2d 848 (N.Y. 1976).

26. Brooklyn Union Gas Co. v. New York State Human Rights Appeal Bd., 359 N.E.2d 393, 398 (N.Y. 1976).

27. Flushing National Bank v. Municipal Assistance Corp. for the City of New York, *supra* note 25, at 855.

28. *See, e.g.,* Alevy v. Downstate Medical Center, 348 N.E.2d 537 (N.Y. 1976).

29. DeFunis v. Odegaard, 416 U.S. 312, 350 (1974).

30. Bakke v. Regents of University of California, 553 P.2d 1152 (Cal. 1976).

31. Id. at 1171.

32. *See* Roemer v. Bd. of Public Works of Maryland, 426 U.S. 736 (1976). *Cf.* Wolman v. Walter, 433 U.S. 229 (1977), with respect to church-related elementary and secondary schools.

33. Gaffney v. State Dept. of Education, 220 N.W.2d 550, 553 (Neb. 1974).

34. Id. at 557.

35. Bloom v. School Committee of Springfield, 379 N.E.2d 578 (Mass. 1978).

36. Americans United v. Rogers, 538 S.W.2d 711 (Mo. 1976).

37. Roemer v. Bd. of Public Works of Maryland, *supra* note 32.

38. Americans United v. Rogers, *supra* note 36, at 718–21.

39. Id. at 723–24.

40. Mallory v. Barrera, 544 S.W.2d 556 (Mo. 1976). The case was a "spinoff" from Wheeler v. Barrera, 417 U.S. 402 (1974), in which the U.S. Supreme Court construed the federal statute as evincing a "clear intention that state constitutional spending proscriptions not be preempted as a condition of accepting federal funds"; Id. at 417.

41. Fox v. City of Los Angeles, 587 P.2d 663 (Cal. 1978); Lowe v. City of Eugene, 451 P.2d 117, 459 P.2d 222, 463 P.2d 360 (Or. 1969), *cert. denied,* 397 U.S. 1042, *reh. denied,* 398 U.S. 944 (1970); Eugene Sand & Gravel, Inc. v. City of Eugene, 558 P.2d 338 (Or. 1976).

42. McGowan v. Maryland, 366 U.S. 420 (1961); Two Guys from Harrison-Allentown v. McGinley, 366 U.S. 582 (1961); Braunfeld v. Brown, 366 U.S. 599 (1961); Gallagher v. Crown Kosher Super Market, 366 U.S. 617 (1961).

43. *See, e.g.,* Kroger Co. v. O'Hara Township, 392 A.2d 266 (Pa. 1978); People v. Abrahams, 353 N.E.2d 574 (N.Y. 1976).

44. Vornado, Inc. v. Hyland, 390 A.2d 606 (N.J. 1978). The New Jersey Supreme Court placed a like emphasis on national precedents in sanctioning the use of public school facilities for religious purposes during nonschool hours; Resnick v. East Brunswick Township Bd. of Education, 389 A.2d 944 (N.J. 1978). *See also* State v. Smith, 247 S.E.2d 331 (S.C. 1978). The Supreme Court of Texas rejected as untenable the argument that the state's Sunday closing law (purportedly an act in restraint of trade) had been preempted by the Sherman Anti-Trust Act; Gibson Distributing Co., Inc. v. Downtown Development Ass'n. of El Paso, 572 S.W.2d 334 (Tex. 1978).

45. Katzenbach v. Morgan, 384 U.S. 641, 651 (1966).

46. People v. Longwill, 538 P.2d 753 (Cal. 1975).

47. State v. Deatore, 358 A.2d 163, 170 (N.J. 1976).

48. Baker v. City of Fairbanks, 471 P.2d 386, 401–2 (Alaska 1970).

49. Miller v. California, 413 U.S. 15, 25 (1973). *See also* Hamling v. United States, 418 U.S. 87 (1974). Despite a strong penchant for activism, the California Supreme Court has declined to reply on independent state grounds in weighing the validity of obscenity legislation; Bloom v. Municipal Court for the Inglewood Judicial District of Los Angeles County, 545 P.2d 229 (Cal. 1976).

50. United Farm Workers of America v. Superior Court of Santa Cruz County, 537 P.2d 1237 (Cal. 1975). *Cf.* Agricultural Labor Relations Bd. v. Superior Court of Tulare County, 546 P.2d 687 (Cal. 1976).

51. State v. Shack, 277 A.2d 369, 371–72 (N.J. 1971).

52. Serrano v. Priest, 487 P.2d 1241 (Cal. 1971).

53. Hawkins v. Superior Court of San Francisco, 586 P.2d 916 (Cal. 1978).

54. People v. Superior Court of Orange County, 434 P.2d 623 (Cal. 1967). *See also* People v. Wheeler, 583 P.2d 748 (Cal. 1978). The Federal Supreme Court has held that a six-member jury is constitutionally permissible in criminal cases; Williams v. Florida, 399 U.S. 78 (1970); Ballew v. Georgia, 435 U.S. 223 (1978).

55. Zeilenga v. Nelson, 484 P.2d 578 (Cal. 1971).

56. Serrano v. Priest, *supra* note 52.

57. Id. II, 557 P.2d 929 (Cal. 1976).

58. Robinson v. Cahill, 303 A.2d 273 (N.J. 1973).

59. Id., 360 A.2d 400 (N.J. 1976).

60. Horton v. Meskill, 376 A.2d 359 (Conn. 1977). *Cf.* Seattle School Dist. No. 1 of King County v. State, 585 P.2d 71 (Wash. 1978); Buse v. Smith, 247 N.W.2d 141 (Wis. 1976); Olsen v. State, 554 P.2d 139 (Or. 1976); Thompson v. Engelking, 537 P.2d 635 (Idaho 1975).

61. Bixby v. Pierno, 481 P.2d 242, 252 (Cal. 1971).

62. Despite significant deviations, the Supreme Court of California selectively follows the federal model. *See, e.g.,* the right to transcript cases, Shuford v. Superior Court of Orange County, 523 P.2d 641 (Cal. 1974); People v. Hosner, 538 P.2d 1141 (Cal. 1975).

63. A parenthetical note by the court is significant in this regard. *See* People v. Collins, 552 P.2d 742, 745 (Cal. 1976).

64. The Supreme Court of Hawaii invoked the state constitution's due process guarantee to ensure that the sentencing court not exercise "wholly unfettered discretion to impose an extended term sentence upon purely retributive considerations"; State v. Huelsman, 588 P.2d 394, 401 (Hawaii 1978).

65. *In re* Podesto, 544 P.2d 1297 (Cal. 1976).

66. People v. Coleman, 533 P.2d 1024 (Cal. 1975).

67. Cooper v. California, 386 U.S. 58, 62 (1967).

68. United States v. Robinson, 414 U.S. 218 (1973); Gustafson v. Florida, 414 U.S. 260 (1973).

69. State v. Kaluna, 520 P.2d 51 (Hawaii 1974). *See also* State v. Barnes, 568 P.2d 1207 (Hawaii 1977).

70. People v. Brisendine, 531 P.2d 1099, 1110 (Cal. 1975). *See also* People v. McGaughran, 585 P.2d 206 (Cal. 1978), questioning the validity of a motorist's detention for a warrant or record check. *Cf.* State v. Opperman, 247 N.W.2d 673, 675 (S.D. 1976), in which the Supreme Court of South Dakota held that, as a matter of state constitutional law, "non-investigative police inventory searches of automobiles without a warrant must be restricted to safeguarding those articles which are within plain view of the officer's vision." The court followed the suggestion of Justice Marshall, dissenting in South Dakota v. Opperman, 428 U.S. 364, 396 (1976), that such a result could be reached under "applicable state law."

71. People v. Norman, 538 P.2d 237 (Cal. 1975).

72. People v. Longwill, 538 P.2d 753 (Cal. 1975).

73. People v. Maher, 550 P.2d 1044 (Cal. 1976).

74. Zehrung v. State, 569 P.2d 189 (Alaska 1977). *See also* State v. Daniel, 589 P.2d 408 (Alaska 1979), applying like principles to closed, locked, or sealed luggage or containers found as a result of a warrantless routine inventory search of an automobile subsequent to the driver's arrest. With respect to the action of federal agents in similar circumstances, *see* United States v. Chadwick, 433 U.S. 1 (1977).

75. Schneckloth v. Bustamonte, 412 U.S. 218, 248 (1973).

76. Id. at 278–80.

77. State v. Johnson, 346 A.2d 66 (N.J. 1975).

78. Id. at 68 n. 2.

79. Commonwealth v. Forde, 329 N.E. 2d 717, 722–23 (Mass. 1975).

80. People v. Ramey, 545 P.2d 1333, 1341 (Cal. 1976). It was not until 1980 that the Federal Supreme Court held that warrantless arrests in the home violate the Fourth Amendment; Payton v. New York, 63 L.Ed.2d 639 (1980).

81. Mapp v. Ohio, 367 U.S. 643 (1961).

82. Miranda v. Arizona, 384 U.S. 436, 504 (1966).

83. Harris v. New York, 401 U.S. 222, 224 (1971).

84. State v. Santiago, 492 P.2d 657, 665 (Hawaii 1971).

85. Commonwealth v. Triplett, 341 A.2d 62 (Pa. 1975).

86. Commonwealth v. Harris, 303 N.E.2d 115, 117 (Mass. 1973).

87. State v. Miller, 337 A.2d 36, 39 (N.J. 1975).

88. State v. Deatore, 358 A.2d 163, 172 (N.J. 1976). The *Harris* rule has been followed in an overwhelming majority of the states. For a listing, *see* one of the dissenting opinions in Commonwealth v. Triplett, 341 A.2d 62, 67 n. 2 (Pa. 1975).

89. People v. Cahan, 282 P.2d 905, 912 (Cal. 1955).

90. People v. Nudd, 524 P.2d 844 (Cal. 1974).

91. People v. Disbrow, 545 P.2d 272, 280 (Cal. 1976).

92. Id. at 291.

93. People v. Isaacson, 378 N.E.2d 78, 84–85 (N.Y. 1978).

94. Benton v. Maryland, 395 U.S. 784 (1969).

95. Ashe v. Swenson, 397 U.S. 436 (1970).

96. Id. at 446.

97. Id. at 443–44.

98. Id. at 452–54.

99. Commonwealth v. Campana, 304 A.2d 432 (Pa. 1973).

100. Pennsylvania v. Campana, 414 U.S. 808 (1973).

101. Commonwealth v. Campana, 314 A.2d 854, 855–56 (Pa. 1974).

102. Pennsylvania v. Campana, 417 U.S. 969 (1974). *See also* Commonwealth v. Walker, 362 A.2d 227 (Pa. 1976); Commonwealth v. Bartolomucci, 362 A.2d 234 (Pa. 1976), examining "duplicitous sentence" questions in contexts not linked to independent state grounds.

103. State v. Gregory, 333 A.2d 257, 261 (N.J. 1975).

104. Id. at 262. American Law Institute, Model Penal Code, secs. 1.07 (2) and 1.07 (3).

105. State v. Gregory, *supra* note 103, at 263.

106. State v. Brown, 497 P.2d 1191, 1198 (Or. 1972). *See also* People v. White, 212 N.W.2d 222 (Mich. 1973).

107. State v. Corning, 184 N.W.2d 603, 605–6 (Minn. 1971).

108. Cousins v. State, 354 A.2d 825, 832–33 (Md. 1976), *cert. denied,* 429 U.S. 1027 (1976). *See also* State v. Treadway, 558 S.W.2d 646 (Mo. 1977).

109. State v. Bessey, 328 A.2d 807, 813, 815 (Me. 1974).

110. State v. Ahuna, 474 P.2d 704 (Hawaii 1970). *Cf.* Ladd v. State, 568 P.2d 960 (Alaska 1977).

111. People v. Anderson, 493 P.2d 880 (Cal. 1972).

112. California v. Anderson, 406 U.S. 958 (1972). *See also* Aikens v. California, 406 U.S. 813, 814 (1972), for an explanation of the Court's action in *Anderson*.

113. Furman v. Georgia, 408 U.S. 238 (1972). The developments in the California case are recounted in Jerome B. Falk, Jr., "The Supreme Court of California, 1971–1972, Foreword: The State Constitution: A More Than 'Adequate' Nonfederal Ground," *California Law Review* 61 (1973): 274–77; and in Wilkes, "The New Federalism," pp. 445–48. *See also* People v. Teron, 588 P.2d 773 (Cal. 1979).

114. Commonwealth v. O'Neal, 339 N.E.2d 676 (Mass. 1975).

115. State *ex rel.* Serna v. Hodges, 552 P.2d 787, 792, 796 (N.M. 1976).

116. *In re* Grant, 553 P.2d 590, 598 (Cal. 1976). *See also In re* Foss, 519 P.2d 1073 (Cal. 1974).

117. *In re* Rodriguez, 537 P.2d 384 (Cal. 1975).

118. State v. Harris, 362 A.2d 32, 37 (N.J. 1976).

119. Ingraham v. Wright, 430 U.S. 651 (1977).

120. Wolff v. McDonnell, 418 U.S. 539 (1974).

121. Id. at 555–56, 561, 567.

122. Id. at 564, 566, 570, 571.

123. Id. at 568.

124. Id. at 582.

125. Id. at 584–89.

126. Id. at 579.

127. McGinnis v. Stevens, 543 P.2d 1221, 1230, 1231, 1236 (Alaska 1975).

128. Avant v. Clifford, 341 A.2d 629, 638, 639, 642, 645, 651–55 (N.J. 1975). The *Wolff* standards prevailed in most states. *See, e.g.,* Bekins v. Cupp, 545 P.2d 861 (Or. 1976); Calkins v. May, 545 P.2d 1008 (Idaho 1976). *But see* California's judicially created "right of access" to the courts accorded prisoners in civil actions brought against them. A remedy was required, the state's highest court averred, to correct a constitutional inadequacy. Although neither a right to appointed counsel nor a right to personal appearance was guaranteed, a majority made plain that the trial court's discretion in withholding either was limited; Payne v. Superior Court of Los Angeles County, 553 P.2d 565 (Cal. 1976).

129. No more than four members of the Court, a minority, have agreed that categorizations premised upon sex are inherently suspect. *See* Frontiero v. Richardson, 411 U.S. 677 (1973). The recurring debate among the justices is well illustrated in Craig v. Boren, 429 U.S. 190 (1976).

130. With respect to discrimination against females in interscholastic sports competition, *see* Darrin v. Gould, 540 P.2d 882 (Wash. 1975). To the contrary, a state ERA has been held subject to an exception for "physical characteristics unique to one sex"; Holdman v. Olim, 581 P.2d 1164 (Hawaii 1978). The absence of an explicit ERA provision and even the lack of an unambiguous equal protection clause need not preclude protection against sex-based discrimination; Peper v. Princeton University Bd. of Trustees, 389 A.2d 465 (N.J. 1978).

131. People v. Ellis, 311 N.E.2d 98 (Ill. 1974).

132. Phelps v. Bing, 316 N.E.2d 775 (Ill. 1974).

133. Craig v. Boren, *supra* note 129, at 204.

134. Id. at 219–22.

135. Stanton v. Stanton, 421 U.S. 7, 17 (1975).

136. Rand v. Rand, 374 A.2d 900, 905 (Md. 1977).

137. *In re* Adoption of Walker, 360 A.2d 603, 605–6 (Pa. 1976).

138. Quilloin v. Walcott, 434 U.S. 246, 255–56 (1978).

139. Caban v. Mohammed, 441 U.S. 380 (1979).

140. Secretary of Commonwealth v. City Clerk of Lowell, 366 N.E.2d 717 (Mass. 1977).

141. Doe v. Dunning, 549 P.2d 1, 4 (Wash. 1976).

142. Henderson v. Henderson, 327 A.2d 60, 62 (Pa. 1974).

143. Orr v. Orr, 440 U.S. 268, 281 (1979).

144. Blackstone described a merger of legal identities: "Husband and wife are one person in law . . . the very being or legal existence of the woman is suspended during the marriage"; 1 *Blackstone's Commentaries* 442.

145. Immer v. Risko, 267 A.2d 481, 483 (N.J. 1970). Subsequently, the court refused to prevent recovery in actions for personal injuries based upon claims of negligence. The justices unanimously declared that "courts are not the keepers of the marital conscience and are not omniscient or inspired to intuit the mysterious and complex ways marriages rise and fall"; Merenoff v. Merenoff, 388 A.2d 951, 962 (N.J. 1978).

146. *See, e.g.,* the action of the Supreme Court of Indiana in Brooks v. Robinson, 284 N.E.2d 794 (Ind. 1972).

147. The Supreme Judicial Court of Massachusetts noted that the rule was "not consonant with the needs of contemporary society" and inconsistent with "the general principle that if there is tortious injury there should be recovery"; Lewis v. Lewis, 351 N.E.2d 526, 531, 532 (Mass. 1976).

148. The Court has refused to intervene in cases affecting homosexuality—Doe v. Commonwealth's Attorney for Richmond, 425 U.S. 901 (1976)—and transsexualism—Grossman v. Bernards Township Board of Education, 429 U.S. 897 (1976).

149. Gaylord v. Tacoma School Dist. No. 10, 559 P.2d 1340 (Wash. 1977).

150. Board of Education of Long Beach Unified School Dist. of Los Angeles County v. Jack M., 566 P.2d 602 (Cal. 1977).

151. Summers v. Anchorage, 589 P.2d 863 (Alaska 1979).

152. Ravin v. State, 537 P.2d 494 (Alaska 1975).

153. Vance v. Bradley, 440 U.S. 93 (1979). The principal state case is Massachusetts Board of Retirement v. Murgia, 427 U.S. 307 (1976).

154. In Nelson v. Miwa, 546 P.2d 1005 (Hawaii 1976), the court did not rule on the basis of the state constitution's equal-protection clause. Instead, it predicated its decision on a legislative finding that, in the context of employment, age is included among those categories said to be inherently invidious.

155. *See, e.g.,* Wurtzel v. Falcey, 354 A.2d 617 (N.J. 1976).

156. Stanley v. Stanley, 541 P.2d 382 (Ariz. 1975); Eaton v. Eaton, 213 S.E.2d 789 (Va. 1975); Chrestenson v. Chrestenson, 589 P.2d 148 (Mont. 1979). To the contrary, *see* Burke v. Burke, 360 A.2d 574 (Vt. 1976).

157. *In re* Quinlan, 355 A.2d 647 (N.J. 1976).

158. Superintendent of Belchertown State School v. Saikewicz, 370 N.E.2d 417 (Mass. 1977).

159. *See, e.g.,* Appeal of Cumberland Valley School Dist. from Final Order of Pennsylvania Labor Relations Bd., 394 A.2d 946 (Pa. 1978) [federal interpretive case law drawn from the private sector applied to the public sector]; Skelly v. State Personnel Bd., 539 P.2d 774 (Cal. 1975) [pretermination safeguards constitutionally required]; Local 1494 of International Ass'n. of Firefighters v. City of Coeur d'Alene, 586 P.2d 1346 (Idaho 1978) [inferential right to strike sustained]; State v. State Supervisory Employees Ass'n., 393 A.2d 233 (N.J. 1978) [scope of negotiations determinations].

160. *In re* Farber and the New York Times, 394 A.2d 330 (N.J. 1978), *cert. denied sub nom.* New York Times Co. & Farber v. New Jersey, 439 U.S. 997 (1978).

3.

RUSSELL S. HARRISON

State Court Activism in Exclusionary-Zoning Cases

INTRODUCTION

Empirical data reported in this chapter clarify the following key issues: Which state courts have been particularly active in hearing and condemning exclusionary-zoning laws? How is the distribution of public opinion on residential segregation, and the extent of actual residential segregation, correlated with the extent of state court activism in attacking exclusionary zoning? Can state court activism produce significant changes in the supply and cost of housing, or do exclusionary-zoning laws have insignificant effects on the distribution of housing? Can state court activism significantly reduce residential segregation by race among metropolitan communities, or does the elimination of exclusionary zoning actually increase racial segregation?

Research on state activity in this field is important, because federal courts—including the U.S. Supreme Court—have shown limited desire to attack exclusionary zoning and because, as this study demonstrates, court rulings on this issue profoundly affect whether people live in segregated or integrated communities. Another reason for this research is to illustrate how a political-system perspective and empirical research methods can help clarify state court decision making in exclusionary-zoning litigation.

The general framework of the political-system perspective is relatively simple. Every political system has certain characteristic internal policy-

Parts of this research appeared in another form in "The Role of State Supreme Courts in Exclusionary Zoning Cases," a paper prepared for delivery at the 1979 Annual Meeting of the Northeastern Political Science Association, Newark, N.J., November 8-10. Helpful comments on this paper were provided by Henry Glick, Ralph Rossum, Robert Seddig, G. Alan Tarr, and M. C. Porter. Assistance was also provided through the Rutgers Research Council and the Rutgers Faculty Academic Study Program scholarship program.

making processes and procedures that are affected by external environmental conditions, and that in turn produce consequences causing "feedback" to the environment. In this research, the central conceptual variable is state court activism involving exclusionary zoning. As used here, *activism* can be defined as a willingness to consider litigation involving exclusionary zoning. Activism regarding exclusionary zoning is affected by the environment of the state legal system and in turn produces certain major consequences or impacts.

Certain exogenous environmental variables affect decision making by state courts regarding exclusionary zoning. Two tasks are necessary to document that empirical relationships exist among these variables. First, these variables must achieve different values in different states or regions. Second, these differences must be generally congruent. In fact, the research reveals that different areas vary not only with respect to state court activism regarding exclusionary areas; they also differ with respect to the degree of metropolitan residential segregation and the degree to which public opinion either condones or condemns residential segregation. Moreover, the research reveals that these differences fit together in a coherent fashion.

Two basic reasons exist for measuring the effects of minimum lot-size restrictions in particular and exclusionary-zoning laws in general, rather than simply assuming their importance. First, many previous judicial impact studies have cast doubt on the effectiveness of court policymaking in producing significant social, economic, or political change along the lines intended by litigants. In fact, some studies indicate that litigation may prove counterproductive. Second, one important study, which attempted to measure how minimum lot-size restrictions affected the distribution of different income groups among metropolitan communities, concluded that minimum lot-size laws have no significant effects on where or how people live. Thus, generalizing from such research, one might conclude that court attacks on restrictive land-use laws are irrelevant. Although they might produce symbolic reassurance for the advocates of court activism in exclusionary-zoning cases, their tangible results might be minimal.

This study, however, demonstrates that such conclusions are erroneous. Minimum lot-size requirements are correlated with the supply and cost of housing, as can be seen from a careful analysis of comprehensive statewide data. Furthermore, minimum lot-size requirements and other exclusionary-zoning laws are even correlated with the extent of residential segregation by race. Where the severity of exclusionary-zoning laws is greatest, the extent of residential segregation is also greatest. Where the extent of exclusionary zoning is less, residential segregation is less.

In summary, the theory to be tested predicts that courts respond to their environments, which includes patterns of public opinion and residential segregation. In addition, courts can act to change their environments. By challenging large minimum lot-size requirements, and other exclusionary-zoning laws, courts can affect where and how people live.

CHARACTERISTICS OF EXCLUSIONARY-ZONING LAWS AND DIFFERENTIAL STATE COURT RESPONSES TO THEM

What are *exclusionary-zoning laws?* Many definitions might be offered, but several are most common. One perspective is that exclusionary-zoning laws are zoning and land-use regulations adopted to maximize certain fiscal objectives, such as low tax rates and high expenditures. Another perspective is that exclusionary-zoning laws are regulations that reduce the supply of housing available for low-income families. Still another perspective is that exclusionary-zoning laws are regulations that result in greater segregation among metropolitan municipalities, by restricting the poor and minorities from gaining access to developing communities that have adopted such laws. Of course, some local officials simply argue that all zoning laws are exclusionary in that they restrict certain types of development, which is a permissible expression of home rule. Another view is that only specific regulations that have been explicitly condemned by courts may justifiably be described as exclusionary.

For purposes of this analysis, the last two definitions tend to beg the issue, since the object of analysis is to understand better why certain courts tend to condemn strict zoning laws, and other courts do not. The first definition is also difficult to apply, because some local officials may say they had specific fiscal objectives in mind by adopting a certain law, and others may keep quiet, regardless of their presumed intentions. Thus a synthesis of the other definitions seems most valuable, namely, that exclusionary-zoning laws may be defined as strict land-use regulations and zoning requirements that have certain de facto empirical consequences:

1. They reduce the supply of available housing, especially housing suitable for low-income families.
2. They raise the median costs of housing in a community.
3. They tend to result in economic and racial segregation among municipalities in metropolitan areas where such laws are prevalent.

Whether a specific law or group of laws has such consequences is of course an open question, as is the issue of whether or not courts will or should condemn such regulations, either for these specific characteristics or for other reasons.

In analyzing zoning laws and zoning cases, it must be noted that zoning and land-use regulations are hardly new.[1] At least some municipalities have been regulating construction practices for decades. However, in the past, zoning laws and land-use regulations were more often adopted by large, highly urban cities such as Boston and New York, rather than by small developing suburban and even rural communities in the metropolitan fringe. Moreover, the primary impact of such laws was usually to separate industrial, commercial, and residential properties from each other, by assigning new construction for each to specific geographical areas within the municipality. Usually, the regulations were written primarily to apply to the quality of multifamily housing, not to the quality or quantity of single-family housing. Furthermore, such laws were seldom if ever adopted—consciously or unconsciously—to ban low-cost housing from the city.[2]

In recent years, however, opponents of strict zoning laws have alleged that new functions and structures have arisen for these laws. These laws are increasingly adopted not by cities, but by new, sparsely populated, relatively affluent suburbs, in the path of metropolitan development. By conscious design or by unconscious impact, they tend to bias who lives where. *Ceteris paribus,* they minimize housing opportunities for the poor and minority families who seek to move outside the old, dilapidated center city or even suburban slums and settle in the newer suburbs. As a result, the adoption of these laws has been a key factor encouraging the recent dramatic growth of residential segregation in many metropolitan areas.[3]

Thus, over time, strict zoning laws have allegedly changed both quantitatively and qualitatively. More importantly, perceptions have spread that such laws are systematically biased. In response, litigation has been launched in many states to attack various forms of allegedly exclusionary zoning.

Much litigation has focused on overt restrictions against single-family, owner-occupied housing. Extensive criticism has been directed against highly restrictive minimum requirements for floor area, setbacks, and frontages;[4] against excessive subdivision specifications that add greatly to the cost of new housing;[5] and against unnecessarily severe building codes that prevent the installation of laborsaving materials or cheaper supplies.[6]

The criticism has been perhaps most successfully directed against minimum lot-size restrictions, however. In the early years after World War II the courts generally accepted such requirements. For example, in 1952 the New Jersey courts allowed Bedminister Township to impose a five-acre minimum lot size to cover 85 percent of its developable land.[7] In 1956, however, the Pennsylvania courts refused to allow four-acre minimum lot sizes.[8] In 1959 the Virginia courts refused to allow a two-acre minimum lot size in Fairfax County.[9] By 1970 the Pennsylvania courts were condemning two- and three-acre minimum lot-size requirements.[10]

Other litigation has been directed against restrictions placed on multiunit rental housing. Some communities have refused to allow zoning for any multiunit housing, either private or public, except by special variance. Such laws have been successfully attacked in cases such as *In re Appeal of Girsh*.[11] Other communities have specifically refused to allow public housing for low- and moderate-income families, and these practices have been successfully attacked in cases such as *DiSimone* v. *Greater Englewood Housing Corporation*.[12] A few communities, while not prohibiting multiunit housing, have made the building regulations and rental stipulations so restrictive that only upper-income families, especially those composed of married adults without children, can obtain apartments. The New Jersey Supreme Court invalidated such restrictions in *Molino* v. *Borough of Glassboro*.[13]

In recent years some attention has shifted to more covert methods of exclusionary zoning. Prohibitions against mobile homes have been successfully attacked in Michigan and Pennsylvania courts.[14] Overzoning for nonresidential usage has been criticized in the famous *Mt. Laurel* case in New Jersey.[15] Excessive growth controls and expensive concessions required for cluster-home developments and planned-unit developments have been recently subjected to legal scrutiny.[16]

The important point in this survey of state court decisions is not that most states have condemned most types of exclusionary zoning. Indeed they have not. Rather, many zoning laws may be seen to have exclusionary results. Thus exclusionary-zoning cases could have been brought in many states, but they were not, and if they were, they met with very different outcomes. In fact, litigation against the various forms of exclusionary zoning has not met with equal success in all states. In some states one finds decided appellate court activism and liberalism, and in other states one finds passivity and restraint.

Like exclusionary zoning itself, state court activism has many interrelated dimensions. One key dimension of the degree to which state courts are active or passive in attacking exclusionary-zoning laws involves how broadly they define due process requirements, equal rights guarantees, and eligibility for standing.

The activist courts have been more sympathetic to certain doctrinal claims. They include arguments that:

1. Exclusionary zoning violates due process guarantees.
2. Exclusionary zoning infringes upon fundamental rights including the right to housing.
3. Exclusionary zoning classifies rights by suspect criteria that include de facto discrimination by wealth and race.
4. The interests at stake in exclusionary-zoning cases are so broad that standing should be generously granted to a wide range of potential litigants.
5. Local government desires to minimize taxes and to maximize services are not sufficient grounds to justify the adoption or application of exclusionary-zoning laws.

6. A long tradition of home rule cannot justify ignoring regional needs for housing when local governments adopt zoning laws.

Activist courts expansively interpret the "due process" requirements that must be met in local zoning decisions: Local zoning is a delegated police power that must be exercised in the public interest and for the community welfare. The relevant public and community must be viewed in terms of the overall metropolitan housing market that extends beyond any one small suburb's corporate borders. Ideally, each community must allow for the construction of a "fair share" of housing suitable to meet the needs of the region's poor and minority families.[17]

Nonactivist courts have used a narrow definition of *general welfare* that is restricted to the individual municipality and fails to encompass the region. They have tended to equate "due process" with "home rule" and have ignored the legitimate interest of state governments in local housing and land-use policy.

Another difference between activist and passive courts is that activist courts are supportive of a wide range of liberal claims concerning "equal rights" guarantees applied to zoning and land use: Housing is a right or interest endowed with fundamental constitutional importance. De facto discrimination by wealth, as well as de facto discrimination by race, is a suspect classification. Where a fundamental right is infringed, or a suspect criterion is used to classify enjoyment of that right, the court must exercise strict scrutiny of the motives and administration of the state or local policies that cause the harm. In exercising strict scrutiny the court cannot permit claims of fiscal pressures to justify local actions in excluding the poor and minorities from its borders. Minimizing local tax rates and maximizing local services are not compelling interests for the locality. Nor can the court accept health justifications as reasonable when the zoning laws make demands far in excess of demonstrable need.[18]

Passive courts react far differently to equal rights claims. They limit suspect criteria only to de jure discrimination on the basis of race, as reflected in the overt displays of prejudice against blacks, which are part of the published public record. They typically ignore the alleged interests of the urban poor and minority groups in suitable housing within their metropolitan area, but outside center-city ghettoes. They recognize concern for local housing values and the local property rate as legitimate bases for zoning restrictions that operate to exclude the poor and minority groups.

Activist and passive courts also differ regarding the issue of standing. Activist courts respond sympathetically to the claim that the interests at stake in exclusionary-zoning cases are so broad that standing should be available to a wide range of potential litigants and liberally construe standing to include a wide range of representatives of the poor, blacks, and other minorities who seek low-cost housing in a community with restrictive zoning laws.

Passive courts are loath to grant standing to the multiplicity of people and organizations affected directly or indirectly by exclusionary-zoning laws. It seems obvious to most courts that a developer who has bought land in a community, and has then been denied permission to build low-cost housing in that community for reasons he or she believes unconstitutional, may have standing to bring suit. It may not seem so obvious that the poor, blacks, and other minority families who now live in communities outside the restrictive community, but who could live in the housing to be built by the developer, should also be granted standing. The activist court would tend to grant standing, especially where the blacks and other minority families are represented in a class-action suit by organizations such as the National Association for the Advancement of Colored People (NAACP). The passive court would not.

Passive courts place multiple roadblocks in the path of litigants seeking to bring suit against exclusionary zoning. Passive courts require potential litigants to show they have a personal harm different from others in their class before standing is granted. For example, litigants are required to show they have personally attempted to purchase or build housing in the community and have been personally denied satisfaction in their attempt. The passive courts also require litigants to have an ongoing suit with the community. Simply having been denied the right to build or purchase in the past would not suffice. Papers must have been filed and continuous litigation pursued. The passive courts further require the litigants to prove they are wealthy enough to afford the housing for which the community is blocking construction. For example, a poor family might be required to prove that some organization was formally committed to subsidize the housing construction, or subsidize their rental payments, if the housing were built. Finally, the litigants are required to prove that a specific exclusionary-zoning law directly prevents any construction of the type of housing to which the litigants seek access and does not simply cause a higher price for each housing unit that in turn denies the litigants access.[19]

The passive courts are more likely to impose these or other restrictive requirements before potential litigants are allowed to present their case on the merits. The passive courts thereby reduce access to the courts and limit the role of the court as a forum for considering and resolving significant social, economic, and political problems of housing scarcity and residential segregation. In general, passive courts follow a principle of "judicial restraint" in deciding what cases and what litigants they will hear.

Figure 3.1 summarizes characteristics that differentiate state court responses to litigants' claims. How broadly state courts grant standing,

Figure 3.1 Court Characteristics That Encourage Activism, Not Passivity, in Attacking Exclusionary Zoning.

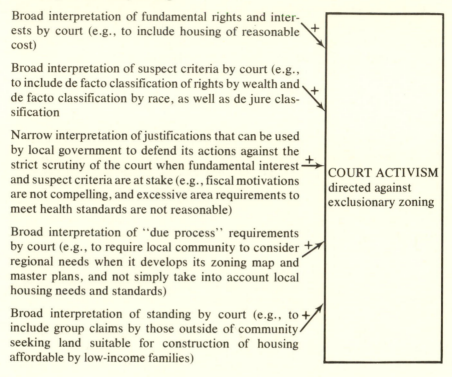

how broadly they construe due process requirements in local zoning cases, how broadly they interpret equal rights requirements—all of these factors determine their reaction to litigant claims attacking exclusionary zoning. The broader the state court's definition of the seriousness of the problem of exclusionary zoning and the proper role of the court in dealing with the problem, the more activist its responses to exclusionary-zoning laws.

Before a strongly activist court, litigants are able to pursue and win boldly innovative arguments. Successful litigation against exclusionary zoning is far more difficult in the face of the adverse attitudes, ideologies, and role conceptions characteristic of the court with extreme passivity and judicial restraint.

However, court activism depends not only on judges' attitudes, ideologies, and role conceptions, but also on litigants' skill. Litigant strategies in bringing cases can also affect whether courts will condemn exclusionary zoning. For example, judicial role conceptions favorable to self-restraint can be overcome by litigants' strategies that minimize the apparent jump required in ruling exclusionary zoning unconstitutional. Litigants who oppose exclusionary zoning can maximize their ratio of court victories to defeats by an incrementalist strategy. Bringing cases into court whose resolution requires only marginally greater activism than in previous cases facilitates positive judicial responses, especially among the more conservative judges.[20] So does focusing on "overt" zoning laws, such as minimum livable floor areas or minimum allowable setbacks, rear yards, and side yards, rather than the more covert exclusionary-zoning methods involving "growth controls" and "non-Euclidian floating zones."[21] Another successful tactic is to focus on exclusionary-zoning laws in "developing communities," rather than in communities that have only a small percentage of land left vacant or that lie in rural areas beyond easy access to jobs and stores and lack present interest for developers.[22] Still another successful tactic is to focus on communities adopting more severe zoning laws. Courts find it easier to condemn zoning laws that obviously make a community more restrictive than in the past, rather than laws that simply perpetuate or codify previous practices within a community.[23]

Similarly, courts find it easier to condemn old zoning laws that are clearly restrictive, rather than new laws that seem to reflect at least nominal intentions to ease restrictions. It is relatively easy to convince courts that a community is being excessively restrictive when it bans all construction for multiunit rental housing or other forms of low-cost residential housing. Many courts have ordered local communities to provide some land somewhere for such housing. What happens when the community rezones the bottom of a quarry for such housing or a swampy marsh? It requires extreme activism for a court to conclude that such action is an impermissible and insufficient local response to the need for low-cost housing.[24]

In general, successful litigation against exclusionary zoning is facilitated by litigant skills in picking clear-cut cases of discrimination, employing the varied legal doctrines that can be used to attack exclusionary zoning, and marshalling extensive proof in support of their claims.[25] In their litigation, however, opponents of exclusionary zoning should rely on state court doctrines to bolster their arguments, not federal court doctrines.

In earlier years the federal courts seemed quite activist in dealing with housing issues. They attacked overt racial zoning,[26] restrictive covenants,[27] and private discrimination in the sale, rental, and leasing of housing.[28] In recent years, however, the personnel of the Federal Supreme Court has shifted, and attitudes of judicial restraint prevail.

The present court has refused to define housing as a fundamental interest, or wealth discrimination as a suspect criterion, and has refused to apply "strict scrutiny" in exclusionary-zoning cases.[29] Moreover, it has not ruled that the failure to define community-housing needs from a regional or metropolitan perspective is a violation of the Due Process

Clause. Furthermore, it has narrowly interpreted standing to exclude many opponents of exclusionary zoning from having their arguments heard on the merits.[30]

However, the fact that the U.S. Supreme Court has not acted to condemn exclusionary-zoning laws does not mean that such laws are above reproach. Rather, it means that legal battles have shifted to the state courts. State courts have broad authority to act on their own against exclusionary-zoning laws, and some state courts have begun to exercise that authority.

Some state courts have become conspicuous for their willingness to play a leadership role in litigation directed against exclusionary zoning. In almost all states the pattern of decisions before the 1960s was passive and restrained, in the sense of extending broad legitimacy to local zoning practices, following the precedent set by the U.S. Supreme Court in *Village of Euclid* v. *Ambler Realty Co.*[31] In a few states the trend toward activism has gone only a short distance, as illustrated perhaps by the Virginia Supreme Court.[32] However, some state courts have displayed noticeable activism in attacking exclusionary-zoning laws in the last decade.

Table 3.1 summarizes the number of notable cases in each state that have raised major issues of exclusionary zoning, according to various surveys of key exclusionary-zoning decisions.

EMPIRICAL CAUSES FOR STATE COURT ACTIVISM

As table 3.1 indicates, a few courts have been especially liberal and activist, creating precedents that are cited by other courts to justify their opposition to exclusionary zoning. The geographic distribution of these courts is distinctive. As illustrated by the activist state appellate courts of New Jersey, Pennsylvania, and Michigan, they are concentrated in the Northeast and the North-Central states.

Why does this noticeable geographical pattern occur? Do environmental differences among the states help explain the differential activism by state courts in exclusionary-zoning cases? Specifically, are activist state courts located in regions where their activism would seem most needed, because metropolitan residential segregation by wealth and race is particularly pronounced? Are these state courts located in regions where judicial activism would seem most acceptable, because public opinion strongly opposes residential segregation by race?

Metropolitan residential segregation refers to racial imbalance among the civil subdivisions within a metropolitan area. It does not refer to differences in racial concentration among neighborhoods within a community, but differences in racial concentration among independent munic-

Table 3.1 A Frequency Distribution of Citations to Notable State Court Cases Involving Exclusionary Zoning, with Totals by State

	Sources of Citations[a]							
	1	2	3	4	5	6	7	TOTAL
State								
New Jersey	5	1	1	8	3	8	5	31
Pennsylvania	5	1	0	6	3	8	5	28
Michigan	2	0	1	3	2	2	1	11
Massachusetts	0	0	1	0	3	3	1	8
New York	0	0	0	1	1	3	1	6
California	0	0	0	0	0	3	1	4
Minnesota	0	0	0	0	1	1	1	3
Ohio	0	0	0	0	0	1	1	2
North Carolina	0	0	0	1	0	0	0	1
Virginia	0	0	1	0	0	0	0	1

[a] Sources of citations:

1. National Committee Against Discrimination in Housing and the Urban Land Institute, *Fair Housing and Exclusionary Land Use* (Washington, D.C.: National Committee Against Discrimination in Housing, 1974), pp. 39–44, "Laws that Exclude Lower-Income Housing."

2. Ibid., pp. 45–46, "Regional Challenges to Exclusionary Zoning."

3. Ibid., pp. 48–49, "Inclusionary Zoning."

4. Daniel Lauber, "Recent Cases in Exclusionary Zoning," in ed. David Listokin *Land Use Controls: Present Problems and Future Reform* (New Brunswick, N.J.: Center for Urban Policy Research, 1974), p. 178.

5. Anti-Exclusionary Zoning Cases, based on inspection of cases reported by LEXIS system, covering the Court of Last Resort for all states, January 1, 1971–April 15, 1980.

6. Computer printout from LEXIS system, reporting cases in last two appellate courts from 1969 to 1979 as of May 4, 1979.

7. Computer printout from LEXIS system, reporting cases in last two appellate courts from 1975 to 1979, as of May 4, 1979.

ipalities and townships. Where a community adopts exclusionary-zoning laws, it often achieves a high level of homogeneity among neighborhoods within the community, but increases heterogeneity between local residents and residents in other parts of the metropolitan housing market. Metropolitan residential segregation measures racial heterogeneity among governmental jurisdictions with autonomous powers over taxing, spending, land use, buildings, subdivisions, and growth policies.

Many previous studies imply that residential segregation is greatest in the southern states of the Confederacy.[33] In fact, the reality does not match the myth. Comparing racial totals in each civil subdivision of every metropolitan area nationwide, the Deep South has the least amount of residential segregation by race.

Part of the explanation is that the South lacks many of the social and economic forces that encourage metropolitan residential segregation. Another key reason is that the South lacks many of the governmental and political forces that encourage metropolitan residential segregation as well.[34] On the other hand, the psychological forces that encourage metropolitan residential segregation—the desire of people of different races to live in different communities—is not the crucial cause of metropolitan residential segregation. Social, economic, governmental, and political forces are far more important causes of exclusionary zoning and residential segregation in metropolitan America.[35] Thus the most prejudiced regions of the country are not necessarily the most segregated areas of the country.

Table 3.2 summarizes the evidence about the correlation of regional location, metropolitan residential segregation by race, and public opinion about residential segregation. The imbalance between actual segregation and popular prejudice is most concentrated in the industrial North, Pacific West, New England, and industrial Midwest.[36] Thus those regions in which the need for action is great, because of extensive exclusionary zoning and residential segregation, also display widespread popular atti-

Table 3.2 Actual Segregation, Popular Support for Segregation, and Differences Between Attitudes and Behavior, by Region

Region	Actual Segregation		Popular Support for Segregation		Differences in Ranks Between Attitudes & Behavior
	% Segregated	Regional Rank	% Prejudiced	Regional Rank	
Industrial North	56.7%	1	13.3%	7	+6
Pacific West	42.1	3	14.1	6	+3
New England	33.5	6	6.3	8	+2
Industrial Midwest	48.0	2	20.9	4	+2
Border South	35.5	4	30.1	2	−2
Midwest Farm	34.6	5	21.3	3	−2
Mountain West	21.4	8	16.9	5	−3
Deep South	26.1	7	36.4	1	−6

Note: Regions are defined by the Michigan Survey Research Center categories. "Actual Segregation" is measured by the mean average for the index of dissimilarity that was computed for each 1970 Standard Metropolitan Statistical Area (SMSA) in the region, comparing the distribution of whites and blacks in each civil subdivision of each SMSA. "Popular support" for segregation is measured by the percent in each region who believed in 1968 that whites have a right to exclude blacks from their neighborhoods. Grateful acknowledgment is extended to the Michigan Research Center and the Rutgers Computer Center for their assistance in obtaining the data on public opinion. The data on metropolitan residential segregation by race were compiled by the author.

tudes that suggest potential legitimacy, support, or at least receptivity towards court activism.

This receptivity to court activism does not occur because strict zoning laws are unpopular. In fact, they are popular, because they are perceived to produce many benefits within particular communities. Local officials believe that by excluding the poor and blacks from their community, they can reduce local tax rates and increase per-capita service benefits. This fiscal motivation is particularly important in the urban, industrial states. These states have a system of local government in which each locality is forced to finance a large share of its total services out of local property-tax revenues. This means that as the proportion of local citizens who are poor increases and the average value of each household's property decreases, either local property-tax rates must increase, or public expenditures per capita must decrease.[37] Thus strict zoning laws are popular, for they are perceived to minimize tax rates and to maximize public services.

The system of local government finance in the urban, industrial states provides incentives for exclusionary zoning; local officials have responded to those incentives, and thus exclusionary zoning is extensive. On the other hand, mass education, public law, and other factors have combined to create popular opposition to racial segregation and public support for equal housing opportunities. This creates a potential conflict of beliefs and values. Public opinion favors strict zoning for fiscal goals but opposes segregation by race. This conflict gives the court leeway in judicial policymaking. It is not forced to oppose one set of strongly held beliefs, without any ability to appeal to a different set of values that can provide legitimacy and support for its actions.

In sum, appreciable fiscal benefits may fall within local communities as a result of exclusionary zoning. On the other hand, the benefits within the community are matched by heavy costs outside the community, including the problems of residential segregation.

In certain urban, industrial states like New Jersey the courts have weighed both the costs and benefits of exclusionary zoning. In the activist state courts the internal benefits from exclusionary zoning have not been deemed sufficient to justify the external costs from these laws.

Figure 3.2 confirms that the identity of the activist state courts is not strictly due to chance. The relatively activist courts can be found in states where the issue of exclusionary zoning has been highly controversial, where a relatively high level of litigation has occurred, and where the quantity and quality of cases condemning exclusionary zoning has been noticeable, based on a review of major state court decisions widely cited as the leading precedents in this policy area.

One finds that the activist state courts are found only in a minority of

Figure 3.2 State Court Policymaking Relative to Environmental Characteristics in Cases Involving Exclusionary Zoning.

	Regions that ranked lower in actual segregation than in popular support for segregation	Regions that ranked higher in actual segregation than in popular support for segregation
Relatively activist state appellate courts	(1) State: 　Minnesota	(7) States: 　New Jersey 　New York 　Pennsylvania 　Massachusetts 　Michigan 　Ohio 　California
Relatively passive state appellate courts	(29) States: 　All 10 Deep 　　South states 　All 5 Border 　　South states 　All 8 Midwest 　　Farm states 　All Midwest 　　Farm states 　　except 　　Minnesota	(13) States: 　Connecticut 　Maine 　New Hampshire 　Rhode Island 　Vermont 　Delaware 　Illinois 　Indiana 　Wisconsin 　Oregon 　Washington 　Alaska 　Hawaii

Summary: Predicted form of relationship   = positive
　　　　　States with successful predictions   = 72% (36 of 50)
　　　　　Statistical significance of relation, using chi-   = 0.01 level of
　　　　　　square test statistic   Probability
　　　　　Pearson's correlation coefficient, for dichotomy   = 0.42
　　　　　　data
　　　　　Sample size   = 50 states

　　The independent variable measures the degree of conflict between the average metropolitan residential segregation in a region (in 1970), compared with popular support for residential segregation (in 1968).

　　The dependent variable measures the presence or absence of multiple (two or more) citations by leading authorities for notable state court cases attacking exclusionary zoning during the period 1969 to 1979.

the states. Moreover, even in those states relatively small numbers of cases explicitly and persuasively attack specific examples of exclusionary zoning. Thus this table certainly does not prove that most state courts oppose exclusionary zoning. They most certainly do not. Rather, this table is simply intended to illustrate, merely for heuristic purposes, what more extended analyses could document more persuasively, namely, that the identity of the relatively activist state courts can be understood better by knowing not simply the facts of the specific cases presented to them, but also the culture and environment of each state. In short, the courts can be viewed usefully, in part at least, as responding to systemic pressures.

By cross-classifying the states, figure 3.2 reveals a visible connection between certain environmental conditions and court policymaking over time. A definite correlation exists among public opinion unfavorable toward residential segregation, the average extent of metropolitan residential segregation in a region, and subsequent judicial activism against exclusionary zoning. The combinations hardly seem chance coincidences. Instead they provide clear evidence that a pattern of environmental pressures helps shape court activism in exclusionary-zoning cases and perhaps judicial activism in other issue areas as well.

Of course, state courts do not blindly follow public opinion or necessarily act even when the need for reform is great. Other branches of government may intervene to obviate the need for court leadership. In addition, other environmental considerations may affect court policymaking. In figure 3.2, for example, one notices that many of the state courts that deviate from the general trend are found in areas with relatively low concentrations of blacks (e.g., Maine, New Hampshire, Rhode Island, Vermont, Wisconsin, Oregon, Washington, Alaska, and Hawaii). The priority of a policy issue on a court's calendar may reflect the political strength of the group that is particularly concerned with the issue. In any case, it certainly seems possible that a wide variety of environmental variables play a role in shaping state court policymaking toward exclusionary zoning. Even environmental pressures that do not affect state court policymaking directly may serve as antecedents for residential segregation and popular attitudes toward segregation, respectively.

In short, empirical evidence can be used to clarify some of the major facilitants for state court activism in exclusionary-zoning cases. The social, economic, and political environment of a state can affect court behavior. But does state court behavior affect the environment?

EMPIRICAL CONSEQUENCES OF STATE COURT ACTIVISM

What difference does it make that certain courts condemn exclusionary zoning? Can attacks on exclusionary-zoning laws effectively combat problems in urban housing markets due to insufficient supply, excessive costs, and an inequitable distribution of housing opportunities?

The past record of judicial policymaking offers little reason to expect that court activism directed against exclusionary zoning will greatly change the supply and cost of available housing or reduce residential segregation in urban housing. Several studies have concluded that just because a court bans a certain behavior as unconstitutional, this action does not mean the behavior will cease.[38] Court decisions condemning public or private behavior as illegal and unjust are often ignored, for example, those regarding public school religious exercises,[39] bookseller censorship practices,[40] school segregation during the 1950s,[41] and police violations of criminal defendants' rights.[42] Even when court decisions are implemented, their implementation may not produce the results desired by the litigants, if the reforms sought are not sufficient to achieve the long-term goals. One example can be found in the cases involving malapportionment and legislative redistricting. Advocates of reapportionment presumably expected that redistricting would greatly increase liberal policies, which did not happen, according to a variety of studies.[43] Another example of frustrated expectations involves the school-integration cases. Many advocates undoubtedly assumed that school integration, among other consequences, would dramatically improve students' academic performances. This has not seemed to happen with great consistency.[44]

Another group of studies casts even more doubt on the general efficacy of court litigation as a means to achieve significant social, economic, and political reform. This research argues that court attempts to solve problems of urban integration and segregation may even prove counterproductive. Federal courts seem to think that court-enforced busing will achieve the intended goal of school integration. However, James Coleman and others argued that the empirical impacts of center-city school integration differ radically from these preconceptions. The long-term result of these attempts to achieve integration is an actual increase in segregation, due to white flight from the center city. Center-city schools may achieve internal balance in racial composition, but only at the cost of increased racial imbalance between center city and suburban school districts.[45]

The relevance of these concerns for this study is underlined by a recent study that argues that exclusionary-zoning laws in general, or minimum lot-size laws in particular, have no significant effects on the supply and cost of housing. Is the author right?[46] Are exclusionary-zoning laws, especially minimum lot-size requirements, irrelevant? A careful analysis of the empirical evidence proves that exclusionary-zoning laws are important, including minimum lot-size provisions. To clarify the impact of minimum lot-size requirements, I report data for New Jersey, one of the states where the courts have been particularly aggressive in attacking exclusionary-zoning laws.

Table 3.3 summarizes correlations between zoning laws and house prices. The sample includes all municipalities in New Jersey with available data on minimum lot-size requirements, median value of owner-occupied housing, and various socioeconomic control variables.

Table 3.3 Effects of Minimum Lot Size on the Price and Supply of Housing

	Independent Variable: Index of Minimum Lot Size		
	Dichotomy Index Measuring Presence of Any Minimum Lot-Size Requirement	Interval Index Measuring Minimum Lot Allowed in Square Feet	Interval Index Weighting Each Observation by the Area of Municipality
Dependent Variable: Median Price of Owner-Occupied Housing			
Equation	0.14**	0.19***	0.16***
1	0.11*	0.19***	0.24***
2	0.15**	0.17***	0.27***
3	0.14**	0.20***	
4			
Dependent Variable: Number of Owner-Occupied Housing Units per Acre			
Equation	−0.13**	−0.19***	
1	−0.14**	−0.19***	−0.32***
2	−0.13**	−0.29***	−0.26***
3	−0.14**	−0.18***	−0.25***
4			

Note: One, two, or three asterisks means that a relationship is statistically significant at a 0.05, 0.01, or 0.001 level of probability, respectively.

Each relationship between minimum lot size and the price of supply of housing is measured by a correlation coefficient. Equation 1 is a bivariate correlation coefficient. Equations 2, 3, and 4 are partial correlation coefficients with controls respectively for median family income, percentage of blacks in the community ten years previously, and percentage of blacks in the county.

The zoning laws are measured using 1967 data. The price and supply variables are measured using 1970 data. The sample covers all New Jersey municipalities with available data.

For a fuller discussion of effects on house prices due to minimum lot-size laws, see Russell Harrison, "Minimum Lot Size Laws and Local Housing Costs in New Jersey" (Paper delivered at the 1981 New Jersey Political Science Association, Jersey City, New Jersey, April 4).

Minimum lot-size requirements are significantly related to the supply and cost of housing. Where minimum lot-size requirements are higher, the average number of housing units per acre is lower. Where minimum lot-size requirements are higher, the cost of the average house is higher. This is true even with controls for average income or percentage of blacks in the local community or in the county.

Other research also indicates that the effects of minimum lot size are clearly significant even taking into account house quality or the supply of available land in the municipality. Moreover, minimum lot-size laws do not affect only the supply of single-family, owner-occupied housing. They also reduce the relative supply of rental housing. In addition, all of these shifts in the supply and cost of housing are even more noticeable when the community has more than one residential zone, especially where those zones require even higher minimum lot sizes. Furthermore, other zoning laws also reduce the supply and increase the costs of housing, such as setback and rear-yard requirements.[47] Thus claims that exclusionary-zoning laws lack any significant effects on the supply and cost of housing must be firmly rejected.

Clearly, exclusionary-zoning laws can lead to residential segregation by wealth. By eliminating or decreasing exclusionary-zoning laws, one can increase the supply of housing suitable for low-income families. However, will this reduce residential segregation by race?

It has been argued that exclusionary-zoning laws operate particularly to keep poor whites out of affluent suburbs. If these laws were eliminated, or at least alleviated, poor whites could then leave center-city locations for the suburbs. These results would not necessarily hold true for center-city blacks. Thus the result of diminished exclusionary zoning would be increased racial segregation among metropolitan communities. This should occur especially in states with limited state aid, aggressive state policies requiring the integration of housing and schools within center cities, and a concentration of public housing in the old core cities.[48]

New Jersey has been and remains a state with limited assistance to local governments, state policies that direct integration efforts against center cities, and a concentration of public housing in the old core cities. Table 3.4 summarizes findings from a survey of zoning laws and racial segregation in New Jersey's twenty-one counties. For each county the degree of residential segregation by race among all the municipalities in that county was computed. Then the average minimum lot size for each community was computed, weighting each lot-size restriction by the number of acres in each municipality.

The evidence is clear. Where the minimum lot size required by local zoning laws is higher, the growth in racial segregation is higher. Where the minimum lot-size requirement is lower, the growth in racial segregation is lower.

Minimum lot-size requirements especially increase the growth of racial segregation where the typical community has many different zones. These include residential zones with even higher minimum lot-size requirements and industrial and commercial zones that exclude all residential housing, especially low-cost housing. When minimum lot-size requirements are combined with other types of exclusionary-zoning techniques, the result is significant growth in racial segregation.

Of course, exclusionary-zoning laws are not the only variables that affect the supply and cost of housing in metropolitan markets. Other variables, such as mortgage rates, also play a role, if only in determining whether consumers can pay the marginal costs added by exclusionary-zoning laws. It should also be noted that the effects of zoning laws are probably far greater in the long run than in the short run. Passing a strict zoning law may have limited impact on construction in the first year. However, the effects of zoning laws are cumulative, and will affect the costs of housing for the life of the units built subject to the laws. In any

Table 3.4 Effects of Minimum Lot-Size Requirements on Growth in Residential Segregation by Race Among Municipalities within County

	Independent Variable: Average Minimum Lot Size for All Municipalities in County, Weighting Each Observation by the Area in Each Municipality	
	Average Minimum Lot Size	Average Minimum Lot Size Multiplied by Average Number of Zones
Dependent Variable: Percent Increase in Residential Segregation by Race		
Equation 1	0.22	0.46*
Equation 2	0.30	0.49*

Note: An asterisk (*) means that the relation is statistically significant at an 0.05 level of probability. Equation 1 measures each relation by a bivariate correlation coefficient. Equation 2 measures each relation with a partial correlation coefficient that controls for certain other possible sources of confounding influences or spurious relations. These include the percentage of minority (Spanish and black), percentage of revenues received by local governments from intergovernmental aid, and the number of municipalities in each county. The independent variables (zoning laws) are based on data for 1967. The dependent variable measures changes between 1960 and 1970 in the coefficient of variation for the percentage of Negroes in each municipality in each county. The sample covers New Jersey's twenty-one counties.

For a fuller discussion of antecedents for intermunicipal residential segregation, see Russell S. Harrison, *Equality in Public School Finance* (Lexington, Mass.: Lexington Books, 1976), ch. 5.

event, the major point is that strict zoning laws disproportionately restrict housing opportunities for lower status families.

In fact, evidence is clear that exclusionary zoning increases racial segregation, not just economic segregation. One reason is that blacks are poorer than whites, looking at incomes and housing equity. Since exclusionary-zoning laws hurt poor families in particular, they hurt blacks in particular. Another possible reason why exclusionary-zoning laws cause racial segregation is their biased application. Minimum lot-size requirements, overzoning for industrial and commercial use, and other types of growth controls are often implemented as a "wait and see" device.[49] Specifically, the municipality waits to see if a developer is willing to build a subdivision particularly attractive to affluent whites, for example, by stressing quality over quantity. If so, the developer obtains a variance and can proceed with development. If the developer seeks to stress construction of housing particularly attractive to poor blacks, no variance is given. Thus highly restrictive land-use regulations and their administrative implementation can cause, both overtly and covertly, the perpetuation and growth of residential segregation by race.

In attacking exclusionary-zoning laws, state court activism is neither counterproductive nor irrelevant. Exclusionary-zoning laws do play an important role in causing distortions in urban housing markets. Reducing the restrictiveness of local zoning and land-use regulations can increase the supply of low-cost housing and reduce residential segregation both by wealth and race.

CONCLUSION

This research documents that state court activism in exclusionary-zoning cases is greatest in areas where the problem of residential segregation is maximum, while public support for residential segregation is minimum. In addition, it documents that the elimination of exclusionary-zoning laws can reduce imbalance in the supply and cost of housing that encourages residential segregation.

The problems of exclusionary zoning and residential segregation are closely connected, especially in certain urban, industrial states of the Northeast. Here state courts have responded to challenges in their environment. They have announced precedent-making constitutional principles for their own states, which are also available to courts in other states confronting similar problems.

What are the precedents announced by the activist state courts? The economic and fiscal self-interest of local communities is not a sufficient reason to justify gross violations of due process and equal rights guarantees. Localities must no longer adopt zoning laws that ignore regional housing needs of the poor, blacks, and other minorities.

NOTES

1. For valuable data on the prevalence of exclusionary zoning laws, *see* Allen D. Manvel, *Local Land and Building Regulation,* The National Commission on Urban Problems, Research Report No. 6 (Washington, D.C.: U.S. Government Printing Office, 1967); Stephen R. Seidel, *Housing Costs and Government Regulations* (New Brunswick, N.J.: Center for Urban Policy Research, 1978); New Jersey Department of Community Affairs, *Zoning in New Jersey, 1967* (Trenton, N.J.: Department of Community Affairs, 1970); id., *Land Use Regulation: The Residential Land Supply* (Trenton, N.J.: Department of Community Affairs, 1972).

2. For an interesting historical perspective on the evolution of zoning laws, *see* National Commission on Urban Problems, "Land-Use Controls: Zoning and Subdivision Requirements," reprinted in *Land Use Controls,* ed. David Listokin (New Brunswick, N.J.: Center for Urban Policy Research, 1974), pp. 19–28.

3. *See* David W. Sears and David L. Faytell, "Black Residential Segregation in American Metropolitan Regions: Some Changes During 1960–1970 Decade," *Public Data Use* 2, no. 3 (July 1974): 35–40. They show that the average increase in racial segregation for a sample of forty-three metropolitan areas was 14 percent and even higher in certain SMSAs like Trenton, N.J., that had a 38 percent increase in racial segregation.

4. *See* Seidel, *Housing Cost and Government Regulations,* app. D, "Legal Limitations on the Use of Zoning Regulations."

5. *See* id., app. C, "Legal Limitations on the Subdivision Control Power."

6. Most of the opposition to unnecessarily severe local building codes centers not in the courts, but in attempts to pass statewide zoning laws to which all localities must adhere.

By June 1975 some twenty-two states had statewide building codes affecting multifamily residential construction, but only fifteen states had statewide codes affecting one- and two-family construction. Of these fifteen states, only nine had a mandatory state code, and four state codes merely provided voluntary guidelines for local governments to adopt if they wished (the other states not reporting their application). Of the nine states with mandatory codes, six used minimum codes to which localities could add more restrictive local amendments, two without state approval. Only three required the adoption of a specific code (Massachusetts, Michigan, and Minnesota). Thus only three states had moved a great distance in ensuring identical building codes among localities. *See* Seidel, *Housing Costs and Government Regulations,* p. 78.

Since 1975 efforts have continued toward bringing greater uniformity into local building codes. New Jersey, for example, implemented a statewide code on January 1, 1977, that had been signed into law in October 1975. However, this law allows local amendments upon appeal. For a description of the New Jersey State Construction Code Act, *see* Sidney Willis et al., "The Municipality's Role Under the New State Uniform Construction Code Act," *New Jersey Municipalities* (January 1976): 12–31.

7. Fisher v. Township of Bedminister, 11 N.J. 111 (1952).

8. National Land and Investment Company v. Kohn, 419 Pa. 504 (1965).

9. Board of County Supervisors of Fairfax County v. Carper, 200 Va. 653 (1959).

10. *In re* Appeal of Kit-Mar Builders, Inc., 439 Pa. 466 (1970).

11. *In re* Appeal of Girsh, 437 Pa. 237 (1970).

12. DiSimone v. Greater Englewood Housing Corporation, 56 N.J. 428 (1970).

13. Molino v. Borough of Glassboro, 116 N.J. 195 (1971).

14. Bristow v. City of Woodhaven, 35 Mich. App. 205 (1971); Green v. Township of Lima, 40 Mich. App. 655 (1972); Shomo v. Denny Borough, 5 Pa. Commonwealth 216 (1972).

15. Southern Burlington County N.A.A.C.P. v. Township of Mt. Laurel, 67 N.J. 151 (1975).

16. Challenges to growth acts have met with little success in federal courts. *See, e.g.,* Golden v. Planning Board of Ramapo, New York, 285 N.E.2d 291 (1972), *appeal dismissed,*

409 U.S. 1003 (1972). *See also* Construction Industry Association of Sonoma County v. City of Petaluma, 522 F.2d 897 (9th Cir. 1975), *cert. denied,* 424·U.S. 934 (1976).

However, the New Jersey courts have given signs of greater sensitivity to problems of exclusionary zoning. *See* Southern Burlington County N.A.A.C.P. v. Township of Mt. Laurel, *supra* note 15, 336 A.2d 713 nn.5 & 20 (1975), and related discussion.

17. *See* id. at 732–34. For an analysis of the "fair-share" plans suggested by the initial *Mt. Laurel* decision and the debate over appropriate court remedies for problems of exclusionary zoning, *see* Jerome G. Rose and Robert Rothman, eds., *After Mount Laurel: The New Suburban Zoning* (New Brunswick, N.J.: Center for Urban Policy Research, 1977), esp. pp. 104–91.

18. *See* Southern Burlington County N.A.A.C.P. v. Township of Mt. Laurel, *supra* note 16, at 723–24, 730–31. For an inventory of the major municipal justifications that have been used to defend exclusionary-zoning laws, as well as the legal and empirical arguments that have been used against them, *see* George Sternlieb and David Listokin, "Exclusionary Zoning: State of the Art, Strategies for the Future," in *Housing in the Seventies,* U.S. Department of Housing and Urban Development, vol. 1 (Washington, D.C.: U.S. Government Printing Office, 1976), 325–50, esp. pp. 331–36.

19. The U.S. Supreme Court has been highly restrictive in granting standing in exclusionary-zoning cases. *See* Warth v. Seldin, 422 U.S. 490 (1975). *See also* Construction Industry Association of Sonoma County v. City of Petaluma, *cert. denied,* 424 U.S. 934 (1976). For useful perspectives on the problem of standing requirements in exclusionary-zoning decisions, *see* David H. Moskowitz, *Exclusionary Zoning Litigation* (Cambridge, Mass.: Ballinger Publishing Co., 1977), ch. 2.

20. Obviously, in those states where the courts have been most activist in the past, it is easier to win cases in the future, since precedents can more easily be cited to bolster arguments. In general, those states where the courts have been most activist in hearing exclusionary-zoning cases are also the states where litigants have been most activist in presenting doctrinal claims attacking exclusionary zoning. They are also the states where the courts are most apt to respond favorably to these claims. These congruities are not coincidences. Instead they reflect the mutual interaction of different components of the state court legal system. Where the courts are responsive to such claims, such claims are brought to court, the court hears them, and the cycle repeats itself, as attention shifts from one to another type of exclusionary zoning.

21. For perspective on growth controls, *see* Moskowitz, *Exclusionary Zoning Litigation,* ch. 7; Seigel, *Housing Cost and Government Regulations,* ch. 9; Fred Bosselman, "Can the Town of Ramapo Pass a Law to Bind the Rights of the Whole World?" in *Land Use Controls,* ed. Listokin, pp. 241–72.

For perspective on floating zones, *see* Jan Krasnowiecki, "Legal Aspects of Planned Unit Development in Theory and Practice," pp. 184–202, in *Land Use Controls,* ed. Listokin; Jacob H. Beuscher, Robert R. Wright, and Morton Gitelman, *Cases and Materials on Land Use,* 2d ed. (St. Paul, Minn.: West, 1976), pp. 604–14.

22. The degree to which the concept of "developing" communities should be narrowly defined has been the subject of heated debate in New Jersey. *See* Jerome G. Rose and Melvin R. Levin, "What Is a 'Developing Municipality,'" and Peter A. Buchsbaum, "The Irrelevance of the 'Developing Municipality' Concept," reprinted in *After Mt. Laurel: The New Suburban Zoning,* ed. Rose and Rothman, pp. 46–70, 71–78.

23. For example, in 1958 Easttown Township, Pennsylvania, won a court case upholding the constitutionality of one-acre minimum lot-size requirements. *See* Bilbar Construction Co. v. Easttown Township Board of Adjustment, 393 Pa. 62, 141 A.2d 851 (1958). Later the township raised minimum lot-size requirements to four acres and blocked development by the National Land and Investment Company of an eighty-five-acre tract. This action was

declared unconstitutional in National Land and Investment Co. v. Kohn, 419 Pa. 504, 215 A.2d 597 (1956).

24. Often a plaintiff landowner in an exclusionary-zoning case never gets to develop the specific property in question. *See* Jan Krasnowiecki, "Zoning Litigation and the New Pennsylvania Procedures," *University of Pennsylvania Law Review* 120 (1972): 1029, 1059–65, 1076–83, 1109. *See also* William L. Brach, "There's a Long, Long Trail Awinding—Mount Laurel from the Developers' View," in *After Mount Laurel: The New Suburban Zoning,* ed. Rose and Rothman, pp. 279–88.

For examples of local governments that have rezoned quarries to swamps to meet court mandates for increased land zoned for low-income housing, *see* Note, "Exclusionary Zoning," *Michigan Law Review* 74 (1976): 760. *See also* Southern Burlington County N.A.A.C.P. v. Township of Mt. Laurel, Slip Decision from the Superior Court of New Jersey, Law Division, Burlington County (Decided July 7, 1978).

25. As part of this effort, it seems useful for litigants to be able to demonstrate that the segregation resulting from exclusionary zoning is so pronounced and consistent that the relationship cannot be dismissed as merely coincidental. Previous research has not clearly documented this widespread belief among opponents of exclusionary zoning, but see the third section of this chapter.

26. *See* Buchanan v. Warley, 245 U.S. 60 (1917).

27. *See* Shelley v. Kraemer, 334 U.S. 1 (1948).

28. *See* Jones v. Alford Meyer Co., 392 U.S. 409 (1968).

29. Village of Belle Terrace v. Boraas, 416 U.S. 1 (1974); Village of Arlington Heights v. Metropolitan Housing and Development Corp., 429 U.S. 252 (1977).

30. Warth v. Seldin, 422 U.S. 490 (1975). However, it must be stressed that federal courts can and will intervene where there is de jure racial segregation; that is, racial discrimination is the obvious motivation for exclusionary zoning. *See, e.g.,* Kennedy Park Homes Association v. City of Lackawanna, N.Y., 436 F.2d 108 (2d Cir. 1971), *cert. denied,* 401 U.S. 1010 (1971); United States v. City of Black Jack, Missouri, U.S.C.A. (8th Cir. 1974), *cert. denied,* 422 U.S. 1042 (1975); Daily v. City of Lowton, 425 F.2d 1037 (10th Cir. 1970).

31. Village of Euclid v. Ambler Realty Co., 272 U.S. 365 (1926).

32. The 1973 decision of the Virginia Supreme Court in Board of Supervisors of Fairfax County v. De Groff Enterprises, 214 Va. 235, 198 S.E.2d 600 (1973), dealt with inclusionary zoning. It resulted in a conservative decision that was described at length by the National Committee Against Discrimination in Housing and the Urban Land Institute, *Fair Housing and Exclusionary Land Use* (Washington, D.C., 1974), pp. 48–49.

The 1959 decision of the Virginia Supreme Court in Board of County Supervisors of Fairfax County v. Carper, 200 Va. 653 (1959), dealt with overt exclusionary zoning. This case resulted in one of the earlier liberal decisions about exclusionary zoning, but was not discussed by the National Committee Against Discrimination.

For an overview of the general evolution of state court attitudes toward exclusionary zoning, *see* Sternlieb and Listokin, "Exclusionary Zoning: State of the Art, Strategies for the Future," pp. 336–41.

33. *See* Norman M. Bradbury, Seymour Sudman, and Galen L. Gockel, *Racial Integration in American Neighborhoods: A Comparative Survey* (Chicago: National Opinion Research Center, 1970), pp. 52–53. They conclude that 31.8 percent of the households in the Northeast live in integrated environments, 25.6 percent of the households in the West, 12.6 percent of the households in the North Central states, and only 11.3 percent of the households in the South. However, their definition of residential segregation and integration is different from ours. They could define all of the households within a metropolitan area as integrated even if each neighborhood and each civil subdivision were extremely segregated from its neighbors. In fact, they label many neighborhoods as having "open integration," even though

they have far less than 1.0 percent blacks, and other neighborhoods in the area have extremely high concentrations of blacks; id., *Racial Integration,* ch. 2.

We do not believe that simply having a few families in a neighborhood, town, or city which live in houses priced similar to those of whites constitutes integration. We certainly do not believe that intergration exists when blacks cannot realistically expect ever to increase their share of the population in a neighborhood, town, or city, even when that percentage share is far below the regional average. *Cf.* id., *Racial Integration,* ch. 1.

34. For a review of some of the major social, economic, political, and governmental antecedents of exclusionary zoning and metropolitan residential segregation, *see* Russell S. Harrison, "Fiscal Zoning and Residential Segregation: Effects of Governmental Fragmentation, State Aid, and Property Taxes on Racial Segregation," in *Equality in Public School Finance* (Lexington, Mass.: Lexington Books, 1976), ch. 5. *See also* Russell S. Harrison, "Exclusionary Zoning, Metropolitan Residential Segregation, and State Ceilings on Local Taxes and Debt" (Paper delivered at the 1978 Annual Meeting of the Northeastern Political Science Association, Tarrytown, N.Y., November 9–11, 1978).

35. For a strong defense of the thesis that "tastes" are a major cause of residential segregation, *see* Gary S. Becker, *The Economics of Discrimination* (Chicago: University of Chicago Press, 1957), pp. 10, 22, 59–62, 129.

36. Many states where public opinion most opposes residential segregation have statutes, commissions, and other legal restrictions against housing discrimination. Thus many states where courts condemn exclusionary zoning and residential segregation are states where the courts are resolving several contradictions. On the one hand, one finds the ideals expressed in public opinion and legally authoritative guidelines. On the other hand, one finds the reality expressed in exclusionary zoning and residential segregation. Whenever contradictions between public morality and current behavior exist, courts may be expected to take a stand to resolve the discrepancy. This is the case not only for the exclusionary-zoning cases, but more generally.

In short, it is not sufficient to study state court behavior as a simple response to the discrete effects both of mass opinion on an issue and of the actual practices of local governments. Rather, one must study the interaction of the two in producing state court responses. In this sense the systemic environment can help explain variation in state court behavior. *Cf.* G. Alan Tarr, *Judicial Impact and State Supreme Courts* (Lexington, Mass.: Lexington Books, 1977), pp. 63–68, 76. Of course, nonsystemic variables also play a role, particularly in shaping the behavior of individual judges.

37. For a discussion of fiscal incentives for exclusionary zoning, *see* Bruce W. Hamilton, "Property Taxation's Incentive to Fiscal Zoning," in *Property Tax Reform,* ed. George E. Peterson (Washington: The Urban Institute, 1973), pp. 125–39, esp. pp. 126–30.

38. *See* Harrell R. Rogers, Jr., and Charles S. Bullock, III, *Law and Social Change* (New York: McGraw-Hill, 1972), pp. 181–209.

39. *See* Kenneth M. Dolbeare and Philip E. Hammond, *School Prayer Decisions: From Court Policy to Local Practice* (Chicago: University of Chicago Press, 1971); Robert H. Birkby, "The Supreme Court and the Bible Belt: Tennessee Reaction to the 'Schemp' Decision," in *The Impact of Supreme Court Decisions,* 2d ed., ed. Theodore L. Becker and Malcolm M. Feeley (New York: Oxford University Press, 1973).

The impact of federal court decisions (for example, the disestablishment cases) on behavior within local institutions (for example, schools) is presumably most limited where state court judges fail to support federal precedents. For a study of conditions that determine the conformity of state court judges to federal precedents, *see* Tarr, *Judicial Impact and State Supreme Courts.*

40. James P. Levine, "Constitutional Law and Obscene Literature: An Investigation of Bookseller Censorship Practices," in *The Impact of Supreme Court Decisions,* ed. Becker and Feeley, pp. 119–38.

41. James P. Levine and Theodore L. Becker, "Toward and Beyond a Theory of Supreme

Court Impact," in *The Impact of Supreme Court Decisions,* ed. Becker and Feeley, pp. 230–44, esp. p. 235. *See* Staff Report, U.S. Commission on Civil Rights, Report of a National Survey of School Superintendents, *Reviewing a Decade of School Desegregation, 1966–1975* (January 1977). *See also* Albert P. Blaustein and Clarence C. Ferguson, Jr., "Avoidance, Evasion, and Delay," in *The Impact of Supreme Court Decisions,* ed. Becker and Feeley, pp. 100–109.

42. *See* Richard J. Medalie, Leonard Zeitz, and Paul Alexander, "Custodial Police Interrogation in Our Nation's Capital: The Attempt to Implement Miranda," in *The Impact of Supreme Court Decisions,* ed. Becker and Feeley, pp. 139–49; Steven R. Schlesinger, *Federalism and Criminal Justice: The Case of the Exclusionary Rule,* monograph (Washington, D.C.: The Heritage Foundation, 1975); Neil D. Milner, *The Court and Local Law Enforcement: The Impact of Miranda* (Beverly Hills, Calif.: Sage, 1971).

43. For negative views of the importance of malapportionment as a cause of state policy outputs, *see* Thomas Dye, "Malapportionment and Public Policy in the States," *Journal of Politics* 27 (August 1965): 586–601; id., *Politics, Economics and the Public* (Chicago: Rand McNally and Co., 1966), pp. 294–95; id., "State Legislative Politics," in *Politics in the American States,* ed. Herbert Jacob and Kenneth Vines (Chicago: Rand McNally and Co., 1965), pp. 157–65; Herbert Jacob, "The Consequences of Malapportionment: A Note of Caution," *Social Forces* 43 (December 1964): 256–61; David Brady and Douglas Edmonds, "One Man, One Vote—So What?" *Transaction* 4 (March 1967): 41–46; Richard Hofferbert, "The Relation Between Public Policy and Some Structural and Environmental Variables in the American States," *American Political Science Review* 60 (March 1966): 73–82.

For different perspectives, *see* Allan G. Pulsipher and James Weatherby, Jr., "Malapportionment, Party Competition, and the Functional Distribution of Governmental Expenditures," *American Political Science Review* 62 (December 1963): 1207–1919; Jack L. Walker, "The Diffusion of Innovations Among the American States," *American Political Science Review* 62 (September 1960): 880–86; Roger Hanson and Robert Crew, "The Effects of Reapportionment on State Public Policy Out-Puts," *Law and Society Review* 8 (February 1973), reprinted in *The Impact of Supreme Court Decisions,* ed. Becker and Feeley, pp. 155–74.

44. *See* David J. Armor, "The Evidence on Busing," *The Public Interest,* no. 28 (Summer 1972): 90–126; Nancy H. St. John, *School Desegregation Outcomes for Children* (New York: Wiley-Interscience Publication, 1975). *Cf.* Thomas F. Pettigrew et al., "Busing: A Review of 'The Evidence,'" *The Public Interest,* no. 30 (Winter 1973): 80–118.

45. James S. Coleman, Sara D. Kelley, and John A. Moore, *Trends in School Segregation, 1968–1973* (Washington, D.C.: The Urban Institute, August 1975). *Cf.* Thomas Pettigrew and Robert L. Green, "School Desegregation in Large Cities: A Critique of the Coleman 'White Flight' Thesis," *Harvard Educational Review* 46 (February 1976): 1–53.

46. *See* Larry L. Orr, *Income, Employment, and Urban Residential Location* (New York: Academic Press, 1975), pp. 74–75. For methodological limitations in his analysis, *see* Russell S. Harrison, "The Role of State Courts in Exclusionary Zoning Cases: Components, Causes, and Consequences of State Court Activism" (Paper delivered at the 1979 Annual Meeting of the Northeastern Political Science Association, Newark, N.J., November 8–10, 1979), pp. 23–26.

47. Data on request from author.

48. John M. Levy, "Exclusionary Zoning: After the Walls Come Down," *Planning* 38 (August 1972): 158–60, reprinted in *Land Use Controls,* ed. Listokin, pp. 179–81. *See also* Robert Schafer, "Conceptual and Empirical Problems in Measuring the Invisible Wall," mimeographed (Cambridge, Mass.: Harvard University, Department of City and Regional Planning, June 1975), esp. pp. 11–15.

49. *See* National Commission on Urban Problems, "Land-Use Controls: Zoning and Subdivision Requirements," in *Land Use Controls,* ed. Listokin, pp. 19–28, esp. pp. 26–28.

PART II.

NONCONSTITUTIONAL POLICYMAKING

4.

LAWRENCE BAUM AND BRADLEY C. CANON

State Supreme Courts as Activists: New Doctrines in the Law of Torts

INTRODUCTION

Images of judicial activism usually involve public law. The classic conception of judicial activism is that of a court finding laws unconstitutional as occurred in the halcyon days of substantive due process or as currently happens in the civil liberties area. Recent commentators also note judicial activism in the courts' assumption of positive policymaking authority as manifested in their development of busing programs to achieve racial balance in schools or their development of minimal standards for prisons and mental hospitals.[1]

But these examples are not the only forms of judicial activism. If it can be viewed as a significant and rather sudden court-engendered alteration in public policy, judicial activism can be found in some other types of court decisions. Courts, for instance, often make radical changes in policy by overruling their own precedents or by substantially modifying or abrogating traditional doctrines that have all the force of precedent. Although this variety of activism can be found in constitutional or other kinds of public law, it occurs much more frequently in the development of the common law where virtually all policy is of judicial origin. Common law doctrines often have important political implications—they determine who gets what, when, and how, to use Harold Lasswell's phrase[2]—but they receive at best only sporadic legislative attention.

One particularly important policy aspect of the common law is tort law. Tort law doctrines have considerable influence on the nature of economic activity because of their function of distributing monetary burdens and benefits to various segments of society. Tort law is more than a vehicle for remedying particular wrongs; it serves as a mechanism for encouraging or discouraging various economic or social endeavors.

For instance, the industrialization of the American economy during the nineteenth century was both facilitated and reflected by dramatic changes in tort law. Classic examples are found in the courts' establishment of the fellow servant, contributory negligence, and assumption of risk doctrines, all employer defenses against liability for work-related employee injury or death. Briefly, workers whose injuries were caused by other workers or by their own partial negligence or who knew (or should have known) of the potential risks attached to their job were denied recovery. The prevalence of such doctrines minimized financial loss and thus encouraged capital investment in industrial enterprises. Stated conversely, these doctrines placed much of the economic burden of industrialization on the shoulders of the working class.[3]

In these and other ways tort law developed in the nineteenth century to encourage industrialization. In the twentieth century, as investment capital became more abundant and the social costs of industrialization became more apparent, tort law shifted direction and began assigning greater costs to business enterprises. One famous example involved the doctrine of privity, which required a contractual relationship between manufacturer and consumer to sustain a product-liability suit. As modern marketing practices interposed one or more middlemen between them, privity effectively foreclosed manufacturer liability for damages caused by unsafe products. In the famous case of *MacPherson* v. *Buick Motor Co.* (1916),[4] the privity requirement was significantly curtailed. The adoption and expansion of *MacPherson* by other courts not only shifted liability away from those least able to bear it, but also encouraged greater attention to making products safer.[5]

The development of tort law in the United States is almost entirely the province of the state appellate judiciary—usually state supreme courts.[6] Although they were sometimes influenced by leading English decisions or by federal cases, most shifts in tort law originated with the state high courts themselves. Historically, prominent state jurists such as Chief Justice Lemuel Shaw of Massachusetts, Chief Justice Charles Doe of New Hampshire, and Justices Thomas Cooley of Michigan and Benjamin Cardozo of New York were the leading figures in the transformation of tort law to meet perceived economic needs. Moreover, despite the increasing federalization of many areas of law, for example, criminal, labor, and commercial law, tort law remains an area where preeminent responsibility for change rests with the state judiciary. Indeed, this is all the more so in recent years as the impact of English decisions has diminished and the development of a federal common law in diversity cases was foreclosed by the *Erie* decision.[7] Nor has tort law become static or has its breadth been reduced as has contract or to a lesser extent property law.[8] In fact, in the post-World War II era tort law is changing more rapidly than ever before and is expanding its scope while doing so.[9] Thus it provides an ideal study of judicial activism by state supreme courts.

This chapter makes such a study. The focus is on dramatic postwar changes[10] in tort law usually accomplished by a single sweeping decision, rather than incrementally, and that by and large have the effect of shifting economic costs from individuals or consumers to manufacturers, providers of services, or other social agencies better able to absorb costs, for example, insurance companies and governmental units. For the most part, the discussion focuses upon tort doctrines that have won widespread adoption and whose development has been largely free of legislative involvement.

The first section looks at state supreme court activism in five areas of tort law: immunities, product liability, family relations, construction defect liability, and procedural issues. These are the areas of most significant postwar change, but a brief discussion of miscellaneous other changes is also presented. A second section recounts the debates over such activism: What is the philosophy of those state supreme courts adopting new doctrines and what is that of dissenters or courts rejecting change? A third section notes and discusses those state supreme courts that have been the cutting edge of tort law activism and also looks at those that are most resistant to such change.

DRAMATIC CHANGES IN TORT LAW SINCE WORLD WAR II

IMMUNITIES

At common law various immunities from tort liability existed. Perhaps the most well known is sovereign or governmental immunity, the doctrine that the government cannot be sued without its consent.[11] The medieval immunity of the English crown was transferred to the states in the colonial period and later extended to cover municipalities.[12] Would-be plaintiffs seeking compensation for torts inflicted by government agencies or employees had to seek relief through private bills in the legislature. In the twentieth century, most states passed legislation creating a claims commission or court similar to the Federal Tort Claims Act of 1946, but they often limited recovery to modest amounts, for example, ten thousand dollars.

Sovereign immunity was almost universally criticized by legal scholars and sometimes even by the courts.[13] Besides noting the irrelevance of its medieval origin, critics argued that it was illogical to deny victims recovery from the state as tortfeasor if they could recover when others had committed the same wrong. Defenses of sovereign immunity were few and often advanced half-heartedly. By the mid-twentieth century, most judges believed that although sovereign immunity was illogical or mischievous, the legislature was the proper body to overturn it or that legislative inaction constituted approval.[14] Sovereign immunity was maintained by tradition and inertia.

About 1960 things began to break.[15] In *Hargrove* v. *Cocoa Beach* (1957),[16] the Florida Supreme Court abrogated immunity for the state's municipalities. Then the Michigan and Illinois high courts made similar decisions. In 1961 California's Court abrogated the doctrine at the state level as well as the municipal one.[17] Afterwards, abrogation decisions occurred rapidly. By 1970 sovereign immunity had been overturned substantially or entirely in eleven states and at the municipal level alone in another eight states through judicial action. The trend continued into the 1970s; by 1978 thirty-three states had abandoned sovereign immunity at the municipal level with about one-half that number doing so in some form at the state level as well.[18] In about ten of these states, the legislature either initially abolished the doctrine or had given substance to a judicial abrogation. In Arkansas the legislature restored sovereign immunity following an adverse judicial decision, and in several other states legislatures modified or put limits upon judicial abrogations.

The greater propensity to abolition at the municipal level often reflected state constitutional provisions that prohibited suits against the state without its consent or expenditures of state funds absent explicit legislative authorization. Twenty-two state constitutions contained one or both such provisions.[19] None, however, contained provisions rendering municipal immunity so rigid. Also, the common law origin of immunity at the municipal level was of relatively less ancient vintage and perhaps of even more questionable logic.[20] Thus high courts in some states found themselves able to abrogate the doctrine at the local level, but constrained at the state level. A few, however, went all the way despite constitutional provisions to the contrary. The Wisconsin Supreme Court, for instance, made the state legally liable for its torts, but recognized that the state courts could not hear such cases except through legislative implementation.[21] Idaho's high court held that the purchase of liability insurance by state agencies effected a waiver of tort immunity.[22]

Another prevailing common law immunity protected charitable organizations from tort liability.[23] Although sustained on several rationales, the primary one was that charitable activity should not be diminished or foreclosed by large adverse judgments. The doctrine of charitable immunity was developed in the mid-nineteenth century and by 1940 had been adopted in all but a handful of states.[24] As the twentieth century progressed it was subject to increasing criticism. Opponents conceded that it may have been justified in the nineteenth century when charities were small and liability insurance nonexistent or in its infancy, but they argued that it was poor public policy in the mid-twentieth century when charities were big business and insurance available.[25] Nonetheless, support for charitable immunity was strong among judges, and many contended that the legislature should make such changes in public policy.

In the 1942 case of *Georgetown College* v. *Hughes*[26] charitable immunity was rejected in the District of Columbia in an opinion written by Judge (later Justice) Wiley Rutledge that devastatingly refuted every argument for the doctrine. In the 1950s fourteen state high courts rethought their position on the doctrine, most citing *Hughes* as the catalyst for making the change. The transformation was virtually completed in the 1960s as another fifteen states abandoned charitable immunity.[27] By 1978 only eight states retained the doctrine.[28] The rapid and almost complete transformation of the law here serves as a prime example of state supreme court activism in the massive postwar reshaping of American tort law.[29]

PRODUCTS LIABILITY

Perhaps the most significant changes in tort law since World War II have occurred in the field of products liability.[30] The result of this rapid evolution in the law has been to alter fundamentally the legal relationship between producers and consumers of goods.

At the beginning of this century, the legal responsibilities of manufacturers for defective products were limited in two important respects. First, manufacturers were liable to persons injured by their products only if negligence were established. Injury itself was insufficient, even if the injury could be traced clearly to a particular product. Second, the liability of manufacturers and sellers of goods was limited to persons with whom they were in privity of contract—in other words, to whom they had directly sold their goods. The privity requirement prevented consumers from suing manufacturers for defective products except in the rare instances when they had dealt directly with each other.[31]

State supreme courts began to chip away at these restrictive doctrines early in this century. Beginning with a 1913 Washington decision,[32] several courts created an exception to the doctrines for defective food and drink. More important, by World War II a majority of the state high courts had adopted the doctrine of the *MacPherson* case[33] (discussed briefly in the introductory section), which made an exception to the privity requirement of any product that "is reasonably certain to place life and limb in peril when negligently made."[34] The effect of this formulation "was to make the exception swallow up the rule"[35] in those states adopting the *MacPherson* doctrine.

In the early postwar period these exceptions to the traditional rules were adopted more widely. Then in the late 1950s state supreme courts began to undertake a wholesale abandonment of the rules themselves. In an extraordinary burst of activity, most of the supreme courts have accepted innovative doctrines that create a new law of products liability.

The change began with the holding by several courts that manufacturers

make an implied warranty of their products' safety to the ultimate consumers. This doctrine overthrew both the requirement of privity of contract and the requirement of negligence. It was first articulated by the
Michigan Supreme Court in 1958.[36] The landmark decision, however, is
Henningsen v. *Bloomfield Motors* (1960),[37] in which the New Jersey
Supreme Court accepted the doctrine directly and clearly with a long
supporting argument.

The new doctrine was particularly important in its elimination of the
privity requirement. Even in the states where the *MacPherson* doctrine
had been accepted, the complete elimination of privity constituted a significant break with existing law. Yet the new rule was adopted rapidly,
achieving acceptance by most state supreme courts in a relatively short
time.

The other major tenet of the Michigan and New Jersey decisions, the
implied warranty to consumers, was just beginning to obtain acceptance
when it was overtaken by an even more radical break with traditional legal
theory. The term *warranty* carries with it some ambiguities and potential
limitations on the right to recover for damages. To transcend these problems, the drafters of the Second Restatement of Torts for the American
Law Institute proposed the formulation that manufacturers simply be
given a strict liability in tort to consumers for damages caused by defective
products. The requirements of both negligence and contractual relationships between producers and consumers were eliminated completely by
the sweeping language of the Restatement section.[38]

The strict liability formulation was first adopted by the California
Supreme Court *Greenman* v. *Yuma Power Products Co.* (1963).[39] Other
states followed with almost unprecedented speed: five in 1965, seven in
1966–67, five in 1968–69, six in 1970–71. By 1976 thirty-seven states had
accepted the strict liability doctrine by supreme court decision. Four
others did so by statute. Most of the remaining states had gone at least
part of the way toward strict liability. Never before had such a momentous
change in tort law swept the American states so rapidly.

At least at the level of legal doctrine, the change in the relationship
between manufacturers and consumers of goods brought about by
the adoption of these two new doctrines is enormous. In a relatively
short time "the courts have effected a veritable revolution in product
liability."[40] Participation in this movement might have been expected from
the most liberal and innovation minded of the state supreme courts. That
even the politically and doctrinally conservative courts hastened to take
part as well is striking.

FAMILY-RELATED ISSUES

A broad range of tort liability issues lies within the family setting. On
four such issues supreme courts in the postwar period have taken activist

roles in upsetting traditional limitations on the right to recover for the injuries.

The first is interspousal immunity. At common law, husbands and wives could not sue each other, because they were considered "one flesh." As this view lost its popularity, another rationale for interspousal immunity developed: the fear that spouses would engage in collusive lawsuits to recover insurance money.

Nonetheless, twentieth-century supreme courts began to abrogate the rule. Between 1914 and 1941 eleven courts eliminated the immunity. In the three decades following World War II thirteen more supreme courts eliminated it, including those of major states such as Illinois, Ohio, New Jersey, and Michigan. More recently, between 1976 and 1980, six additional courts decided to allow suits between spouses. By now interspousal immunity is clearly the minority rule, and few supreme courts have reaffirmed the rule in recent years.[41]

The abrogation of interspousal immunity reflects a highly activist approach in two respects. First, the immunity was an ancient part of the common law and thus not lightly changed. In addition, public opinion as reflected in legislative action had not been supportive of the policy change. Only in New York has the legislature acted to abolish the immunity. In four other states legislation has reaffirmed that immunity. In Illinois the reaffirmance came only three years after a Supreme Court decision had eliminated interspousal immunity.

The second issue is the right of wives to recover for loss of consortium. Under the common law a husband whose wife was injured could sue for loss of her consortium, meaning her companionship, affectionate relations, and services. No parallel right existed for a wife whose husband was injured; the husband had a property right in his wife, but the wife had no such right in her husband.

The traditional rule survived nineteenth-century changes in the legal status of women within marriage, which could have led to equalization of the husband's and wife's position in this regard.[42] Indeed, the first judicial challenge to the rule did not come until 1950, when the federal Court of Appeals for the District of Columbia established the wife's right to sue for loss of consortium in that jurisdiction.[43] For several years after 1950 most of the supreme courts that considered the issue reaffirmed the traditional prohibition on the wife's action, but gradually the tide turned. By 1980 the high courts of twenty-five states had established the wife's right of action, including ten that earlier had disagreed with the District of Columbia decision. Six other states adopted the change by statute. Several supreme courts have reaffirmed their support for the traditional doctrine in recent years, but their position gradually has been losing ground.[44]

The direction of supreme courts' action on this issue in recent years demonstrates their activism in support of tort plaintiffs. Changes in the status of women perhaps made it inevitable that the positions of wife and husband be equalized in most states. But this equalization could have been brought about through abolition of the action for loss of consortium, considered by many to be rather antiquated. Instead, most supreme courts have chosen to equalize the law by expanding tort liability, as they have done in so many other areas of tort during the past few decades.[45]

A third issue is immunity of parents and children from lawsuits by each other. Unlike interspousal immunity, this rule is not of ancient vintage. The first adoption came in Mississippi in 1891.[46] From that time on there was a steady stream of adoptions, eventually totalling more than forty. Several states newly established the immunity as late as the 1960s. The main rationale for the immunity was that to permit suits between children and parents would threaten family harmony.

In the 1960s and 1970s state supreme courts began to abrogate parent-child immunity, and they did so with considerable speed. The abrogation process started with a Wisconsin decision in 1963.[47] Other states joined in, allowing suits between parents and children generally or in the specific but common case of automobile accidents. By 1980 the immunity had been cut back or abolished in more than twenty states, and the process could be expected to continue. As with some other immunities, a major impetus for change here has been the widespread holding of liability insurance. Although insurance created fears of intrafamily collusion, it also made lawsuits within the family lose some of the adversary character that had concerned supporters of immunity.

A final and somewhat different kind of family issue concerns prenatal injury. The courts traditionally barred recovery for injuries that were suffered before birth, whether the child was born alive with the injury or the injury resulted in the death of the fetus. The bar to recovery was based largely on the legal nonexistence of the injured party at the time of injury.

The process of change began with a 1946 decision by the federal District Court for the District of Columbia that allowed recovery for prenatal injuries to a child.[48] Three years later the Minnesota Supreme Court upheld an action for the wrongful death of a child, based on prenatal injuries; the court also ruled that a child who remained alive could sue for personal injuries.[49] Other states quickly followed, allowing actions for personal injuries, wrongful death, or both. By 1973 twenty-one supreme courts approved of actions for wrongful death, seventeen for personal injury.

In its 1973 abortion decision the U.S. Supreme Court held that a fetus is not a person under the Fourteenth Amendment.[50] A few state supreme court judges have cited the abortion decision in support of their opposition to allowing recovery for prenatal injuries.[51] Nonetheless, the ruling did not halt or reverse the trend toward allowance of recovery; since 1973 some additional state supreme courts have joined the trend.

LIABILITY FOR DEFECTS IN CONSTRUCTION

Another significant judicially generated postwar shift in doctrine occurred in the area of liability for injury caused by defective construction. At common law the liability of contractors or builders was limited by two doctrines. The "accepted work" doctrine held that contractors were released from liability for injuries to third parties (absent fraud or willful negligence) caused by negligence once their work was accepted by the party engaging them. Acceptance was denoted by payment in full or a formal release. Similarly, builder-vendors of homes were immunized against liability to purchasers (again with the above exceptions) by the ancient doctrine of caveat emptor.

Both doctrines were shaped in and suited to a simpler era. A century or two ago it was usually possible for a purchaser to inspect a prospective home and determine how safe or sound it was. But today hidden wiring and gas lines, complex built-in appliances, the availability of potentially toxic construction products, and so on virtually dictate that the average buyer of a new home accept on faith that it meets minimal safely standards. A similar problem faces individuals or firms in assessing the quality of construction or other improvements contracted. Nonetheless, the doctrines were not without twentieth-century defenders. They obviously served the construction industry and those who financed it. Moreover the doctrines also minimized litigation and thus appealed to judges. With the postwar mass production of subdivisions, however, liability for construction defects became a focal point of judicial conflict. The first repudiations of the accepted work doctrine occurred in Pennsylvania and Delaware in 1949.[52] In the mid-1950s New York's highest court handed down a very persuasive opinion.[53] By 1960 eight state appellate courts had rejected the doctrine and subsequently an additional sixteen have done so, for a total of twenty-four in all. Although rejection is now the majority position, the trend here has not been entirely unidirectional. In the 1950s seven state high courts that had not previously considered the issue adopted the accepted work doctrine and two more did so in the 1960s. Combined with those states that had previously adopted the doctrine, it prevails in eighteen states.

Caveat emptor was modified or curtailed by the development of a tort doctrine usually known as builder-vendor implied warranty.[54] It was first adopted by the Colorado Supreme Court in 1964,[55] although three appellate courts had a few years earlier come to a similar substantive position by applying legal fictions to property law.[56] Immediately, other state high courts began adopting the doctrine; twelve did so in the 1960s and nineteen more in the 1970s. Only four appellate courts have rejected builder-vendor implied warranty, and only one has done so since 1966. In 1969 the California Supreme Court went so far as to hold financiers liable for breaches of the implied warranty when the builder-vendor became insolvent, but no other court has seen fit to impose such far-reaching liability.[57]

PROCEDURAL ISSUES

Each of the four areas discussed above involved substantive issues, those concerning the conditions under which tort liability exists. During the postwar period, the state supreme courts' activism also extended to what we may call "procedural issues," that is, the conditions for bringing and arguing tort cases. Activism regarding two such issues has been especially notable.

The first is the statute of limitations for medical malpractice claims. Typically, malpractice statutes have limited actions to a certain period "after the cause thereof accrued." The courts traditionally interpreted this period to begin at the time of the treatment allegedly responsible for a patient's injury; the result was to deny recovery to patients who did not discover the injury until a later time. Between 1917 and 1936 this interpretation was abrogated by the courts in three states and overturned by legislation in a fourth. It was replaced by the "discovery rule," under which the statute of limitations began to run only when the patient discovered the problem or reasonably could have been expected to discover it. But no other courts moved away from the traditional rule for more than two decades.

The process of change was renewed in 1959, when the Pennsylvania Supreme Court adopted the discovery rule for cases in which foreign objects had been left in patients.[58] Other states followed, adopting the rule either in general terms or only in foreign objects cases.[59] By 1974 the courts of twenty-five states had accepted the discovery rule in a fifteen-year period.

The popularity and rapidity of this change are notable because the courts involved had to upset a settled interpretation of a statute, and this is a more radical break than an alteration of the common law.[60] Some courts shrank from this step, but most were willing to assert themselves in support of what they regarded as an equitable result.

The second procedural issue concerns arguments by counsel in trial. In the early 1950s courts began to rule on a technique of plaintiffs' attorneys in which they would suggest to a jury that an injured party be allowed a certain amount of money per day for pain and suffering damages. This "per-diem formula" often helped to produce large awards to plaintiffs. For this reason it has been attacked as prejudicial.

The response of the state supreme courts to this technique in the 1950s and 1960s is interesting, because the issue was essentially new, unconstrained by precedent. The New Jersey Supreme Court made a strong argument against the formula in 1958,[61] and several courts followed its lead. But about two-thirds of the courts considering the issue chose to allow use of the per-diem formula. In this respect, as in so many others, the general trend has favored the legal position of tort plaintiffs.

OTHER ISSUES

These examples hardly exhaust the cases in which state supreme courts have taken innovative action to change the tort law. The list of tort law issues on which one or more courts have established new rules at variance with traditional law is long and diverse. One commentator discovered more than thirty-five questions on which state supreme courts overruled their own earlier positions during the ten years from 1958 to 1967, including issues such as the liabilities of multiple tortfeasors contributing to an injury, the application of the contributory-negligence rule, and a driver's duty to a "guest" passenger.[62] It is doubtful that the pace or breadth of innovation have slowed substantially since that time. Across the whole range of the law of torts, state supreme courts have played an activist role in overturning existing doctrines and developing new law favorable to plaintiffs.

THE DEBATE OVER TORT LAW ACTIVISM

Most changes in tort law wrought by state supreme courts in the postwar years were enveloped in controversy. Much of this controversy, of course, was substantive: was the new position more logical or did it make better policy than the old one? But a steady undercurrent of debate focused not on the changes themselves but on the idea that the courts were making such changes at all. From time to time books, law review articles, and even judicial opinions would address the phenomena of significant judicially mandated changes in the law of torts. To some critics this was nothing short of judicial policymaking or judicial activism and thus beyond the function of the courts. Defenders often conceded the activism charge, but argued that such change was within the normal purview of the courts.

This section briefly highlights the debate over judicial activism in tort law. The main focus is on what appellate judges themselves have said in their opinions or in law review articles they have written on the subject.[63] Occasionally, however, pertinent points by legal commentators are noted. Essentially, the debate has three focuses. The first is the question of who should make policy, judges or legislators? The second asks about the courts' relationship to the law, upholder of precedent or modernizer? The third is the issue of how willing the courts should be to follow trends and/ or the weight of legal authority.

WHO SHOULD MAKE POLICY, JUDGES OR LEGISLATORS?

The most frequent criticism of significant judicial change in tort law is that it violates the legislature's function of making public policy. This criticism also gives courts making such changes the greatest pause. On several occasions state supreme courts have indicated a favorable attitude toward changing tort doctrines, but have refrained from accomplishing it out of deference to the legislature.[64] When such changes have been made, dissenting justices often have accused the majority of a violation of separation of powers. As the elected representatives of the people, only the legislature, it is argued, possesses any warrant to alter public policy.[65] Moreover, legislative hearings and debate are subject to factual and argumentative presentations by all interested citizens and are thus superior to lawsuits as a vehicle for generating sound and reasoned changes in policy.[66]

Obtaining legislative consideration of a tort law issue, however, is often a vain hope, and some state high courts, losing patience after years of waiting, have announced new policies on their own.[67] This has been justified by noting that the legislature was simply too pressed with other business to put tort reform issues on its agenda[68] or by arguing that nonconsideration manifested a legislative belief that if certain legal doctrines were unjust, the courts would correct them.[69] Alternately, some courts have engaged in policy innovation as a means of agenda setting. They have made the change and pointedly noted that if the legislature disagreed with it, the lawmakers were free to restore the status quo.[70] Indeed, the California, Illinois, and Minnesota high courts went so far as to stay the effect of some decisions until a date following the next legislative session, subject to whatever statutes were then in force.[71]

At times, a state supreme court would argue that its policy changes were in harmony with legislative intent. This was done by noting that the philosophy inherent in some recently passed laws was analogous to that in the court's new tort policy,[72] that the court's decision merely followed the direction of recent legislative enactments in a particular tort area,[73] or that the court's action was consonant with legislative committee recommendations even though they had never been adopted by the session as a whole.[74]

Of course, such justifications were not available to courts when the legislature had explicitly rejected tort law reform. Many state high courts then bowed to the lawmakers' will.[75] Others went ahead and defied the legislature anyway. Various rationales were expressed, but the case was put most succinctly by Chief Justice Thomas Grady of Washington.

. . . legislators are faced with strong opposition to change by those who are the beneficiaries of such a rule [charitable immunity], and proponents of a change find efforts to secure corrective legislation futile. When such a situation arises and the courts become convinced that the rule should no longer exist, there is justification for action to be taken by them.[76]

Most commonly, state supreme courts saw no need to be concerned with legislative consideration of a tort law reform. Virtually all tort policies, they pointed out, were of judicial origin and had not been enacted or even considered by the lawmakers in the first place. Thus if the courts were to alter substantially or replace such doctrines, it was hardly a usurpation of legislative authority; the growth of the common law has always been the province of the judiciary. As the Washington Supreme Court said in abrogating charitable immunity, "We closed our doors without legislative help and we can likewise open them."[77]

In somewhat similar vein, arguments reminiscent of mechanistic jurisprudence were adopted to refute the usurpation charge. The new tort law position, a court would announce, was not a manifestation of activism, but merely a discovery of the true law, a correction of an error the court had made in the past. The court was not making new policy but simply finding the law.[78]

These rationales were not without judicial critics. Conceding the judicial origin of tort law doctrines, dissenting justices argued that they were nonetheless manifestations of public policy and thus were properly in the legislative realm. Two wrongs do not make a right, they said. Moreover, the early adoptions of such doctrines were accomplished by judges who were not consciously engaged in policymaking but were trying to apply the common law as they understood it.[79]

THE COURTS' ROLE: MAINTENANCE OF STARE DECISIS OR MODERNIZATION?

Another rhetorical battleground involved the venerable doctrine of *stare decisis*, the idea that precedents once adopted should not be overturned. Many dissenting justices and not a few majorities worried about the disruptive impact an abrupt change in the law would have, not only on those concerned with the tort doctrine immediately at stake, but with those relying on other legal doctrines subject to reformist criticism. Arguments over stare decisis occurred at two levels. When the precedent was old, dating from the nineteenth or early twentieth century and not recently reaffirmed after serious consideration, only a small number of justices expressed concern about overruling it. They could nonetheless be vociferous. Chief Justice John Bell of Pennsylvania argued repeatedly that stare decisis was the "basic principle and fundamental precept upon which the House of Law was built and maintained"[80] and that it should always be applied except for irreconcilable precedents or when the original reason for the rule of law no longer existed.[81]

However, when the precedent was more recent, concern about abandoning it was much more widespread. Here reaffirmation was often the case—a manifestation of lawyers' willingness to push for reform and the courts' reluctance to accede to such pressure quickly. When the courts finally did decide that change was necessary, dissenters decried the impact of such a shift on lower courts and clients. "The judicial wastebasket," said one, "should not be filled with precedents only a few years old."[82]

Many state supreme courts defended the overturning of precedent by explaining that technological, economic, or social conditions[83] had changed so significantly since the establishment of the original doctrine that alterations in legal doctrines were necessary to render justice. Often the court would engage in a detailed accounting of nineteenth- and twentieth-century conditions as they related to the tort doctrine at issue. The Arkansas Supreme Court made a typical argument when abrogating interspousal immunity: "Whenever an old rule is found unsuited to present conditions or unsound, it should be set aside and a rule declared which is in harmony with those conditions."[84] A few courts were more militant. The New Jersey Supreme Court declared: "The law should be based upon current concepts of what is right and just and the judiciary should be alert to the never ending need for keeping its common law principles abreast of the times."[85] In short, courts should be committed to substantive justice as well as legal stability and must be willing to readjust public policy to balance the former with the latter.

In defending the overruling of more recent precedents, courts argued that the common law was always changing with the times—and ever more rapidly nowadays with increased technological and social change—and thus a degree of uncertainty in the law was inevitable.[86] Pressures for reform themselves created this uncertainty. The only way of restoring stability, it was sometimes argued, was for courts to adopt tort law reforms.[87] Disturbing or inequitable impacts of such adoptions were often minimized by rendering prospective rather than retroactive decisions.[88]

Not everyone agreed with the philosophy. Some disputed the underlying assumption that the common law was or should be constantly changing to parallel economic or social changes—at least to the extent that it came around to denying its earlier development abruptly. This was not growth but merely a seesawing backward and forward. Even when the outmoded nature of the original tort doctrine was conceded, many argued that the courts were obligated to protect the integrity of the common law.[89] In other words, courts found the law; they did not make public policy.

ARGUMENTS ABOUT TRENDS AND THE WEIGHT OF AUTHORITY

Both sides in the activism versus restraint debate relied on current legal trends or the weight of authority to buttress their position. Obviously, early in the history of a tort reform, courts seeking to reject the reform would note the weight of authority and courts seeking to justify an adoption would note a trend; that is, in the last few years the reform had been adopted in so many jurisdictions or by some prestigious courts. Some-times, an opinion would throw in the weight of legal scholarship (which almost always favored reform) as well.[90] Justices favoring the status quo would then deplore "trendiness" or reliance on scholarly commentary as a gross form of judicial activism.[91] Some state high courts were cautious in this respect. Although they rejected reform proposals in their minority days, they clearly hinted that they were sympathetic and were likely to switch positions once the reform attained majority status.[92] Others were bolder. The New Mexico Supreme Court responded to a criticism that it was "playing follow the leader," by asserting that there is "nothing wrong [with this] if the leader is going in the right direction."[93] Once a reform attained a majority position, of course, the shoe was on the other foot. Then the reformers argued for following the weight of authority, and the old guard protested that numbers should not matter.

THE ROLE OF PARTICULAR SUPREME COURTS

Postwar activism in tort law has not been limited to a few state supreme courts. When the states are ranked by the speed with which their highest courts have adopted new tort doctrines, we do not find a few states regularly among the early adopters and others consistently at the bottom. Indeed, on seven major doctrines first introduced since the war, almost half of the states have been among the first five adopters of at least one doctrine.[94] Robert Keeton identified thirty supreme courts that overruled at least one traditional tort doctrine during a single decade from 1958 to 1967.[95]

But courts have differed in their roles in the tort law revolution over the past three decades. One measure of the relative activism of state supreme courts is the set of rankings shown in table 4.1. Each supreme court[96] was ranked from 1 to 50 according to the speed with which it adopted each of fourteen postwar innovative doctrines, with all adoptions through 1975 counted. The mean rank for all of the doctrines comprises a supreme court's ranking in table 4.1.[97]

ACTIVIST COURTS

A few state supreme courts are notable for their recent leadership in tort law reform. These courts have been the most willing to advocate innova-tive positions and to reassess established doctrine. Perhaps the leading activist courts have been the supreme courts of California, Michigan, and New Jersey; their leadership is indicated by their positions among the top four courts in our rankings.

The California Supreme Court was the first to promulgate a general doctrine of strict liability in tort, thereby initiating the single most dramatic legal change in tort law.[98] Moreover, it also was among the first five adopters of four other tort reforms. Indeed, the California Court has been extraordinarily bold in its reassessment of tort law. This boldness is best reflected in the 1975 decision that eliminated the traditional contributory

Table 4.1 Rankings of State Supreme Courts in Propensity to Tort Law Activism in the Postwar Years

State	Rank of Average Tort Innovation Adoption	State	Rank of Average Tort Innovation Adoption
1. New Jersey	12.6	26. Florida	27.9
2. Michigan	14.5	27. Delaware	28.1
3. Kentucky	15.1	28. Arkansas	28.4
4. California	16.7	29. S. Carolina	28.6
5. Louisiana	18.1	30. Maryland	29.8
6. Pennsylvania	19.8	31. Mississippi	31.0
7. New York	19.9	32. North Dakota	31.3
8. Washington	20.4	33. South Dakota	31.5
9. Ohio	21.7	34.5 Idaho	31.6
10.5 Minnesota	21.8	34.5 Nebraska	31.6
10.5 New Hampshire	21.8	36. Nevada	31.7
12. Connecticut	22.0	37. Arizona	31.8
13. Illinois	22.3	38. N. Carolina	34.5
14. Oklahoma	23.0	39. Rhode Island	35.0
15. Oregon	23.1	40.5 Kansas	35.8
16. Texas	23.3	40.5 W. Virginia	35.8
17. Iowa	24.0	42. Alaska	36.1
18. Wisconsin	24.7	43. Hawaii	36.3
19. Colorado	24.9	44. Montana	37.0
20. Indiana	25.0	45. N. Mexico	37.4
21. Tennessee	25.5	46. Vermont	37.7
22. Georgia	25.8	47. Virginia	38.6
23. Utah	27.0	48. Massachusetts	41.1
24. Alabama	27.1	49. Wyoming	44.7
25. Missouri	27.2	50. Maine	46.6

Note: Rankings are based upon the adoption of fourteen innovations in tort doctrine. They include eleven of the twelve major innovations discussed in the text (all but the abrogation of parent-child immunity), as well as three others: the right of privacy, the *Baxter* doctrine that advertisement of a product's safety warrants its safety, and the Connecticut rule that landlords are liable for failure to remove ice and snow from walkways.

A court was given a rank of 1 if it was the first adopter of an innovation, a 2 if the second adopter, and so on. A court was not ranked for an innovation if it was precluded from acting by the adoption of a statute. Courts not adopting an innovation are ranked 50 (or slightly lower if one or more courts were not ranked). The average ranks shown in the table are means of all ranks for individual innovations.

negligence rule by overthrowing a century-old interpretation of statute.[99]

The California Court's leading role in tort law has been part of a more general liberal activism in the postwar period. Its innovation in tort law has been matched by its work on due process and equal-protection issues in constitutional law.[100] This record can be traced in large part to liberal appointments by the three governors who served between 1942 and 1966. But the most important figure in the court's tort activism during this period was Roger Traynor, who joined the court in 1940 and retired as chief justice thirty years later. Traynor, one of the great figures of the law in this century, wrote many of the court's innovative opinions on tort doctrine. Most significantly, he spurred the court forward through an early advocacy of changes in the tort law; for instance, he advocated strict liability in tort in a 1944 opinion, nearly two decades before his or any other court adopted that position.[101]

The New Jersey Supreme Court made the 1960 decision that was the key step in the elimination of the privity requirement in warranty, a decision viewed by some as the effective beginning of strict liability.[102] The New Jersey Court also has been quick to adopt tort innovations, and it has been unusually willing to overrule traditional doctrines to support tort plaintiffs.

This line of policy does not seem to stem from the general liberalism found in the California Supreme Court. Indeed, on issues of criminal procedure the New Jersey Court was a critic rather than a supporter of the Warren Court's innovations.[103] But the court is notable for its members' enthusiastic support for judicial activism. In a survey taken in the late 1960s, its justices were far more willing than those of three other supreme courts to embrace lawmaking as an appropriate judicial function.[104] Their acceptance of activist roles undoubtedly reflects the leadership of Arthur Vanderbilt and Joseph Weintraub, chief justices during most of the postwar period. In tort law, the court's activist proclivities have been reflected in early support for doctrinal changes favorable to plaintiffs; the result was a strongly liberal policy.

The Michigan Supreme Court attracted attention in 1958 as the first court to break with the privity requirement in warranty.[105] It also has adopted other innovative doctrines early. Its activism was reflected in an unusual persistence in seeking to abrogate the immunity of governmental entities despite the strong support of the Michigan legislature for that immunity.[106]

The court's activism dates only from 1958. That year is significant, because it marked the accession of a liberal majority to the court as a result of appointments by longtime Democratic Governor G. Mennen Williams. Before Williams's appointments, the court was composed of Republicans and relatively conservative Democrats. Afterwards, the court came to acquire a liberal tinge that was reflected in its tort decisions. As one commentator said, the court's new majority preferred "rough justice" over "ancient rules."[107]

These three courts provide too few cases to generalize about the sources of tort activism in the postwar period. However, they suggest that a general activist tradition and ideological acceptance of the direction of change contribute to high levels of activism. Where these two factors combine, as in California, a position of leadership in development of the law perhaps is inevitable.

RESTRAINTIST COURTS

Just as certain courts can be identified as leading activists in tort law, other courts stand out for what might be called their "restraint" in this area. Some supreme courts explicitly have refused to accept much of the doctrinal change in support of tort plaintiffs that has occurred in the postwar period. Among these advocates of restraint are the supreme courts of Maine, Kansas, Nebraska, Virginia, and North Carolina. Notably, all of these courts rank in the bottom one-third in table 4.1.

These states all are nonurbanized and may be characterized as politically conservative. In general, their high courts' support for restraint probably stems chiefly from justices' ideological disagreement with the liberal tinge of recent tort innovations. Although rural areas often are identified with resistance to innovation,[108] it is not clear that nonurbanism translates directly into resistance to judicial innovations.[109]

Until very recently Massachusetts would have been counted among the leading restraintist courts. In our rankings the Massachusetts Supreme Court stands close to the bottom, and it was notable for its vocal opposition to many doctrinal changes in tort. This position is striking, because Massachusetts is very different from the other states that have been slow to accept new doctrines in the postwar period: it is a highly urbanized state, one whose politics arguably are the most liberal in the country. What were the sources of its court's support for judicial restraint?

These sources seem to lie in the court itself. The Supreme Court of Massachusetts is a prestigious and self-confident court, whose luminaries have included some of the giants of American law such as Lemuel Shaw and Oliver Wendell Holmes, and it has frequently played an activist role in policymaking. This role extended to the law of tort is an earlier period; Massachusetts, for instance, led the states with its proclamation of tort immunity for charitable institutions in 1876.[110] But this and other innovations of that period were favorable to defendants and thus conservative.

In more recent times the court seemed to adhere to its conservatism, and as the direction of legal change reversed, the court became a supporter of restraint rather than activism. This history suggests that at least in extreme cases a court may develop a tradition strong enough to withstand the impact of a succession of personnel changes. Yet the strength of tradition should not be exaggerated; since 1975 the Massachusetts Supreme Court has begun to take a newly activist position in support of change in the tort law.[111] As a result, no longer can this court be regarded as a bulwark of opposition to tort activism.

NONMAINSTREAM COURTS

Among the supreme courts that have adopted few of the postwar tort innovations, by no means all have resisted change directly. For some courts, the most frequent response to new doctrines has been a non-response—an absence of any rulings on these doctrines. Most illustrative of the states in this category are Alaska, Hawaii, Idaho, Montana, New Mexico, North Dakota, and Vermont.

This nonresponse might be viewed as an alternative strategy of judicial restraint. The Supreme Court of Maine, an advocate of judicial restraint when it does rule on tort innovations, also has remained silent on several innovative doctrines. But some of the courts listed above, like those of Idaho and North Dakota, have rejected none of the recent innovations. Moreover, of these courts, only the Supreme Court of New Mexico possesses substantial control over its docket. The other courts, working in systems without intermediate appellate courts, would have relatively great difficulty in avoiding legal issues brought by litigants.

Thus it appears that the nonresponse of courts in these states primarily reflects the absence of demand. These states all have low populations and nearly all are relatively rural. The first characteristic could be expected to limit the quantity of relevant litigation. The second may limit attorneys' sophistication about or awareness of legal innovations that might be presented for consideration to the courts. Because of these characteristics, supreme courts in states such as Montana simply may have few opportunities to express positions on innovative doctrines. If this is the case, they may be seen as existing in legal systems that are not conducive to innovation, not in systems that actively oppose innovation.

OTHER STATES

No supreme court has been perfectly consistent in its responses to tort innovations. But it has been possible to categorize some as relatively activist, restraintist, or uninvolved. In contrast, some state supreme courts are virtually impossible to categorize because of the variation in their behavior. On some tort questions they have been among the early supporters of innovation, and on others they have been notable for their resistance to change.

The Wisconsin Supreme Court is a good example. In the 1960s this court was unusually willing to question and overturn its traditional positions on tort issues; in seven cases it reversed itself. But during the same period the Wisconsin Court rejected innovative doctrines on issues such as the discovery rule for medical malpractice and the per-diem formula for pain and suffering damages. A similar pattern exists for the Mississippi Supreme Court. It was among the leaders in the adoption of the per-diem rule, builder-vendor implied warranty, and the abrogation of charitable immunity. But it refused to depart from sovereign immunity, and it rejected the discovery rule as well. Both Wisconsin and Mississippi rank in the middle one-third of the supreme courts in overall tort law innovativeness.

Supreme courts such as these two reflect the multiple influences on judicial activism. Innovativeness on a particular issue depends in part on the speed with which appropriate cases reach a court and the content of the cases that do arrive. Judges may view two innovations in a field differently on ideological or other grounds. Even minor changes in a court's membership may affect its collective attitude toward tort doctrines. For these reasons it is understandable that a particular court's position varies. Perhaps it is a consistent response to innovations that is remarkable where it occurs.

CONCLUSION

One important theme developed in this chapter is the lack of uniformity in the states' responses to demands for change in tort law. Some state supreme courts have led the process of policy change, and others have lagged behind or actively opposed change. Some of their justices have championed the new wave of doctrinal support for tort plaintiffs, and others have offered principled arguments for maintenance of the status quo. Certainly, the tort law policies of state supreme courts are no exception to the general rule of diversity in public policy among the states.

Yet more impressive than this diversity of response has been the general pattern of activism. Nearly all of the state supreme courts have taken part in the uprooting of traditional tort doctrines, and most have played an active role in this process. As a result, the body of tort law in this country is fundamentally different from what it was a little more than a generation ago. A set of doctrines that limited the legal rights of injured persons has been uprooted and replaced in large part with new rules that support recovery for injuries.

This process underlines the continuing importance of tort law as a field of active policymaking by state appellate judges. The work of the state courts in tort law is particularly significant, because they are relatively free from competition and control. Although the federal courts play a major role in establishing doctrine on civil liberties issues, they have not sought to make independent policy in common law fields since *Erie* v. *Tompkins*[112] was decided in 1938. State legislatures are increasingly important participants in tort policymaking,[113] but even today they allow their courts considerable autonomy in molding the law of torts. As a result, authoritative legal rulings on tort issues are made primarily by the state supreme courts.

More generally, of course, the activity of the state supreme courts in tort law provides further evidence of their importance as policymakers. This book attests to the growing interest of scholars in the work of this relatively neglected level of the court system. Our inquiry suggests the value of further investigation in the areas of significant activity by the state supreme courts to understand more fully their role in the policymaking process.

NOTES

1. The most critical assessment of the "new" activism is Donald Horowitz, *The Courts and Social Policy* (Washington, D.C.: Brookings Institution, 1977).

2. Harold Lasswell, *Politics: Who Gets What, When and How* (New York: McGraw-Hill, 1936).

3. For a detailed discussion of the making and impact of employer defense doctrines in the nineteenth curtury, *see* Lawrence Friedman and Jack Ladynski, "Social Change and the Law of Industrial Accidents," *Columbia Law Review* 67 (1967): 50–82.

4. MacPherson v. Buick Motor Co., 111 N.E. 1050 (N.Y. 1916).

5. For a detailed discussion of the rise and fall of the doctrine of privity, *see* Edward H. Levi, *An Introduction to Legal Reasoning* (Chicago: University of Chicago Press, 1949), pp. 8–27; William Prosser, "The Assault Upon the Citadel," *Yale Law Journal* 69 (1960): 791–848.

6. In this article the term *state supreme court* is used generically to describe the state's highest court regardless of its actual nomenclature.

7. Erie RR. Co. v. Tompkins, 304 U.S. 64 (1938). Since the 1920s the U.S. Supreme Court had decided virtually no tort cases of substantive significance. The Court of Appeals for the District of Columbia, however, decides some such cases and consequently is an independent influence in the development of tort law.

8. *See, e.g.*, Grant Gilmore, *The Death of Contract* (Columbus: Ohio State University Press, 1973).

9. *See* Robert E. Keeton, *Venturing to Do Justice: Reforming the Private Law* (Cambridge, Mass.: Harvard University Press, 1969).

10. We define postwar changes as those adopted by most states since 1943. In some cases, however, early development of doctrinal change preceded World War II.

11. The doctrine is not peculiar to tort law but extends to contracts, administrative law, and so on. But it has prevailed longer and is less easily minimized in tort law.

12. Some state supreme courts, especially when considering municipal liability, did not apply the doctrine to injuries occurring in proprietary functions, for example, when a city operated a swimming pool, as opposed to those occurring in governmental functions, for example, in the course of police or firefighting operations.

13. *See* the discussion in William L. Prosser and John Wade, *Torts: Cases and Materials*, 4th ed. (Mineola, N.Y.: Foundation Press, 1971), pp. 1122–23; Kenneth Culp Davis, *Admin-*

istrative Law and Government, 2d ed. (St. Paul, Minn.: West, 1975), p. 11. *See also* United States v. Lee, 106 U.S. 196 (1882).

14. *See, e.g.,* Larsen v. Yuma County, 225 P. 1115 (Ariz. 1924); Madison v. City and County of San Francisco, 234 P.2d 995 (Cal. App. 1951).

15. Sovereign immunity had never been extended to the municipal level in New Jersey. In New York municipal immunity was curtailed by statute in the 1940s.

16. Hargrove v. Town of Cocoa Beach, 96 So.2d 130 (1957).

17. Muskopf v. Corning Hospital District, 359 P.2d 457 (1961).

18. Many courts limited liability to negligence or nonperformance of duty that the governmental agency owed on an individual basis; failure to perform duties owed the public in general, for example, maintenance of a bridge, did not engender liability.

19. Note, "Sovereign Immunity—Contract Obligations Can Be Enforced Against the State of Oklahoma in Ordinary Actions at Law," *Tulsa Law Review* 11 (1976): 459–63.

20. The first case was Russell v. Men of Devon, 100 Eng. Rep. 359 (1798). The court ruled for the county on the grounds that it had (in England at that time) no corporate existence or treasury.

21. Holytz v. City of Milwaukee, 115 N.W.2d 618 (1962).

22. Gates v. Pickett and Nelson Constr. Co., 432 P.2d 780 (1967).

23. In a few states the doctrine did not apply to "strangers" (those who had received no benefits from the charity); in a few others the doctrine protected only donations or trust funds (as opposed to receipts from charitable money-making activities).

24. Only the Minnesota and New Hampshire supreme courts had rejected it. In seven states, no appellate court had considered the doctrine.

25. About 90 percent of the charitable immunity cases involve hospitals or other nonprofit medical institutions.

26. Georgetown College v. Hughes, 130 F.2d 810 (1942).

27. In two states the doctrine was repudiated by legislative action. In New Jersey the legislature reinstated the doctrine following judicial abrogation.

28. In another five states some vestiges of the doctrine remained.

29. For a more detailed description of the abrogation of charitable immunity and its impact, *see* Bradley C. Canon and Dean Jaros, "The Impact of Changes in Judicial Doctrines: The Abrogation of Charitable Immunity," *Law & Society Review* 13 (1979); 969–86.

30. Developments in product-liability law have been particularly complex. For fuller discussions, *see* William L. Prosser, "The Fall of the Citadel," *Minnesota Law Review* 50 (1966); 791–848; Richard A. Epstein, *Modern Products Liability Law* (Westport, Conn.: Quorum Books, 1980).

31. It also meant that if a person bought a defective product that subsequently was used by and caused injury to another party, that party could make no claim on the seller for injury.

32. Mazetti v. Armour & Co., 135 P. 633 (1913).

33. MacPherson v. Buick Motor Co., *supra* note 4.

34. Id. at 1053.

35. William L. Prosser, *Handbook of the Law of Torts*, 4th ed. (St. Paul, Minn.: West, 1971), p. 643.

36. Spence v. Three Rivers Builders & Masonry Supply, Inc., 90 N.W.2d 873 (1958).

37. Henningsen v. Bloomfield Motors, 161 A.2d 69 (N.J. 1960).

38. Restatement (Second) of Torts, sec. 402A (1965).

39. Greenman v. Yuma Power Products Co., 377 P.2d 897 (1963).

40. Robert L. Rabin, *Perspectives on Tort Law* (Boston: Little, Brown & Co., 1976), p. 141. On the practical impact of these legal changes, *see* James L. Croyle, "An Impact Analysis of Judge-Made Products Liability Policies," *Law & Society Review*, 13 (1979): 949–67.

41. One strongly worded reaffirmance was made by the Delaware Supreme Court in Alfree v. Alfree, 401 A.2d 161 (1979).

42. *See* Barbara A. Brown et al., *Women's Rights and the Law* (New York: Praeger, 1977), p. 118.

43. Hitaffer v. Argonne Co., 183 F.2d 811 (D.C. Cir. 1950).

44. In the 1970s Fourteenth Amendment equal-protection issues or state's equal-rights amendment issues have impinged upon the consortium question. *See, e.g.*, Hopkins v. Blanco, 320 A.2d 139 (Pa. 1974).

45. California's Supreme Court initially abolished consortium rather than extend a cause of action to wives—West v. City of San Diego, 353 P.2d 929 (1961)—but later restored the consortium action for both spouses—Rodriguez v. Bethelehem Steel Corp., 525 P.2d 669 (1974).

46. Hewlett v. George, 9 So. 885.

47. Gollier v. White, 122 N.W.2d 193.

48. Bonbrest v. Kotz, 65 F. Supp. 138.

49. Berkennes v. Corniea, 38 N.W.2d 838 (1949).

50. Roe v. Wade, 410 U.S. 113, 156–59 (1973). *See* Rand Eric Kruger, "Wrongful Death and the Unborn: An Examination of Recovery After Roe v. Wade," *Journal of Family Law* 13 (1973): 99–114.

51. Justus v. Atchison, 565 P.2d 122, 130–31 (Calif. 1977); Mone v. Greyhound Lines, Inc., 331 N.W.2d 916, 921 (Mass. 1975) (Braucher, J., dissenting).

52. Foley v. Pittsburgh-Des Moines Co., 68 A.2d 517 (Pa. 1949) and *Hunter v. Quality Homes*, 68 A.2d 620 (Del. 1949).

53. Inman v. Binghampton Housing Authority, 143 N.E.2d 895 (1957).

54. Caveat emptor is a doctrine of contract and property law. It was not repudiated by the development of the tort remedy, but the latter carved out a large exception to it. In a few states the warranty rested in property or contract law rather than in tort. In Louisiana, with its civil law background, caveat emptor never prevailed, and a remedy similar to builder-vendor implied warranty was traditionally available.

55. Carpenter v. Donohue, 388 P.2d 399.

56. The fiction, in brief, was that the defect rendered the property transfer less than fully complete. *See* Vanderchried v. Aaron, 140 N.W.2d 819 (Ohio App. 1957).

57. Connor v. Great Western Savings and Loan Association, 447 P.2d 609 (Cal. 1968). Appellate courts in four states explicitly rejected *Connor*, and the California legislature subsequently passed legislation overturning its holding.

58. Ayers v. Morgan, 154 A.2d 788 (1959).

59. The foreign-objects cases are surprisingly numerous in the appellate reports. Presumably their number reflects the likelihood that a patient who discovers a surgically implanted foreign object will take legal action; still, the frequency of these cases is vaguely unsettling. In the same way the case law on defective food and drink includes a strikingly large number of decisions concerning soft drinks with superfluous and undesirable contents. An afternoon's perusal of these decisions can be sufficient to convince the reader to abstain from consumption of soft drinks—not because certain of the ingredients cause cancer in laboratory animals, but because those animals' cousins may themselves be among the unintended ingredients.

60. *See* Levi, *An Introduction to Legal Reasoning*, pp. 6–7.

61. Botta v. Brunner, 138 A.2d 713.

62. Keeton, *Venturing to Do Justice*, pp. 169–76.

63. The following are articles about activism and restraint in the common law written by appellate court judges: James D. Cameron, "The Place for Judicial Activism on the Part of a State's Highest Court," *Hastings Constitutional Law Q.* 4 (1977): 279–93; Robert Leflar, "Appellate Judicial Innovation," *Oklahoma Law Review* 27 (1974): 321–46; Jack G. Day,

"Why Judges Must Make Law," *Case-Western Reserve Law Review* 26 (1976): 563–93; Albert Tate, Jr., "The Law-Making Function of the Judge," *Louisiana Law Review* 28 (1968): 211–34; Walter V. Schaefer, "Precedent and Policy," *University of Chicago Law Review* 34 (1966): 3–25.

64. Allen v. Wilkenson, 243 A.2d 515 (Md. 1968); Maki v. Frelk, 239 N.E.2d 445 (Ill. 1968).

65. *E.g.*, Frechtman v. Stover, 199 N.E.2d 354 (Ind. 1964).

66. Rowland v. Christian, 443 P.2d 561 (Cal. 1968) (Burke, J., dissenting); Pierce v. Yakima Valley Memorial Hospital, 260 P.2d 765 (Wash. 1953) (Hill, J., dissenting).

67. *E.g.*, Hungerford v. Portland Sanitarium, 384 P.2d 1009 (Or. 1963); Colby v. Carney Hospital, 254 N.E.2d 407 (Mass. 1969).

68. *E.g.*, Battalla v. State, 176 N.E.2d 729 (N.Y. 1961). *See also* Tate, "The Law-Making Function of the Judge"; Cornelius J. Peck, "The Role of Courts and Legislatures in the Reform of Tort Law," *Minnesota Law Review* 48 (1963): 265–312.

69. *E.g.*, Williams v. City of Detroit, 111 N.W.2d 1 (Mich. 1961).

70. Wawak v. Stewart, 449 S.W.2d 922 (Ark. 1970); Holytz v. City of Milwaukee, 115 N.W.2d 618 (Wis. 1962). *See also* Robert E. Keeton, "Creative Continuity in the Law of Torts," *Harvard Law Review* 75 (1962): 462–509.

71. Muskopf v. Corning Hospital District, 359 P.2d 457 (Cal. 1961); Molitor v. Kaneland Community Unit District, 163 N.E.2d 89 (Ill. 1959); Spanel v. Mounds View School District, 118 N.W.2d 795 (Minn. 1962).

72. *E.g.*, Green v. Superior Court, 517 P.2d 1168 (Cal. 1974).

73. *E.g.*, Dole v. Dow Chemical Co., 282 N.E.2d 288 (N.Y. 1972).

74. Battalla v. State, *supra* note 68.

75. *E.g.*, Martino v. Grace-New Haven Community Hospital, 148 A.2d 259 (Conn. 1959); Schulte v. Missionaries of LaSalette Corp., 352 S.W.2d 636 (Mo. 1961).

76. Pierce v. Yakima Valley Memorial Hospital, *supra* note 66, at 775 (Concurring opinion). *See also* Neeley v. St. Francis Hospital, 361 P.2d 155 (Kan. 1964).

77. Pierce v. Yakima Valley Memorial Hospital, *supra* note 66, at 774. Fleming James, "Tort Law in Midstream: Its Challenges to the Judicial Process," *Buffalo Law Review* 8 (1959): 315–44, details in chapter and verse the judicial origin of virtually all major controversial tort policies.

78. *E.g.*, Parker v. Port Huron Hospital, 105 N.W. 1 (Mich. 1960); Hargrove v. Town of Cocoa Beach, *supra* note 16.

79. Flagiello v. Pennsylvania Hospital, 208 A.2d 193 (Pa. 1965) (Jones, J., dissenting); Pierce v. Yakima Valley Memorial Hospital, *supra* note 66, at 765.

80. Niederman v. Brodsky, 261 A.2d 84, 90 (1970). *See also* Webb v. Zorn, 220 A.2d 853 (1966).

81. Flagiello v. Pennsylvania Hospital, *supra* note 79, at 214–15.

82. Cochran v. Keeton, 252 So.2d 313, 318 (Ala. 1971) (Lawson, J., dissenting).

83. The Virginia Supreme Court even noted that metaphysical concepts had changed in the twentieth century and accordingly rejected the "one flesh" rationale behind interspousal immunity. *See* Surratt v. Thompson, 183 S.E.2d 200 (Va. 1971).

84. Missouri-Pacific Trans. Co. v. Miller, 299 S.W.2d 41, 46 (1957).

85. Schipper v. Levitt and Sons, 207 A.2d 314, 325 (1965).

86. *See, e.g.*, Pierce v. Yakima Memorial Hospital, *supra* note 66; Flagiello v. Pennsylvania Hospital, *supra* note 79.

87. This argument is made most forcefully by Keeton, "Creative Continuity in the Law of Torts."

88. *See, e.g.*, Parker v. Port Huron Hospital, 105 N.W.2d 1 (Mich. 1960); Colby v. Carney Hospital, 254 N.E.2d 407 (Mass. 1969).

89. *E.g.*, West v. City of San Diego, 353 P.2d 929 (Cal. 1961) (Peters, J., dissenting); Surratt v. Thompson, *supra* note 83 (Cochran and Harman, JJ., dissenting).

90. *E.g.*, Humber v. Morton, 426 S.W.2d 554 (Tex. 1968); Cochran v. Keeton, *supra* note 81.

91. Cochran v. Keeton, *supra* note 82, at 318. *See also* Niederman v. Brodsky, *supra* note 80, at 90 (Bell, CJ., dissenting).

92. *E.g.*, Stranlendorf v. Walgreen Co., 114 N.W.2d 883 (Wis. 1962); Puhl v. Milwaukee Auto Ins. Co., 99 N.W.2d 163 (Wis. 1960).

93. Stang v. Hertz Corp., 497 P.2d 732, 735 (1972).

94. The doctrines are the abrogation of sovereign immunity, abrogation of the "accepted-work" doctrine, the acceptance of the per-diem formula, allowance of wives' actions for loss of consortium, establishment of builder-vendor implied warranty, abrogation of privity in warranty, and establishment of strict products liability.

95. Keeton, *Venturing to Do Justice*, pp. 176–79.

96. Adoptions of doctrines in published decisions by lower courts also were counted where the state supreme court was silent. Thus strictly speaking, the rankings are of court systems rather than of supreme courts. But only a small minority of the counted adoptions were by lower courts.

97. The rankings for each supreme court should be regarded as only approximate. A more complex and equally meaningful set of rankings that takes into account the specific years in which a tort law innovation was adopted puts the state high courts in slightly different positions. *See* Bradley C. Canon and Lawrence Baum, "Patterns of Adoption of Tort Law Innovations: An Application of Diffusion Theory to Judicial Doctrines," *American Political Science Review* 75 (1981): 975–87.

98. Greenman v. Yuma Power Products Co., *supra* note 39.

99. Li v. Yellow Cab Company of California, 532 P.2d 1226. *See also* Connor v. Great Western Savings and Loan Assn., *supra* note 57.

100. On the court's activism generally, *see* the annual review of its work in the *California Law Review*, *e.g.*, "The Supreme Court of California, 1976–1977," *California Law Review* 66 (1978): 137–49.

101. G. Edward White, *The American Judicial Tradition: Profiles of Leading American Judges* (New York: Oxford University Press, 1976), ch. 13; Harry Kalven, Jr., "Torts: The Quest for Appropriate Standards," *California Law Review* 53 (1965): 189–206. The 1944 case was Escola v. Coca Cola Bottling Co., 150 P.2d 436.

102. Henningsen v. Bloomfield Motors, *supra* note 37.

103. *See* Bradley C. Canon, "Organizational Contumacy in the Transmission of Judicial Policies: The Mapp, Escobedo, Miranda and Gault Cases," *Villanova Law Review* 20 (1974): 50–79.

104. Henry Robert Glick and Kenneth N. Vines, *State Court Systems* (Englewood Cliffs, N.J.: Prentice-Hall, 1973), pp. 69–73. *See also* Richard Lehne, *The Quest for Justice: The Politics of School Finance Reform* (New York: Longman, 1978), esp. pp. 42–46.

105. Spence v. Three Rivers Builders and Masonry Supply, Inc., *supra* note 36.

106. J. B. Jones, "Government Immunity in Michigan: The Effects of Uncertainty" (Paper delivered at the 1978 meeting of the Midwest Political Science Association, Chicago, Illinois, April 18–21).

107. S. Sidney Ulmer, "Politics and Procedure in the Michigan Supreme Court," *Southwestern Social Science Quarterly* 46 (1966): 375–84. *See also* Glendon A. Schubert, *Quantitative Analysis of Judicial Behavior* (Glencoe, Ill.: Free Press, 1959), pp. 129–42; Malcolm M. Feeley, "Another Look at the 'Party Variable' in Judicial Decision-Making: An Analysis of the Michigan Supreme Court," *Polity* 4 (1971): 91–104.

108. On the findings of innovation studies, *see* Everett M. Rogers with Floyd Shoemaker,

Communication of Innovations: A Cross-Cultural Approach, 2d ed. (New York: Free Press, 1971).

109. Our analysis of state supreme court responses to tort innovations before World War II shows that many in relatively rural states were quick to adopt new doctrines favorable to plaintiffs. *See* Canon and Baum, "Patterns of Adoption of Tort Law Innovations: An Application of Diffusion Theory to Judicial Doctrines." Indeed, in the postwar period two rural states, Kentucky and New Hampshire, are among the top ten adopters of tort innovations. This suggests caution in explaining courts' restraintist positions by citing their rural location.

110. McDonald v. Massachusetts General Hospital, 120 Mass. 432 (1876). More generally, *see* Leonard Levy, *The Law of the Commonwealth and Chief Justice Shaw* (Cambridge, Mass.: Harvard University Press, 1959).

111. Most notably, the Massachusetts Court was the first state supreme court to allow a child to sue for loss of a parent's consortium; Ferriter v. Daniel O'Connell's Sons, Inc., 413 N.E.2d 690 (1980). *See also* Sorensen v. Sorensen, 399 N.E.2d 907 (1975); Brown v. Brown, 409 N.E.2d 717 (1980).

112. Erie v. Tompkins, 304 U.S. 64.

113. One good example of the role of state legislatures is the widespread statutory adoption of the comparative negligence rule as a substitute for the traditional rule of contributory negligence. *See* Li v. Yellow Cab Co., *supra* note 99, at 1232.

5.

HENRY R. GLICK

Supreme Courts in State Judicial Administration

State court organization and management has a long history of decentralization and judicial independence. Usually considered an important part of local government, state trial courts and clerk's offices have been staffed, managed, and frequently organized by local judges and other officials with little obligation and frequently no inclination to follow external standards of judicial administration. Only some states have authorized supreme courts to supervise other judges closely, and even those with some power meet varying resistance from lower courts throughout the state. Administration in the fifty state court systems varies tremendously, and considerable differences also exist in the organization and management of county or regional courts within individual states. Realistically, the term state judicial *system* often has meant little other than the presence of dozens of trial courts linked to the appellate hierarchy during infrequent instances of judicial review.

Localism and judicial decentralization still characterize many state judiciaries. But there also is a growing and increasingly influential national movement to reorganize state courts within a streamlined judicial hierarchy with rules of procedure, budgeting, staffing, and records management all standardized and supervised by state officials under active leadership of the state supreme court.[1]

Stimulated by reform ideas generated by national organizations such as the American Judicature Society, American Bar Association, Institute for Judicial Administration, and the National Center for State Courts, state bar association leaders and other reform activists are seeking to transform state courts into genuine hierarchies of judicial cohesion and authority. Fueled by a law-business ethic that sees courts as efficient producers of decided cases, reformers want to establish firm management control.

Increasing the power of supreme courts to supervise state judicial systems adds to the courts' policymaking role and furthers state centraliza-

109

tion. We also may speculate that a shift in judicial focus and loyalty from local politics to state supreme courts will increase the force of supreme court case decisions throughout a judicial system. Although the move toward centralized judicial systems under the leadership of state supreme courts has been in the wind for a decade or more, genuine shifts in political power are just now taking place in many states, and they deserve careful examination over the coming years.

GOALS IN STATE COURT REFORM

Court reform includes a number of specific policies that emphasize cohesive judicial organization and supreme court leadership.

CONSOLIDATION AND SIMPLIFICATION OF COURT STRUCTURES

Reformers believe that state courts ought to be streamlined into a few types of courts to eliminate their disorganized appearance and the confusion about which courts hear what cases (overlapping jurisdiction). The reform model advises that each state should have a supreme court; possibly an intermediate court of appeals, depending upon state population and the crush of cases; one type of trial court of general jurisdiction; and one or two types of trial courts of limited jurisdiction. Traditional systems that include separate divorce courts, family courts, small claims courts, traffic courts, juvenile courts, and others should be consolidated into a single county court that would decide all of these cases. Reformers believe this would improve the prestige of courts and make them easier to understand, use, and supervise.

CENTRALIZED MANAGEMENT

The reform view is that state supreme courts should have the final authority and provide leadership in state judicial administration. Combined with court consolidation, placing the power to manage the courts at the apex of the judicial pyramid will develop cohesion and statewide rationality in court operations. Supreme courts themselves will not actively supervise other judges, but will work through state court administrators appointed by supreme courts. State administrators will have a sufficiently large staff, budget, and authority to scrutinize the work of the lower courts. Their job will be to gather complete records on the flow of cases in the trial courts, conduct research on problems faced by the courts, provide information and advice to local judges and administrators, and conduct in-service training programs for state judicial personnel. Local court officials are expected to pay close heed to direction coming from the top of the judicial system.

CENTRALIZED RULE MAKING

One proposal calls for giving state supreme courts the final authority to make all rules of judicial procedure and evidence and to regulate the practice of law. Rule making is intended to replace widely varying methods throughout the state and to transfer this power from state legislatures, where it traditionally has been placed, to state supreme courts. This would give the judicial branch control over its own internal operations and elevate the courts as a more equal branch of government.

CENTRALIZED JUDICIAL BUDGETING

Another reform ideal—centralized judicial budgeting—is one of the most important and controversial in the reform package. Traditionally, judicial budgets have been part of the executive budget, and governors have been able to screen judicial requests before the legislature has reviewed the budget. In many states, local courts also have the responsibility for making their own budget requests. In the eyes of reformers this derogates the judicial branch and makes it dependent on the executive branch. It should be replaced, they argue, with power vested in the state supreme court to make a single budget for the entire judicial system that would be transmitted directly to the legislature without executive interference. The financial independence of local courts also would be substantially reduced, and state judges would have to become more attentive to state judicial administrative leadership.

FULL STATE FINANCING FOR COURTS

State courts receive their financial support from many sources, including some state money, local funding, and court fines and fees. Like the budgeting process, current financing encourages decentralization and independence, since local trial courts and clerks are not dependent upon state supreme court recommendations and approval for the source of their money. It also permits much local variation in financial support for courts. Full state financing is designed to buttress the power of state supreme courts, standardize local financial support, and elevate the importance of courts in the eyes of state officials.

MERIT SELECTION OF JUDGES

Another feature of state court reform is to substitute merit selection procedures for partisan ones. Under merit selection (Missouri Plan), potential judges are initially screened by a panel of lawyers and laymen who present a limited number of candidates to the governor for each judicial vacancy. Governors are required to select judges from this list, and after serving for one year, a new judge must be approved by the voters for a longer term. The screening panel is expected to be oriented to professional legal values in choosing the best possible people for the courts. The plan assumes that legal standards of excellence in education, training, judicial experience, and proper judicial attitudes will replace partisan emphasis on party loyalty and political experience as the criteria for becoming a judge. Merit selection is expected to improve the image of the courts and upgrade the quality of decision making and judicial conduct. Judges chosen according to merit also are expected to support centralized professional judicial administration and will be insulated from local political considerations in managing the courts.

POLITICAL STAKES IN REFORM

All of these changes in state judicial administration are important to various elites and groups interested in state court reorganization. Reformers tend to include high-status business lawyers, state bar association leaders, and various middle-class, good-government organizations such as Leagues of Women Voters, Chambers of Commerce, local service clubs, and others. They usually have a nonpartisan, business-efficiency perspective of the proper role of government. From their point of view, changes in court structure, judicial management, and selection of judges promise to rationalize and standardize the courts and make them more predictable and efficient.

Their general goals of reform also imply support for many specific changes in judicial procedure and local legal practices. For example, reducing delay in processing cases is very high on the reform agenda. Various procedures have been tried, including transferring judges to busy districts, having compulsory pretrial and preappeal conferences where attorneys are urged to reach informal settlements, adopting statewide speedy trial laws that require criminal cases to be decided within a certain number of days, changing court calendaring methods for scheduling and moving cases through the judicial process, improving record keeping, using new jury-selection procedures, and other techniques. All of these methods require people at the local level to change their ways of conducting judicial business. In addition, new statewide standards of personnel selection and in-service training programs are expected to sharpen the skills of local court employees in various tasks. Reformers also generally agree that the greatest improvement will come about when state supreme courts and professional court administrators lead the courts.

Attractive as these goals may seem, they are not universally appealing. Administrative changes and centralization in the supreme court mean controversial shifts in political power from local to state government. For example, attempts to transfer funding and budgeting from cities and counties to state government will produce fundamental changes in the officials and agencies that determine management. Changes in funding sources directly imply changes in policy direction and requirements for compliance with state guidelines. Court clerks who serve both county government and the trial courts also stand to lose some of their functions and influence as managers of the court bureaucracy and gatekeepers in processing cases. A recent report of the National Center for State Courts also reveals that state courts are among the last governmental agencies to adopt merit or civil service personnel systems or equal-employment opportunity,[2] leaving the staffing of local courts to traditional patterns of personal and political-party patronage. New proposals to establish statewide merit and affirmative-action selection of court employees, therefore, promises to upset many well-established and customary local influences in the trial courts. Although court personnel probably will continue to be selected from local citizens, their political attention, policy orientation, and career strategies must increasingly shift from local to state government.

Merit selection of judges also creates much political conflict in the states, since local political parties fear that they will lose influence over a plentiful and attractive source of political patronage. Various urban social groups, especially nonwhites and other minorities, also frequently believe that merit selection is simply a smokescreen to eliminate local popular influence and give judicial positions to higher status whites.

Court reform also arouses the opposition of many lawyers who make their living in daily use of the local trial courts. Accustomed to existing procedures, customs, and personnel, they often oppose changes that will require them to learn new routines and formal rules and to develop new informal pathways through the local judicial system.

PATTERNS OF STATE COURT REORGANIZATION

Nearly all of the states have court administrators working with the supreme court in various areas of judicial management, but the powers of state officials vary tremendously across the country. Reformers have been successful in some areas, and the role of certain state supreme courts is increasing, but other reforms still are unpopular with legislatures, governors and others who are directly affected by changes in judicial organization.[3] Compromise is the typical outcome in battles over the courts.

Court reformers have been fairly persuasive in gaining adoption of streamlined and consolidated court systems. In place of long chains of trial courts of general and limited jurisdiction, many with names and legal functions drawn from old England, about twenty states have combined their many different courts into one or two types of trial courts that include the jurisdiction of many previous courts. Overlapping jurisdiction has been removed, since the same court now hears a much wider variety of cases.

Merit selection of judges also is catching on in the states. Surveys of changes in judicial selection show that when a state changes its current method of selecting judges, it adopts the Missouri Plan. Throughout American history the states have adopted different methods of judicial selection depending on what generally was in vogue at the time—legislative election, gubernatorial appointment, partisan election, nonpartisan election—and it is clear that merit selection is most popular today.[4] Even at the federal level, where senatorial courtesy and party power have been well established for many years, merit selection got an initial (but probably short-lived) start under the Carter administration.[5] A dozen years ago about ten states used merit selection; today about half of the states use the Missouri Plan for some judges, and the trend is toward its greater use.

Court reform has achieved less success in other areas of judicial management and centralization. About three-quarters of the courts have obtained the power to transfer judges to other courts to help reduce case backlogs, and most have wide authority to make uniform rules of procedure and evidence and to scrutinize the practice of law. Supreme courts probably have achieved these particular powers, because they are considered insignificant by other political elites and groups who are jealous of their own political influence. These two reforms, for example, affect mainly the internal operations of the courts and have little impact on other critical powers such as court budgeting and finance and the management practices of the lower courts.

The politics of court reform generally shows that the less impact court changes have on personnel, nonjudicial political power, and basic court organization, the more likely they are to be adopted.[6] According to this conclusion, court consolidation and merit selection appear to be very controversial. Although they often are controversial, they also are more palatable when merit procedures are implemented gradually, and court personnel are assured that no one will lose his job. Rule-making powers and transferring judges to promote efficiency are less controversial and are approved more often than other changes. However, about half of the states have retained giving state legislatures the power to veto judicial rule making by a simple majority vote. Compromise and checks and balances still characterize many of these reforms.

State supreme courts and court administrators have less impact on other areas of judicial management. In half of the states, supreme courts have no authority to supervise the management practices of local courts. They cannot review budgets or finance, purchasing, capital improvements, or case management, nor can they implement statewide personnel systems. Only one-quarter of the states have placed the budget-making power in the hands of state supreme courts, but in half of them governors still have the power to review and revise judicial requests. The other states have a variety of practices. In some states the executive branch prepares the judicial budget based upon requests of various courts throughout the state, and in other states no formal judicial input whatever goes into the budget-making process. Governors apparently reject few judicial requests, but that probably is due to their extensive influence and control before the preparation of formal budgets for the legislature.

State financing still is in the future for most states. Less than ten state court systems receive 80 percent or more of their funds from state money, and in over thirty states the state governments contribute less than 40 percent of the judicial total. This means that local funding and court fines and fees contribute most of the judicial funding in most of the states.

The powers of state court administrators also are limited in most of the states. A few states provide almost no staff or budget for administrative operations. The court administrator in these few states is little more than an administrative clerk and occasional troubleshooter for the supreme court. In a half dozen other states, however, court administrators have extensive powers including the ability to require trial courts to submit caseflow data and budget finance information, and they may establish statewide personnel systems and approve local court expenditures. In the large majority of states, though, state court administrators are more likely to be a source of information and ideas for administration than powerful supervisors of the state courts. They may gather statistics on the movement of cases through the courts and engage in research on judicial management, and they may do some long-range planning on the future needs of the courts. Administrators also provide information and assistance to local courts upon request. But even in these areas, small staffs and budgets are likely to limit the scope and impact of their activities.

EXPLAINING PATTERNS OF STATE COURT ADMINISTRATION

Summaries of state administrative arrangements make it clear that no universal or nationwide package of reforms has been adopted in the fifty states. Moreover, the more we gather information on judicial administration, the more we find that individual trial courts employ many methods for coping with what reformers believe are serious problems in the judicial process. However, except for the promotional writing of reformers, which exhorts others to adopt reform goals, and summaries of current state court practices, little systematic research is being conducted on the role of state supreme courts in administrative policymaking, and few explanations are being given for variations in judicial management practices in the fifty states. Some excellent reports on the politics of adoption of reforms have been written for one or a few states, giving us a general picture of how and why reforms get through state legislatures, but we do not have a very clear idea of what accounts for management arrangements in the states.

In recent years political scientists have become interested in understanding the dynamics of state policymaking, not only how policy is made and who is influential, but also the content of policy and differences among the states in the kinds of policies selected. An important concern has been the adoption of policy innovations or the new ways states cope with problems. Court reform also can be viewed as the politics of adopting innovative policies by state government. Reform requires many new methods of administration and court organization, and considerable conflict arises over change.

A major thrust of most innovation research has been to identify major social, economic, and political factors that explained patterns of policymaking among the fifty states. Jack L. Walker and Virginia Gray discovered, for example, that the wealthier, industrial, and more politically competitive states were more likely to adopt various policy innovations.[7] Research on city governments by Michael Aiken and Robert Alford found that older cities with high ethnic populations and little in-migration were more likely to adopt public housing and urban-renewal policies.[8] These researchers theorized that various patterns of communication among political elites are important for policy adoption. Walker suggested that regional patterns of emulation exist in which administrators seeking solutions to problems compare their own situations and needs with the solutions of nearby states with which they identify most closely. Aiken and Alford hypothesized that older, more stable cities are more likely to adopt innovations due to well-established, predictable patterns of communication among affected groups and political leaders.

Some of the previous research on policy innovation dealt with a variety of policies, while other studies concerned single issues. Both have advantages and problems. Studies of many issues provide a general perspective of state innovation but also may link policies that have little relevance to one another and are produced by different political forces. Studies of single issues provide important detail but miss the overall scope and pattern of state policymaking.

The policies examined here deal only with the courts, not with general patterns of state policy innovation. However, as described earlier, court reform contains several separate components that make this area of public policy somewhat more complex than research on single issues. Court reform often has been assumed to be a single, all-inclusive public policy, since reform groups often sponsor a reform package designed to produce a model state court system. But some features of reform are more attractive than others. Therefore, it is an open question whether all or even most innovations occur together or if patterns of innovation separate court reform into distinctive parts. This issue is important also because of the highly visible role of national organizations of court reform that seek similar programs in all fifty states. Assuming the importance of national communication and strategies to achieve court reform, individual state variations in innovation are especially interesting. Finally, patterns of innovation in the courts can be related to general experiences in state policy innovation to determine how judicial politics relates to the rest of state policymaking.

A number of hunches or hypotheses could be made about innovations in judicial administration. Two possibilities are examined here that reflect different perspectives about why reforms are adopted in the states. The first comes from an important theme in the judicial reform movement itself. It suggests that the adoption of merit judicial selection closely parallels the adoption of other administrative reforms. Some reformers go further and believe that merit selection actually must be adopted first if other reforms also are to be adopted. They argue that only when judges are freed from the influence of local politics (that is, popular elections) can they become oriented toward quality judicial administration. Judge-administrators may have to make locally unpopular decisions to obtain maximum resources for the courts or they may have to create new rules of procedure to improve court efficiency, all of which may upset local lawyers, court employees, and others who prefer traditional court operations. But if they are subject to recall at election time, judges may be reluctant to exercise independent judicial leadership. Therefore, merit selection that guarantees a long-term or life appointment will substantially insulate judges from these improper forces and will provide new opportunities for creative judicial management.[9]

The second hypothesis is related to much previous research about state government. It suggests that instead of being closely tied to or limited to other features of the judiciary, reorganization of the courts and the movement to centralize judicial administration is connected to broader features of state government and to state social, economic, and political systems. For example, the urban industrial states have a greater number and variety of competing political demands as well as the resources to meet and respond to modern problems. They are more likely to tax heavily, spend more, and, as mentioned, adopt many more policy innovations to deal with various problems.[10]

Just as state legislatures and administrative agencies are likely to initiate novel approaches to government and management in the urban states, court systems in these same states also are more likely to change to respond to growing quantities and wider varieties of litigation.[11] A related but contrary hypothesis, however, is that competition between the two political parties, which contributes to policymaking particularly in the urban industrial states, will prevent innovation in judicial administration. Mindful of the patronage value of court positions, for example, well-organized political parties may try to prevent court reorganization and centralization promoted by political competitors in state bar associations and the judicial branch.

Each of these hypotheses provides different ideas about what produces change in judicial administration. They are not necessarily mutually exclusive, but they do tap theoretically different sources of political influence on change in state judicial administration. The first one suggests that change is contained within the judiciary itself. The second idea proposes that judicial organization and management, although usually viewed as a very distinctive and largely insulated area of state government, is affected by many of the same forces that determine other features of government organization and policymaking.

Information about innovations in state judicial administration and other data is available in a number of sources. Relevant material for all fifty state judicial systems has been collected in the following areas: characteristics of the office of state court administrator, state court structure, powers of judicial management, control of judicial misconduct, and education available in judicial administration. Information about judicial merit selection and other features of state political, social, and economic systems for each of the fifty states includes data on when merit selection was adopted and how extensively it is used in each of the states; measures of state wealth, education, urbanism, and industrialization; governmental size, development, and modernization; and competition between the two major political parties. These data permit the careful testing of propositions about judicial reform.[12]

The first hypothesis links merit selection to other innovations. To test the effects of merit selection, the date it was first adopted in a state, and how extensively it currently is used were related, using simple correlations, to a number of specific administrative innovations. Simple correlations range between 0 and ±1, indicating high positive or negative relationships. If merit selection usually is found with other innovations, the correlations should be positive and closer to 1 than 0. If merit selection must be adopted before other innovations can occur, the date for merit adoption should correlate highly with each of the other innovations.

The results of this test reveal that all of the administrative innovations occur almost independently of when states first adopted the merit recruitment of judges and its current usage in the fifty states. The highest correlations (0.24 and 0.34) occur with measures used to indicate control over judicial conduct (the date judicial removal and misconduct commissions were created). Most other relationships are in the positive direction, suggesting a possible link between recruitment and administrative innovation, but the strength of the relationships is extremely small.

This means that states that select judges through partisan election and gubernatorial and legislative appointment are just as likely to have adopted innovations in court management and judicial organization as states with merit selection. Moreover, for the administrative innovations for which dates of adoption or dated comparisons are available, such as court modernization and rule-making powers of the state supreme court, it is clear that the recruitment method used has practically no impact on when innovations were incorporated into state judicial systems.

Since few judges in any of the fifty states have extensive backgrounds as administrators, some even maintaining that they have no taste for court management,[13] it appears that judges in those states with the most advanced mechanisms for centralized management would, at a minimum, have a superior opportunity to assert themselves in modern judicial administration. The relationships indicate that these states are not necessarily the merit selection states.

It is worth noting that the only significant relationship, although very weak, occurs between merit selection and the creation of judicial removal commissions. A possible explanation is that unlike other administrative arrangements, removal commissions are tied ideologically only to the personal qualities of judges themselves, not to management or budgeting or the rule-making power of the courts. Therefore, it is likely that this administrative change has little impact on other political values or consequences for the positions and powers of other officials and groups. When merit selection has been accepted in a particular state, additional merit evaluation of incumbents also is probably acceptable. Nevertheless, we must bear in mind that the connection between these two variables is very small.

These results might appear to suggest that the politics of judicial selection is an independent political issue in the states or that it at least is not connected to other features of court reform. The evidence indicates, however, that merit selection frequently *is* proposed with certain court changes, but is abandoned in political compromises. Political parties, judicial incumbents, and interest groups that benefit from the status quo may not object strongly to structural change in the courts if they do not affect job security, the number of judgeships, and existing patterns of patronage in the selection process. Therefore, they may withhold support for organizational reform until merit selection is withdrawn. Describing the process as "the major concession," observers of court reform explain:

It seems that in nearly every effort to unify state court systems, there is a concomitant attempt to obtain a merit plan for selecting judges. However, such proposals frequently meet with strong resistance. Indeed, the opposition generally is so intense that merit selection usually becomes the first major element associated with the unification package to be compromised or eliminated entirely. . . . [I]t is clear that this package may contribute to the defeat of a unification package if the two concepts are united.[14]

From the perspective of the advocates of judicial reform, it is regrettable that merit selection often is rejected as politically unacceptable, but the significance of these political outcomes here is that court reorganization and modern court management frequently *are* adopted in states that do not adopt merit selection. Therefore, the first hypothesis that links judicial administration to judicial selection must be rejected.

The other hypothesis examined here is that state social, economic, and political systems are more responsible for innovations in judicial administration and court organization. To test this alternative explanation, the administrative innovations were related to the other data that tap numerous characteristics of the fifty states. The first step was to get a workable handle on the large quantity of information. Before relationships could be examined, the administrative innovations were factor analyzed. This process reduced the number of variables included in the analysis from fourteen items to four composite or summarized factors. Each state received a numerical score describing its characteristics on each factor or dimension of judicial administration. The scores were then used in correlations with the states' socioeconomic and political characteristics.

The four factors or dimensions of innovation discovered are named according to their most prominent features. "Centralized Judicial Management" includes financial and staff support for the state court administrator, power of the supreme court to supervise the lower courts, centralized judicial budgeting, and higher state funding for court management. "Court Consolidation and Simplification" refers to the extent that trial and appellate courts have been integrated into a streamlined, coherent hierarchy with few separate types of courts. "Judicial Education and Qualification" is a combination of the presence of in-service state training programs, university education in judicial administration, and the existence of judicial removal commissions in the states. "Judicial Rule Making" describes the state supreme court's power to devise and require implementation of judicial rules of procedure.

Since factor analysis produces four separate factors, it is clear that court reform is not a single, unified dimension of state public policy. Certain parts of the court reform model tend to be adopted together, whereas other parts follow different patterns completely. It also means that many states are likely to select certain reforms but to shun others. New York, for example, ranks very high in adopting centralized judicial management and high judicial education and qualifications standards, but has rejected court consolidation. Other states also select some but not other features of reform. A ranking of the fifty states in each category of judicial reform is presented in table 5.1.

Additional correlation analysis (multiple regression) helps to explain the patterns of policy adoption in the fifty states. Table 5.2 summarizes the relationships between the merit selection variables and the various state social, economic, and political characteristics and the four major factors or dimensions of state judicial administration. The numerical scores in the main body of the table depict the strength of the relationship between each combination of variables. The possible range is from 0 to ±1.00. As before, a high score indicates a strong relationship, and a low score refers to a very weak relationship. The R^2's at the bottom of the table reveal the percentage of variation in the judicial administration factors that can be explained or accounted for by all of the variables combined listed to the left of the table. Again, a high number indicates that much variation is explained, whereas a small number reveals that the variables are not successful in explaining many differences in state scores in that particular aspect of judicial administration.

The table confirms, first, that judicial selection is not strongly related to judicial administration. The effect of this variable may seem somewhat unclear, since date of adoption and extent of current use of merit selection often are related in opposite ways to the factors of judicial administration. However, in most instances the relationships are small and/or not statistically significant. As concluded earlier, the findings show that the fifty states either adopt or reject modern court management methods and administrative arrangements without regard to the method of judicial selection.

Other relationships are more important. The strongest ones are found for variations in "Centralized Judicial Management," where we see that states that score high in other areas of governmental development (general policy innovation and the relative size of state government) also are most likely to have developed the agencies and procedures for state leadership in judicial management. As described earlier, the components important for this factor include strong support for the office of state court administrator and a significant management and budgeting role for the state supreme court. The high coefficients suggest that centralized judicial management requires facilities, specialized staff, and general governmental support similar to other areas of state policy innovation, all of which are more apparent in states with relatively large and specialized governments. Clearly, more than any other elements of judicial administration, the factor of centralized judicial management is an integral part of general patterns of state policy leadership and the size and apparent complexity of government.

It also is significant that centralized judicial management is the *only*

Table 5.1 The Fifty States Ranked in Categories of State Court Reform

	Centralized Judicial Management		Court Consolidation and Simplification		Judicial Education and Qualifications		Judicial Rule Making	
1.	Alaska	3.410	Iowa	1.882	New York	2.548	New Jersey	1.376
2.	Hawaii	2.845	N. Carolina	1.784	Pennsylvania	2.116	Colorado	1.362
3.	New Jersey	1.621	Illinois	1.708	California	1.803	W. Virginia	1.064
4.	New York	1.504	Kansas	1.487	New Jersey	1.416	Wyoming	1.018
5.	Rhode Island	1.219	Florida	1.327	Michigan	1.321	Kentucky	1.009
6.	N. Carolina	1.005	Arizona	1.202	Florida	1.074	Maine	.975
7.	Maryland	.835	Oklahoma	1.122	Colorado	1.049	Idaho	.948
8.	Vermont	.572	California	1.041	Illinois	.969	Florida	.906
9.	Colorado	.568	Idaho	.996	Missouri	.936	Pennsylvania	.899
10.	Virginia	.428	S. Dakota	.993	Indiana	.689	Michigan	.870
11.	Wisconsin	.414	Kentucky	.950	Tennessee	.678	Arizona	.861
12.	Connecticut	.409	Washington	.809	Oklahoma	.509	Washington	.787
13.	New Mexico	.386	Hawaii	.738	Louisiana	.483	New Mexico	.729
14.	Delaware	.261	Maryland	.604	Washington	.476	N. Dakota	.720
15.	Michigan	.256	Wyoming	.503	Georgia	.423	Hawaii	.637
16.	Idaho	.236	Virginia	.454	Kentucky	.397	Indiana	.591
17.	Tennessee	.177	Nevada	.376	Alaska	.319	Utah	.561
18.	Maine	.173	Wisconsin	.282	Texas	.299	S. Dakota	.533
19.	Illinois	.155	Connecticut	.191	Wisconsin	.254	Montana	.502
20.	N. Dakota	.062	Oregon	.189	Ohio	.184	Arkansas	.491
21.	Utah	.014	Ohio	.174	Utah	.174	Oklahoma	.480
22.	S. Carolina	-.023	Alaska	.053	Arizona	.166	Alabama	.428
23.	Louisiana	-.031	Vermont	-.014	Connecticut	-.021	New Hampshire	.401
24.	W. Virginia	-.058	New Mexico	-.037	Maryland	-.041	Alaska	.166
25.	Oregon	-.128	Louisiana	-.108	Alabama	-.165	Rhode Island	.148

#	State	Score	State	Score	State	Score	State	Score
26.	California	-.165	Georgia	-.151	S. Carolina	-.185	Massachusetts	.087
27.	Pennsylvania	-.227	W. Virginia	-.155	Oregon	-.269	Delaware	-.007
28.	Kentucky	-.319	Missouri	-.205	Kansas	-.280	Maryland	-.130
29.	Alabama	-.366	Maine	-.208	N. Carolina	-.284	Texas	-.150
30.	Nebraska	-.367	Colorado	-.220	New Hampshire	-.306	Connecticut	-.155
31.	Arkansas	-.393	Utah	-.224	Massachusetts	-.318	Ohio	-.199
32.	Washington	-.401	Alabama	-.270	Nebraska	-.371	Missouri	-.304
33.	Florida	-.411	Massachusetts	-.321	New Mexico	-.524	Nevada	-.332
34.	New Hampshire	-.428	Texas	-.326	Minnesota	-.565	Iowa	-.334
35.	S. Dakota	-.458	New Hampshire	-.367	Idaho	-.580	Vermont	-.351
36.	Kansas	-.502	Mississippi	-.495	Mississippi	-.609	Nebraska	-.406
37.	Nevada	-.511	Pennsylvania	-.593	Arkansas	-.657	S. Carolina	-.458
38.	Arizona	-.531	New Jersey	-.721	Delaware	-.701	Mississippi	-.679
39.	Oklahoma	-.542	Montana	-.730	N. Dakota	-.716	Illinois	-.679
40.	Ohio	-.571	New York	-.732	Wyoming	-.781	N. Carolina	-.818
41.	Massachusetts	-.728	N. Dakota	-.760	Virginia	-.798	Kansas	-.821
42.	Missouri	-.788	Nebraska	-.828	S. Dakota	-.814	Georgia	-.902
43.	Iowa	-.925	Michigan	-.972	Maine	-.830	Wisconsin	-.906
44.	Mississippi	-.925	Rhode Island	-1.054	Hawaii	-.848	Maine	-1.052
45.	Wyoming	-.945	S. Carolina	-1.178	W. Virginia	-.874	Virginia	-1.208
46.	Indiana	-.962	Indiana	-1.276	Iowa	-.880	Tennessee	-1.564
47.	Minnesota	-1.081	Tennessee	-1.610	Vermont	-1.033	California	-1.662
48.	Georgia	-1.189	Minnesota	-1.612	Nevada	-1.284	Louisiana	-1.702
49.	Montana	-1.220	Delaware	-1.735	Rhode Island	-1.665	Oregon	-1.760
50.	Texas	-1.343	Arkansas	-1.962	Montana	-1.928	New York	-1.975

Note: The number next to each state is the factor score of the state on the overall dimension of judicial reform. The numbers range from high negative numbers and indicate the state's policy on each dimension. A high positive number indicates that a state has most of the characteristics of the ideal model favored by court reformers. A high negative number indicates that a state lacks most of the favored characteristics.

Table 5.2 Regression Coefficients for State Characteristics and Factors of Judicial Administration

State Characteristics	Factors of Judicial Administration			
	I CENTRALIZED JUD. MGT.	II COURT CONSOL. AND SIMPLIF.	III JUDICIAL EDUC. AND QUALIF.	IV JUDICIAL RULE MAKING
	Beta	*Beta*	*Beta*	*Beta*
Merit Judicial Selection				
Date of adoption	0.27	−0.22	0.13	−0.26
Current use	−0.23	0.39	0.30	0.12
Socioeconomic				
Median family income	0.26	0.21	−0.17	−0.26
% population in industrial employment	0.03	−0.16	0.19	0.07
% population urban	a	0.03	0.06	0.15
Median education	−0.35[b]	0.13	−0.11	0.19
Governmental Development				
Legislative professionalism	−0.05	0.14	0.40[b]	−0.19
Policy innovation	0.51[b]	−0.27	0.19	−0.06
State employees/10,000 population	0.70[b]	−0.14	−0.30[b]	0.20
Political Competition				
Average % Democrat vote—governor	a	−0.03	0.15	−0.21
% membership lower house from majority party	−0.02	a	−0.21	0.06
	R^2 0.66	R^2 0.37	R^2 0.66	R^2 0.19

a. Variable excluded from the regression equation; scores insufficient for necessary computer evaluation.
b. These coefficients are significant at or very near the 0.05 level.

factor of judicial administration that is strongly related to the size and general innovative character of state government. Most likely, this is due to the location of the court administrator as a *state* administrative agency with state employees, a state budget, and a capitol address. Moreover, although judicial administration occurs under the supervision of the supreme court, the court administrator's office is structurally similar to state agencies in the executive branch. Like other parts of the bureaucracy, the judicial administrator carries out state programs and coordinates local governmental action within the framework of state public policy.

The other features of judicial administration are more in-house or separate judicial structures. They do not require typical bureaucratic organizations with their permanent staff, budgets, and routines. In particular, "Court Consolidation and Simplification" and "Judicial Rule Making" pertain primarily to reorganization of existing judicial institutions and behavior, not to the role of administrative agencies. Similarly, "Judicial Education and Qualifications" refers to upgrading the skills of existing court personnel within the context of established court systems. These aspects of judicial administration are more esoteric and focus primarily on local judicial organizations. In addition, reflecting the generally conservative outlook in the judicial process, judges and other court personnel frequently do not welcome external pressure to change, but prefer traditional techniques of managing the local judiciary. Therefore, most administration in local courts may not reflect other patterns of state government. Offices of the state court administrator, however, are likely to grow and develop as do other state agencies that benefit from incremental increases in state budgets, number of state employees, and their expanding political functions.

Innovations in judicial education and qualification are positively related to legislative professionalism. This suggests a common state interest in developing experienced personnel capable of leadership and skilled management in both branches of government. Other features of state judicial administration are predominantly tied to the judiciary itself and do not seem to be connected to the legislature or the executive branch and are not linked to other features of state governmental systems. It also is worth noting that competition between political parties has no effect on administrative innovations. This finding parallels much other state policy research that has discovered that political parties do not have much impact on the precise content of state public policy.

Much variation still is left unexplained by this analysis, especially in court consolidation and simplification and judicial rule making. Although these aspects of judicial administration appear to be more separated from other elements of state government, we still may wonder why certain states move in the direction of reform goals and others retain traditional judicial systems. One possible explanation might be that simply not much variation in innovations remains among the states. Perhaps reformers have been so successful that nearly all of the states have identical judicial systems and nothing is left to explain. But that is not the case. Despite the movement toward consolidation and simplification of state court organization, for example, many differences still exist among the fifty states. It also is difficult to imagine what some of the states have in common other than their particular court system. For instance, except for having traditional and complex court systems, New York, Arkansas, Indiana, Michigan, and Tennessee seem to have little else in common. Perhaps other variables exist, or perhaps individual state political histories, the unusual strength of certain interest groups that oppose change, or other local factors affect the state courts. Future searches for common threads may provide more clues.

THE IMPACT OF CENTRALIZED STATE JUDICIAL ADMINISTRATION

It is clear that certain states are more likely than others to adopt centralized judicial management and to reorganize parts of the state judicial process. However, we do not know what effect these changes have on trial or appellate judicial procedure or the output of the courts. A number of issues in state judicial administration require further attention. Perhaps the most important one concerns the basic political relationships among state courts. A few studies of individual states strongly suggest that changes made at the state level will have limited impact, because strong traditions of local justice lead trial judges to reject outside influence in their own court operations. They see supreme court judges as colleagues, not as bosses.[15] A different possibility, however, is that if centralized budgeting and state financing are adopted, local judges will have few alternatives but to follow the directives of state supreme courts. Sources of finance and budget approval could change the orientations of lower court judges. A comparison of management practices in states with and without strong centralization may be illuminating.

Another issue in state judicial administration is the transmission of innovations. For innovations to have an impact, judges must be made aware of them and must be convinced or coerced to adopt them. Given the traditionally decentralized and independent character of the judicial process, coercion is extremely unlikely; therefore, persuasion and compromise are the likely methods that probably will achieve change. We need to learn how information is transmitted from supreme courts to other judges, how much effort supreme courts place on having changes adopted, and how they are received by other judges.

Supreme court leadership also may be only one of several sources of information and influence in judicial administration. Others include informal communication among trial judges, attendance at regional and national conferences on judicial management, and newsletters from national reform organizations. State supreme courts do not have a monopoly on the flow of information and actually may have to compete with others for influence over "their" state courts.

Although little research on state court management exists, one study of trial court innovation suggests that professional administrators and supreme court leadership are not the major factors responsible for producing change in the courts.[16] According to the hypotheses of court reformers, we would expect that professional administrators propose most changes for the trial courts. The evidence suggests, however, that professional administrators are not even working in the courts when most new ideas are developed and implemented. Instead, hiring an administrator is an innovation itself that comes *after* many other changes already are in place. Perhaps rather than providing leadership, administrators are brought in to handle routine management tasks at the direction of trial judges and perhaps local legal elites who are responsible for court innovation. The research also shows that the degree to which local courts are integrated into reorganized state judicial systems has practically no effect on trial court innovation. The power of state supreme courts to supervise the trial courts was not examined in this research, but the findings suggest that supreme court leadership may not affect local practices.

The future role of state supreme courts is unclear. Leadership in court reform usually has come from various private national organizations and the federal Law Enforcement Assistance Administration (LEAA). Many changes in local criminal courts and police departments in particular have been endorsed and funded by LEAA. National reform organizations also have received federal grants to experiment and to conduct research in judicial administration. However, it seems likely that in the Reagan years less federal money will be available for judicial reform, and state governments probably will have to pick up more of the costs of state and local courts. This possibly could strengthen the role of supreme courts in supervising judicial administration. But state contributions to the judiciary never have been very great, nor have the courts been a high priority for state government. Faced with other rising costs stemming from cutbacks in federal grants, state governments probably will rely even more on local governments to pay for the courts. Few states have vested major powers of judicial administration in their supreme courts and judicial administrators. Increasing the role of local governments probably will strengthen already influential local officials and judges in controlling the courts.

Advocates of state judicial centralization may have to work even harder to increase the power of state supreme courts in this new area of public policy.

NOTES

1. Russell R. Wheeler and Howard R. Whitcomb, eds., *Judicial Administration* (Englewood Cliffs, N.J.: Prentice-Hall, 1977); Larry Berkson, Steven Hays, and Susan J. Carbon, eds., *Managing the State Courts* (St. Paul, Minn.: West, 1977).
2. National Center for State Courts, *Equal Employment Opportunity in the Courts* (St. Paul, Minn.: National Center for State Courts, North Central Regional Office, 1979).
3. Larry Berkson and Susan Carbon, *Court Unification: History, Politics, and Implementation* (Washington, D.C.: U.S. Government Printing Office, 1978).
4. *See* Henry R. Glick and Kenneth N. Vines, *State Court Systems* (Englewood Cliffs, N.J.: Prentice-Hall, 1973); Henry R. Glick, "The Promise and Performance of the Missouri Plan: Judicial Selection in the Fifty States," *University of Miami Law Review* 32 (1978): 509–41.
5. Henry R. Glick, "Federal Judges in the United States: Party, Ideology, and Merit Nomination," *Loyola of Los Angeles Law Review* 12 (1979): 767–806.
6. Beverly Blair Cook, "The Politics of Piecemeal Reform in Kansas Courts," *Judicature* 53 (1970): 274–81; Lois Morrell Pelekoudas, "Judicial Reform Efforts in Ten States, 1950–1961" (Ph.D. diss., University of Illinois, 1963).
7. Jack L. Walker, "The Diffusion of Innovations Among the American States," *American Political Science Review* 63 (1969): 880–99; Virginia Gray, "Innovation in the States: A Diffusion Study," *American Political Science Review* 67 (1973): 1174–85; Jack L. Walker, "Comment: Problems in Research on the Diffusion of Policy Innovations," *American Political Science Review* 67 (1973): 1186–91.
8. Michael Aiken and Robert R. Alford, "Community Structure and Innovation: The Case of Public Housing," *American Political Science Review* 64 (1970): 843–64.
9. Laurance M. Hyde, Jr., "Good Judges are Made . . . ," in *Justice in the States, Addresses and Papers of the National Conference on the Judiciary,* ed. William Swindler (St. Paul, Minn.: West, 1971); Dorothy W. Nelson, *Judicial Administration and the Administration of Justice* (St. Paul, Minn.: West, 1974); Steven W. Hays, *Court Reform: Ideal or Illusion?* (Lexington, Mass.: Lexington Books, 1978).
10. Thomas R. Dye, *Politics, Economics and the Public* (Chicago: Rand McNally and Co., 1966); id., *Politics in States and Communities* (Englewood Cliffs, N.J.: Prentice-Hall, 1975); id., *Understanding Public Policy,* 3d ed. (Englewood Cliffs, N.J.: Prentice-Hall, 1977); Walker, "Diffusion of Innovations"; Gray, "Innovation in the States"; Herbert Jacob and Kenneth N. Vines, eds., *Politics in the American States,* 3d ed. (Boston: Little, Brown & Co., 1976).
11. Burton M. Atkins and Henry R. Glick, "Environmental and Structural Variables as Determinants of Issues in State Courts of Last Resort," *American Journal of Political Science* 20 (1976): 97–115.
12. A detailed description of the collection and organization of the data is available in Henry R. Glick, "Innovation in State Judicial Administration: Effects on Court Management and Organization," *American Politics Quarterly* 9 (1981): 49–69.
13. Hays, *Court Reform.*
14. Berkson and Carbon, *Court Unification,* pp. 139–40.
15. Hays, *Court Reform.*
16. Lucinda Long, "Innovation in Urban Criminal Misdemeanor Courts," in *The Potential for Reform of Criminal Justice,* ed. Herbert Jacob (Beverly Hills, Calif.: Sage, 1974).

6.

CARL BAAR

Judicial Activism in State Courts: The Inherent-Powers Doctrine

This chapter deals with an area of law in which courts behave sharply contrary to the expectations of students of public law and the judicial process. If political scientists were to rank the nation's courts by the extent to which they have displayed judicial activism, the U.S. Supreme Court would rank high over the past several decades. The lower federal courts, both district and appellate, would also be high on the scale, as they increasingly develop creative responses to litigants challenging the operation of numerous state laws and departments. The state courts would generally rank below the federal courts in degree of judicial activism, although certain leading state supreme courts are recognized for their increasing involvement in major policy issues and their willingness to challenge legislative and administrative action. At the bottom of the scale would be the state trial courts, which are usually studied as components of a larger civil or criminal justice process with an often passive, peripheral, and indistinct role.

Yet if one were to examine the doctrine of inherent powers and especially its use "to provide needed court personnel, facilities and equipment,"[1] the ranking would be completely reversed. In inherent-powers cases, state trial courts have for many years been willing to challenge executive and legislative authorities, issue mandatory writs to elected and appointed officials, and even hold those officials in contempt. Numerous state supreme courts have approved the inherent-powers doctrine and applied it against administrative and legislative officials. A number of state supreme courts have been more cautious than the trial courts; yet all levels of courts in the states have been more active in this area than have the federal courts. The federal district courts have been virtually silent in using the doctrine of inherent powers to mandate necessary resources; appellate judges have taken steps to avoid even touching the issue; and the Supreme Court has never considered it. As a result, state trial courts, backed by state supreme courts, have developed and extended an area of law that has allowed the judiciary to take carefully measured and circumscribed action without precedent in the federal courts.

How is it that in this field state courts have moved in where the federal courts have feared to tread? It is not a matter of substantive jurisdiction—the inherent-powers doctrine has common law and constitutional roots shared by courts of the nation as well as the states. It is partly a matter of practical politics—the disputes that give rise to inherent-powers lawsuits are more common at the state trial court level. More than this, however, it is a different set of priorities and strategies that are shared by state courts and largely rejected by federal courts. These state court priorities and strategies have often led political scientists to see state courts as relatively passive and uncreative, because political science research has focused on issues of lower priority for those courts. Federal courts have given priority to policy divergence with the political branches of government, and state trial courts have emphasized the need for judicial efficacy in the face of resource dependencies. As a result, federal courts have used a consensus approach to issues of judicial efficacy and a conflict approach on high-priority policy matters; the state trial courts have done the opposite. Many state courts are therefore strongly activist in orientation, if we focus on a field of law closer to what those courts identify as their core values and activities. We then find a level of judicial activism that requires us to rethink our analyses of judicial politics.

SCOPE AND DEVELOPMENT

Inherent powers, according to the manual used by the National Judicial College,

consist of all powers reasonably required to enable a court to perform efficiently its judicial functions, to protect its dignity, independence and integrity, and to make its lawful actions effective. These powers are inherent in the sense that they exist because the court exists. . . .[2]

Following from this broad statement comes its application in matters of resource dependency: "Courts have the inherent power to incur and order paid all expenses reasonably necessary to the efficient operation of the court or to performance of its judicial functions."[3] This rule means that if a court can show that a particular expenditure is required (that is, reasonably necessary) for carrying out its judicial functions, that court can issue an order (most commonly a writ of mandamus) forcing fiscal authorities to appropriate and disburse the money.

The inherent-powers doctrine can be anchored in both constitutional and legislative necessity. If a state constitution requires that a given court exercise jurisdiction in certain cases, and funding authorities provide appropriations too small to hire and reimburse adequate support personnel to process the cases, the fiscal authorities may be ordered to do so. If state statutes give the court authority to select and set salaries of support personnel, a city or county government cannot directly or indirectly override the statutory authority delegated to the court.[4] Constitutional necessity also carries with it a broader notion of the "judicial power." By creating a court or set of courts and vesting in it judicial power, state constitutions have implicitly granted the judiciary the traditional powers of a court, established over centuries of Anglo-American legal history. Judicial power is valued, because it provides a check on governmental abuse of authority. To provide that check, the courts must not be dependent on other branches of government, but must "shield [their] ability to judge independently and fairly."[5] By this logic, derived from the principle of separation of powers, American state courts have extended the inherent-powers doctrine from its "limited antecedents in England"—for example, the power to punish contempt before the court—so that the doctrine can now be invoked to mandate legislative action.[6]

Inherent powers are now in widespread use in many if not most states in the United States. Leading cases have come out of the courts of last resort in Michigan, Massachusetts, Pennsylvania, Washington, Indiana, Colorado, and Texas. Opinion writers and commentators have also cited endorsements and applications of the doctrine in the courts of last resort in Arizona, Arkansas, California, Florida, Illinois, Kentucky, Maine, Minnesota, Missouri, Montana, Nebraska, Nevada, New Jersey, New York, Ohio, Oregon, South Dakota, and Wisconsin—some twenty-five states in all. Only the Supreme Court of Alabama has opposed inherent powers in principle and has done so over a strong dissent by its chief justice.[7] Because "the appellate cases are merely the tip of the iceberg,"[8] it is likely that inherent powers have been used by trial courts in other states as well.

Although the doctrine has become more prominent in the past twenty years, it has been established for some time. Pennsylvania used it in 1838 and 1857; Michigan in 1855; Indiana in 1893, 1894 and 1940; Missouri in 1873 and 1874; Wisconsin in 1874 and 1912; Nevada in 1902; Montana in 1909; and California in 1930. What has happened from the earlier cases to the modern cases of the last twenty years is that the scope of litigation has expanded. The earliest cases established "the inherent power to provide and require payment for food and lodging of jurors."[9] Later cases established the court's control over allocation of physical space, including office and storage space for the court clerk. Cases then established judicial authority to mandate funds for furniture, building repairs, and even air conditioning for a court in Wisconsin. Twentieth-century cases primarily involve support personnel and the court's inherent power to obtain necessary positions, fill them, and obtain adequate salaries. Earlier cases dealt with court secretaries, deputy clerks, and court reporters; more recent cases have dealt with court administrators and with juvenile and adult probation officers. Thus as court functions and the range of support personnel has increased, the doctrine has been extended. But more important, it has been extended beyond the dispute over a particular room or person to authorize mandating of tens of thousands (and even millions) of dollars covering the whole range of necessary court services.

The modern history of inherent powers in state courts must begin with the Colorado case of *Smith* v. *Miller* in 1963.[10] The case arose out of a dispute between the trial judges of El Paso County and the county board of commissioners over the scope of judicial authority to set salaries of court secretaries. The board refused to approve the salary schedule recommended by the court, so the court (in the person of visiting trial judge John Mabry) issued a writ of mandamus. The county commissioners appealed to the Colorado Supreme Court, which upheld the trial judge. The supreme court's opinion, quoting Mabry at length, vindicated the independence of the judiciary; "it is the genius of our government that the courts must be independent, unfettered, and free from directives, influence, or interference from any extraneous source." Checks and balances are essential, the court agreed, but do not require that "a coordinate department of government" such as the courts "be compelled to depend upon the vagaries of an extrinsic will."[11]

The *Smith* v. *Miller* decision had a wide impact. Because it limited the discretion of county boards to allocate local funds (courts typically take a visible fraction of county government staff and expenditures), county officials began to support a shift to state funding of the courts, and by 1970 Colorado became only the eighth state to adopt general state financing of its court system. Meanwhile, the lawyer for the El Paso County judges, Jim R. Carrigan, was invited to lecture on inherent powers at the fledgling National College of State Trial Judges, then located at Boulder, Colorado, in the summer of 1964. By 1970 some two thousand judges had discussed the topic, and Carrigan had prepared five editions of a handbook compiling relevant principles and precedents.[12] Each edition asked its readers to notify the author and the college of additional cases—including unreported or even unlitigated cases—and the booklet continued to expand. A generation of judges has been able to instruct and encourage one another in the use of inherent powers, so the doctrine has not only flourished but has matured as jurisdictions draw the lines between judicial, legislative, and executive authority.

By the late 1960s the most prominent battleground was in Michigan, where the Circuit Court of Wayne County was fighting the Board of County Commissioners. The circuit judges filed a complaint in the Wayne County Circuit Court on April 2, 1968, alleging that the county board had not provided "a sufficient number of court employees with adequate and reasonable compensation in order to permit and expedite the efficient administration of justice."[13] The judges asserted the inherent power to provide these resources by court order. The case was tried by a circuit judge from adjacent Oakland County, who held on October 15 that the judges "were entitled immediately to appoint 11 additional probation officers. . . ; a judicial assistant at a minimum salary of $25,000 per annum; [and] 8 additional law clerks," and mandated payment of their salaries from the county treasury.[14] The judgment also required that the county pay for the lawyer retained by the judges to prosecute the case.

In December 1969 the Michigan Supreme Court attempted to fashion a compromise, allowing the circuit court to mandate the judicial assistant (that is, court administrator) but not the probation officers and law clerks.[15] The plaintiff judges asked for and received a rehearing, following which the supreme court reversed its earlier compromise decision and adopted *per curiam* the December 1969 concurring opinion of Justices Eugene Black and John Dethmers that had rejected the attempt at compromise.[16] On September 30, 1971, the same day it released its new majority opinion in the *Wayne County* case, the Michigan Supreme Court also held in *Judges of the 74th Judicial District* v. *Bay County* that a judicial district is not bound by a collective bargaining agreement executed by the county board to set the salaries of the court employees.[17] That second case was not based directly on inherent powers, but on the constitutional status of the court as a state rather than a local agency. But both cases taken together affirmed the supreme court's stand on the authority of state trial courts to direct their own internal affairs and even mandate funds when necessary to assure a required level of judicial service.

In 1970 inherent powers first received national attention as the result of a suit in Philadelphia. Vincent A. Carroll, the President Judge of the Court of Common Pleas, sued Mayor James Tate on June 16 for $5,230,817, representing funds that the court requested for fiscal 1970–71, but the city-county government refused to appropriate the funds. On September 30 the trial judge ordered payment of $2,458,000 to the court, including major items for adult and juvenile probation, data processing, apprehension of fugitives, courtroom personnel, attorney and arbitration fees, and law clerks. Four months later the Pennsylvania Supreme Court affirmed and modified the order, setting a figure of $1,365,555, reduced to reflect the fact that the fiscal year was more than half over.[18] There was no unanimity over specific program expenditures (for example, a bail project was disallowed, because it was useful but not reasonably necessary), but there was strong support for the principle that the courts could overrule the funding decisions of elected representatives if those decisions obstructed the efficient operation of a court:

Unless the legislature can be compelled by the courts to provide the money which is reasonably necessary for the proper functioning and administration of the Courts, our entire judicial system could be extirpated, and the Legislature could make a mockery of our form of Government. . . .[19]

These three cases illustrate how inherent-powers issues have shifted from early controversy over badges of judicial status (for example, adequate courtrooms and control over needed space) and uncontrollables such as jury lodging and fees to maintenance and development of a wide variety of management functions and staff personnel. At the same time the doctrine has led to an expanded variety of both colorful and conscientious behavior in state trial courts. In 1973 Wayne County Chief Judge Joseph A. Sullivan called each of the county commissioners before him in open court the morning after they again rejected the court's budget requests. He asked each one how he voted. The commissioners who supported the budget were excused; the opponents were held in contempt, although not jailed. On August 6, 1976, Los Angeles Municipal Judge Joseph R. Grillo arrested a county auditor who had refused to issue airline tickets to the judge. The tickets, already approved in the previous budget, would have allowed the judge to go to Sacramento to lobby for additional municipal judgeships that county officials opposed. Grillo sentenced the auditor to two days in jail for contempt, later rescinding the order after the issue of the judiciary's control of its own budget had been joined.[20] In the early 1970s an elected Republican county clerk in southern Illinois, at odds with the Democratic-controlled county board, found the telephone line item cut from his budget. Having previously used litigation to establish his role as a provider of essential court services, the clerk resorted to different tactics. He called an afternoon news conference on the courthouse steps, at which time he released a number of carrier pigeons—his alternate method of official communication. The television cameras rolled, and the telephone item was restored within the week.

These and other colorful incidents often obscure the preparation that precedes most inherent-powers actions. For example, in January 1973 the Morgan County (Alabama) Commissioners rejected the secretarial salaries recommended by the three circuit judges (from $4,680 to $7,200 a year) in favor of a uniform pay scale that gave clerk-typists $348 a month. Following the resignation of one judge's secretary in March, the three judges agreed to "make inquiry in their geographical areas as to the reasonable and fair worth of legal secretaries." They "inquired of four other courts in the area, of numerous attorneys in the circuit, and of the larger industries as to secretarial pay. The court then convened and made a detailed finding of fact," fixed the salaries, and directed the county commission to pay them.[21] The case law in most states requires that the trial court build a record that includes full justification of mandated items.

Trial judges are sensitive to the political consequences of activism in use of inherent powers. An Indiana judge whose court has vigorously used the mandate sees it only "as a last resort." Even then it produces the "worst possible publicity, especially because we're elected." A Louisiana judge joked that inherent powers means one thing the first four years of a judge's term and something else during the two years preceding re-election. In Alpena County, Michigan, a trial judge was defeated at the polls following an inherent-powers conflict. So, however mundane we may regard the circumstances of much inherent-powers litigation, it has very real consequences for the judges involved. They place themselves in a vulnerable position to defend what they see as the independence and effectiveness of the courts. They may not choose to exercise their hard-won independence to develop creative applications of equal protection that upset established conventions of state and local government, but they will fight for it nevertheless, preserving the principle for the future.

THE ROLE OF STATE SUPREME COURTS

In all but a handful of inherent-powers cases, the state supreme courts are not directly involved. Battle lines are drawn between trial courts and fiscal authorities, and the state supreme court participates as part of its appellate review function. In this setting most state supreme courts have tried to act as mediators or compromisers. They have done so in two principal ways: (1) legal development: clarifying the legal doctrine and putting strict guidelines on its use, and (2) administrative supervision: using the supreme court's superintending or rule-making authority to prevent unilateral application of inherent powers by a trial judge alone. The first approach is used by the state supreme courts during the adjudication process; the second is used outside that process.

The law-development function was most impressively exemplified by the Supreme Court of Washington in the 1976 *Juvenile Director* case.[22] Earlier in 1976 the court had ruled seven to two that the Washington State Bar Association was responsible to the supreme court and therefore the doctrine of separation of powers forbade the state auditor from auditing funds collected by the bar.[23] The court's opinion had no precedent in any other state and was an unexpected extension of inherent-powers reasoning to limit a statewide agency. Ironically, the inherent-powers language was *obiter dicta;* the court had already held that the legislature had not intended to designate the state bar association as a "state agency."

By June, however, the Supreme Court handed down a landmark decision of the opposite kind in a more routine inherent-powers case. A Superior Court judge had issued a writ of mandate directing the Lincoln County Board of Commissioners to increase the salary of the county director of juvenile services. The court unanimously reversed, holding that the trial court had not met its burden of proof. The court upheld the doctrine of inherent powers, but argued that it was of sufficient importance that it could be invoked only with great care. The majority opinion of Justice Robert F. Utter was an impressive piece of scholarly work, drawing heavily from secondary sources including M.J.C. Vile's treatise on *Constitutionalism and the Separation of Powers* and developing one of the most thoughtful justifications for inherent powers ever written by an American court. It went beyond notions of the judiciary as a separate branch of government to develop criteria for when checks by one branch over another are and are not appropriate. The opinion never mentioned the *Washington State Bar Association* case, although Justice Utter wrote the majority opinion there as well, before changing his views.

Once inherent powers is linked to basic constitutional principles, it becomes too heavy an instrument to use for raising the juvenile director's salary. Thus the Washington Supreme Court majority increased the burden of proof to the highest level available in civil cases: "clear, cogent and convincing evidence." Four of nine justices, on the other hand, preferred the traditional "preponderance of the evidence" test and held that even that burden was not met by the trial court. There is no sign that other states will join in raising the burden of proof for inherent-powers cases. In that sense Washington's decision was unusual. In another sense Washington's decision was a typical albeit more successful attempt to do two things: (1) strengthen inherent powers by developing a more fully justified basis for its use; and (2) place practical restrictions on its use by trial courts so that it is invoked only in times of clearest and most pressing need.

Other state supreme courts have actively but carefully played a law-developing role. In 1972 the Massachusetts Supreme Judicial Court used an obscure incident involving $86 to entrench inherent powers in that state's jurisprudence.[24] A Superior Court judge had incurred the $86 bill by purchasing a tape recorder and three tapes to avoid cancelling a court session for lack of a stenographer. The county treasurer refused to pay, and the retailer sued. The Massachusetts high court upheld the trial judge's authority, but avoided the rhetoric of earlier cases. As one commentator described the decision, it "wisely avoids . . . verbal combat" with county officials by labelling "the inadequacies of facilities and personnel as the enemy." Moreover, "no evil motives are ascribed to the other branches. Thus the court enhances the view of inherent power as a protective device

employed on behalf of the populace and not as a ploy in an intergovernmental power struggle."[25]

Other states have wrestled with the need for balancing judicial authority
with competing claims of other branches of government. In April 1976 the
Minnesota Supreme Court refused to extend inherent powers to allow a
district court to set the minimum salary of the court clerk. The court
upheld the practical necessity concept for inherent powers, but called for
"due consideration for equally important executive and legislative functions."[26] In *Carroll* v. *Tate,* the Pennsylvania high court supported the use
of inherent powers in a million-dollar judgment, but not before reviewing
the specific budget items in dispute and disallowing some items requested
by the plaintiff common pleas judge.

Increasingly, the law-developing role of state supreme courts has been
combined with an administrative supervisory role, so that state supreme
courts that want to mediate local inherent-powers conflicts can more
effectively do so. In these instances, state supreme courts use their administrative and superintending authority to either prevent litigation or establish procedures for channelling litigation. In so doing, these state supreme
courts exercise significantly more administrative authority over state trial
courts than the U.S. Supreme Court exercises over the federal district
courts.

The first use of administrative authority by a state supreme court
occurred in Michigan, as a result of the *Wayne Circuit Judges* case. In its
first run at the case in December 1969, the Michigan Supreme Court
attempted a compromise during the adjudication process. Its majority
opinion emphasized the need to show "necessity" rather than "reasonableness" alone and rejected most of the trial judges' demands. But the
compromise decision did not hold, and the stronger views of the two
concurring justices prevailed on rehearing. However, on November 9,
1971, a month after the new decision came down and the same date on
which a further rehearing was denied, an administrative order was entered
providing

that no judge of a subordinate court may hereafter, by peremptory writ or otherwise, order the expenditure of public funds for any judicially required purpose
until such judge has submitted his proposed writ or order to the constitutional
office of Court Administrator, and has obtained due approval thereof by that
office.[27]

The Michigan administrative order substantially cut down the use of
inherent-powers litigation and hence the opportunity for Michigan trial
courts to issue orders against local funding authorities. What had been a
part of the litigation process became part of the administrative process.
This conversion followed two steps. First, the state court administrator

issued guidelines in November 1973 implementing the supreme court order. The guidelines required that all courts provide their local appropriating body with a line-item budget with adequate documentation to justify new or additional expenditures; that "all available local communication and good faith efforts to reach acceptable resolution be exhausted"; that "a comprehensive written statement" setting out the court's "reasonable and necessary" requirements be prepared if an appropriating body takes "unilateral action" that endangers the administration of justice; and that any proposed order name an administrative official (for example, clerk or treasurer) rather than a governmental body (for example, county board).[28] The thrust of the guidelines is to reduce the level of conflict and encourage settlement of disputes outside the judicial process.

Following the guidelines, a second element has been important. The state court administrator's office has not merely reviewed the material submitted by trial courts, but has done its own investigation and mediation—often to the dismay of the trial judges. In 1975 the state court administrator's office rejected a trial court's application for an order, in spite of the trial court's thorough effort at good-faith communication and thorough documentation of the need for salary increases for support personnel. The state office had two personnel specialists study the matter and concluded that the salaries proposed by the trial court were out of line with comparable salaries in that county or in comparable courts elsewhere in the state.[29] In 1976 an austerity program in Genessee County resulted in the layoff of twenty-three court employees. The trial court asked the supreme court to issue an order for additional funds. In response the state court administrator held a fact-finding session in the county and negotiated a compromise whereby the county board approved funds to rehire seven of the twenty-three employees.[30] No court order was ever issued. In these and other cases state-level intervention avoided the use of court orders, even where trial judges and court officials might have preferred to issue an order and join the conflict. Thus although the Michigan Supreme Court's opinion in *Wayne County Judges* did not restrict trial courts to the same degree as the Washington Supreme Court's opinion in the *Juvenile Director* case, the administrative order issued by the Michigan Court had substantial impact in practice, due to the willingness of state court administrative personnel to monitor and mediate local conflicts rather than simply back up the local judges. A matter of judicial independence was transformed into a matter of management review.

A similar process took place in Massachusetts following the September 1972 decision in *O'Coin's* v. *Treasurer of the County of Worcester,* the case of the $86 tape recorder. On November 8, 1972, the Supreme Judicial Court promulgated Rule 3:23, requiring prior approval by a chief judge before any individual trial judge can contractually bind a state or local

funding authority. A denial can be appealed by the trial judge to the chief
justice of the Supreme Judicial Court. The process is designed to stimulate
joint action by the judiciary and discourage individual judges from acting
alone.[31] It has also led to involvement of statewide court administrative
personnel in mediation efforts between trial judges and local officials.[32]
One commentator's conclusion shows the parallel between developments
in Massachusetts and Michigan:

Inherent power need not be inevitably associated with conflict and friction. Rather
it should be viewed as an important tool which, if established with a minimum of
rhetoric, can be woven into a procedural framework within which judicial status
can be enhanced and judicial influence effectively applied.[33]

A related but somewhat different approach was taken in Indiana, the
state in which the inherent-powers doctrine has been most extensively
used over the years and has been the most controversial. Trial courts had
long challenged county budget decisions and were usually upheld by the
state supreme court (for example, in 1940, 1955, and 1966). By 1976 the
use of the mandate was a way of life in some Indiana counties. In Vigo
County a court mandated funds to pay for an unlisted phone number for
the judge's personal residence, to pay for the judge's Indiana Judges
Association dues, to purchase new robes, and to purchase coffee and
coffee pots; the Vigo County auditor reported that court mandates
exceeded $100,000 a year for each of the previous four years.[34] In Marion
County (Indianapolis) a court mandated its entire budget "without following the normal budgetary process."[35] In Lake County the budget submitted
by the court to the county council contained on the last page a statement
signed by a presiding judge that the items contained therein were necessary
for operation of the court; no prior effort had been made to persuade
county officials. Lake County judges went even further, and for the first
time in any state extended the inherent-powers doctrine to the county
prosecutor, who won a $250,000 mandate on the grounds that his personnel
were officers of the court.[36]

In the midst of growing public and local government complaints (one
judge was defeated in a spring 1976 primary), the Indiana Legislative
Council established "the interim study committee on the Power of Certain
Branches of Government to Mandate Funds." After its creation on March
31, it held three meetings (in May, June, and July), unanimously approving
a constitutional amendment that read:

. . . notwithstanding any other provision of this constitution, the General Assem-
bly may by law regulate, limit, or abolish the power of the courts to order any
governmental units or officials to appropriate funds, or to disburse unappropriated
funds, for the operation or maintenance of the courts.[37]

The legislative committee realized that a 1962 constitutional amendment in New York with similar intent had been subsequently modified in the New York courts, so that the inherent-powers doctrine would prevail. But the committee felt its "notwithstanding" clause would preclude a similar interpretation in Indiana.

Before the 1977 legislative session convened, the Indiana Supreme Court issued an emergency order on November 1 adopting Trial Rule 60.5, clarifying the scope of mandate authority and providing procedures for review of a court order. "Mandate will not lie for extravagant, arbitrary or unwarranted expenditures nor for personal expenditures," stated the rule. "Prior to issuing the order, the court shall meet with the mandated party to demonstrate the need for said funds." The procedures for reviewing an order differed sharply from those in Michigan and Massachusetts. Because Indiana had created a state court administrator's office only one year before, the Supreme Court could not opt for an administrative screening procedure. Instead, its procedures spelled out how a mandate appeal would be adjudicated in court, including a procedure for appointing a special judge to try the case. (Note however that a special judge would only be appointed if the mandated party filed a petition asking that the trial not be held before the court that issued the order.) Thus an adversary process was maintained, not replaced by a conciliation process. What the Supreme Court rule did was make the existing adversary process more explicit and rational.

The new procedure was immediately put to work. On January 3, 1977, two Lake County small claims court budgets of over $200,000 each were mandated. On April 18 a special judge entered a decree reducing the sums to $176,000 and $173,000, still a substantial amount of money for two court divisions with a total case load of thirty-five thousand. A month later, on May 18, the Indiana Supreme Court affirmed the special judge's findings.[38]

Activity in other counties subsided, however, and even Lake County had been without mandate litigation in the two years since 1977. As a result, no legislative action has been taken on the proposed constitutional amendment, although it was introduced again in the 1979 legislative session. The Supreme Court's intervention, exercised through its rule-making rather than adjudicating function, had signalled both to the trial courts and the legislators its desire for a rational and moderate exercise of the inherent powers of the courts. At the same time, the Supreme Court did not back away from its support of lower court use of the mandate even when prohibitory legislation was pending.

Thus the state supreme courts, particularly in those states where inherent-powers controversies have been most intense, have carved out major roles. They have been willing to use administrative supervisory authority to impose their policy preferences on lower courts. At the same time, they have tried to reduce the use of inherent powers—and the level of conflict that occurs when it is used. In this sense the state supreme courts are highly active within the court system, but more restrained than the trial courts in their willingness to challenge other branches of government. They have used inherent-powers cases as a way to both reiterate the independence of the judiciary and extend their own control over the trial courts.

INHERENT POWERS IN THE FEDERAL COURTS

The notion that a court has the inherent power to have its lawful orders enforced is a principle that applies in federal as well as state courts. Yet no suit has ever been filed asking that federal authorities provide funds for essential federal court activities. The closest thing to an inherent-powers conflict, pitting a federal trial judge against another branch of government, arose in the spring of 1963, when Chief Judge Sylvester Ryan of the Southern District of New York enjoined the General Services Administration (GSA) from executing planned alterations of the federal courthouse in Foley Square. He claimed authority to indicate where in the courthouse judicial branch personnel could and could not be moved. The federal judiciary's response was immediate and conciliatory. Within twenty-four hours the Judicial Council of the Second Circuit set up a three-person committee (including then-Judge Thurgood Marshall) to handle negotiations between the chief judge and the GSA. After a compromise was reached that apparently gave Ryan what he wanted, the injunction was lifted.[39] No judgment was entered or opinion written on the matter by any court; in fact, the injunction was not issued as part of any pending case. The incident may have been unique; even in the years before 1939 when the Justice Department administered the courts, there is no indication of federal judges issuing orders to provide necessary resources.[40]

The U.S. Supreme Court dealt with one inherent-powers case that could provide a basis for mandating funds. The case was *Ex Parte Peterson,* decided June 1, 1920, with Justice Louis Brandeis delivering the majority opinion (the three dissenters filed no opinion). The court held that a federal district court has the inherent power to appoint an auditor to simplify issues before a jury and to impose costs on the parties. In Brandeis's words: "Courts have (at least, in the absence of legislation to the contrary) inherent power to provide themselves with appropriate instruments required for the performance of their duties."[41] Where *Ex Parte Peterson* diverged from similar state cases was that the cost of the needed resource—the auditor—was borne by the parties in the cases and not by public funds. In a footnote Brandeis observed that Massachusetts (since 1878) and Maine (since 1897) required that auditor's fees be paid by the county. In contrast, wrote Brandeis, "Congress has made no provision for paying from public funds either the fees of auditors or the expense of the stenographer." Rather than even consider mandating congressional payment, the justice concluded that "the power to make the appointment without consent of the parties is practically dependent upon the power to tax the expense as costs."[42] Although the issue of taxing costs has been raised on a number of later occasions in the federal courts—even in a recent case involving the Environmental Defense Fund,[43] the Supreme Court has never faced the question of mandating a funding authority for any part of the disputed costs.

EXPLAINING STATE COURT ACTIVISM

What accounts for the prevalence of inherent-powers cases in state courts and their virtual absence in the federal courts? A number of reasons—some structural, some administrative, some functional—combine to provide an explanation for the sharp differences in the degree of judicial activism displayed by state and federal courts in this field. Five explanatory factors are discussed in this section. The first three are structural and administrative; they derive from the way state courts have been organized and financed in the past. Court organization and financing are gradually changing; therefore, to the extent that these three state-federal differences account for the high degree of state judicial activism, that activism is likely to become a thing of the past. The other two explanatory factors reflect continuing functional differences between state and federal trial courts; to the extent that those two factors are important, judicial activism in inherent-powers cases is likely to persist. After this section outlines the five factors, the next section discusses the future prospects of inherent powers and considers the extent to which state trial court activism will continue.

First, state and federal courts have different bases of funding. State courts have largely been funded by local governments; state funding predominantly covers fixed expenses such as judges' salaries, and local governments—in practice, counties—fund relatively variable expenses for support personnel, equipment, and facilities. In contrast, the federal courts have a single funding source, the U.S. Congress. Thus, as Geoffrey Hazard has argued, an inherent-powers case in a state trial court not only pits the judiciary against the other branches of government, but also a state agency against a local agency. The court is therefore defending not only judicial independence, but the authority of the state constitution and state statutes in the face of local political opposition.[44] Our review of inherent-powers conflicts suggests that most of them involve local funding agencies and not the state legislature or governor. One would expect state trial courts to be far more reticent to challenge the state legislature than a county board—

as reticent as federal trial courts have been about challenging the appropriation authority of the congress.

Second, different bases of funding have given rise to different administrative strategies. The federal judiciary emphasizes a consensus approach in presenting its financial needs to Congress, but state trial courts often adopt the adversary posture that befits a conflict approach. The federal courts' congressional relations on budget matters have been handled with great care over the years. For over twenty years Hugo Black testified annually before the House Appropriations Subcommittee in defense of the Supreme Court's budget. Longtime Subcommittee Chairman John Rooney often praised Chief Justice Earl Warren for things such as using less expensive limousines than did comparable executive officials. When the lower federal courts' budgets began running into trouble in the mid-1950s in Rooney's subcommittee, the Judicial Conference of the United States replaced a more patrician, Princeton-educated judge with a Chicago trial judge who was a product of that city's Democratic machine. That judge, William J. Campbell, established cooperative relations with Rooney that persisted for over a decade.[45] When Campbell left the chairmanship of the Judicial Conference Budget Committee, he was replaced by an Ohio federal judge who was an old friend of the ranking minority member of the subcommittee. Other judges have since succeeded to the Budget Committee chairmanship, usually chosen with similar needs in mind.

In contrast, state trial courts are less likely to have institutionalized their relations with local and with state agencies. Appearances before local funding authorities are viewed as demeaning—"going hat in hand" to those whose very actions could be challenged by parties before the court. A trial judge may in fact be an old political adversary of state or local legislators; thus many state court administrators are cautious about involving judges in legislative relations.[46] Most important, the fragmentation of state and local funding authorities makes it more difficult for state trial courts to evolve specialized committees and experienced spokesmen, as have the federal courts. A local trial court will have fewer judges to choose from in designating a person to appear before the county commissioners. Experienced and effective middlemen are often unavailable. Individual trial judges, faced with a less stable political environment, resort to an approach they know best—the adversary process.

Third, state trial courts are faced with tighter external fiscal controls than federal trial courts. Previous discussion suggests that court-county board conflicts often arise out of line-item budgets, in which nonjudicial authorities can set the salary level of a single employee or approve the purchase of a single piece of equipment. Under those circumstances the number of potential conflicts is multiplied far beyond the total dollar sums involved. In contrast, control over the federal court budget is placed by statute in the Administrative Office of the United States Courts (AOC), a judicial branch agency. The AOC often exerts tight (some trial judges would say excessive) central control over the judicial budget, but its control is not subject to challenge as a violation of inherent powers. Furthermore, the AOC has sufficient authority to transfer funds across line items that it can meet a crisis in an individual trial court.

Fourth, a higher volume and variety of litigation and judicial functions are found in state than in federal courts. As a result, trial court administration is more complex, personnel more diverse, and government involvement more widespread in state than in federal courts. State court budget requests are therefore less routine, and the funding decisions of state and local governments are more likely to affect what trial courts do than are the funding decisions of the U.S. Congress. Both the essential and the innovative work of state trial courts may be heavily impacted by funding decisions. The essential and innovative work of federal trial courts is less likely to be impacted by congressional funding decisions.

State trial courts deal more extensively with routine high-volume litigation—violations and misdemeanors, small claims, uncontested divorces. Much of this litigation involves parties that are less articulate and less wealthy than parties in federal court; in fact, some state trial courts may take on the character of social agencies.[47] Consider the increasing variety of programs and personnel within the ambit of state trial courts—probation officers, marriage counselors, pretrial release programs, diversion programs, juvenile detention facilities, arbitration programs, neighborhood legal centers, offices for collection and disbursement of child support, and professional administrators and management analysts. Some of these programs and roles are being developed by innovative metropolitan courts; others have been established for decades. Because many are peripheral to traditional adjudicative functions, they are not as well shielded by norms and conventions from external interference or domination. But as they grow in importance—because they provide essential dispute-processing services for the diverse clientele of state trial courts—state judges remain wary of executive and legislative actions that could compromise these programs and personnel.

Federal trial courts are relatively free from these needs and problems. They employ probation officers, but few other professional staff. They have no trial court administrators, although court clerks, often with legal training, may function as court administrators, especially in larger centers. Computerized management-information systems exist in only a few courts, funded through pilot projects of the Federal Judicial Center, a national judicial branch body. Federal trial courts have specialized bankruptcy judges, but otherwise lack the variety of small claims, civil, family, and juvenile matters that have led state courts into expanding their nonadjudication services. Federal judicial activism is still confined largely to the exercise of adjudicative functions.

Following from these state-federal differences in court activities and functions is a fifth difference: federal trial courts are better able to mobilize counsel to provide support for their activism. Judicial activism in federal courts focuses on major policy issues in adjudication. Therefore, the federal trial judge can call on the resources of the litigants and the lawyers whose success in pursuing a claim may depend upon their legal and empirical research and upon their skill in devising feasible and creative remedies. State trial courts, on the other hand, often work in areas where attorneys are either peripheral to or absent from the judicial process. Some state court functions (small claims courts are the best example) are explicitly designed to facilitate the bringing and resolving of disputes without lawyers. In this setting state judicial activism focuses on maintaining and improving the operation of courts and court programs in which lawyer participation is either low (for example, small claims, juvenile, and adult probation) or fleeting (for example, high-volume criminal cases). The core activities of the state trial court are therefore more directly exposed to executive and legislative intervention, because the court is less able to depend on others to mobilize resources on its behalf. The litigation bar is unavailable as an immediate support for judicial initiative and is therefore less effective as a buffer against legislature and executive.

The fourth and fifth factors suggest essential differences in the organization and function of state and federal trial courts that have led state courts to a high level of judicial activism in adjudicating inherent-powers cases. The issues that arise in inherent-powers cases are important to state trial courts, because the dependence of trial courts on external funding authorities is more closely linked to the exercise of essential court activities. Actions of state and local fiscal authorities are more likely to impact on state trial court priorities and values than congressional budget action is likely to impact on federal trial court priorities and values. When the core values and activities of a court are threatened, an activist court is more likely to adopt a conflict rather than a consensus strategy. Thus activist federal courts have challenged state, local, and federal authorities when adjudicating major policy issues arising out of the federal constitution; these same courts have been conciliatory and careful on questions of funding and resources. Meanwhile, activist state courts have challenged state and local authorities when the loss of necessary administrative autonomy and fiscal resources threatens their standing as part of a separate branch of government; these same courts are often cooperative and supportive in their relations with local officials charged with enforcing community norms.

PROSPECTS FOR THE INHERENT-POWERS DOCTRINE

To what extent will administrative changes in the state courts increasingly limit the use of the inherent-powers doctrine? Will inherent-powers cases soon be read as legal history, recounting the petty squabbles that characterized the era of strong local governments in the mid-twentieth century? The gradual shift from local to state financing of courts is likely to reduce the amount of inherent-powers cases. The adoption of state supreme court rules, as in Michigan and Massachusetts, that emphasize conciliation and the intervention of administrators, is also likely to reduce inherent-powers litigation. So is the adoption of global budgets for an entire state court system, free from the detailed external line-item controls that have given rise to inherent-powers cases.

These trends therefore suggest a decline in inherent-powers litigation. However, there are strong indications that the doctrine will persist and will be used. The differences between federal and state trial court organization and functions are, if anything, growing more pronounced. State trial courts are growing more accustomed to housing support services, diverse technologies, and professional nonlawyer personnel and to developing dispute-resolution and enforcement processes that operate without lawyers. Therefore some of the major concerns that gave rise to judicial activism in inherent-powers litigation remain. If state authorities are more generous with public money than local authorities, less conflict would arise. But in the post-Proposition 13 era, few would predict that outcome.

Current developments in individual states already indicate that the inherent-powers doctrine is likely to have some use at the state level, so the shift from local to state financing of courts will not render the doctrine obsolete. For example, Alabama's 1973 Judicial Article not only provided for state rather than local funding of the courts, but also included inherent-powers language:

Adequate and reasonable financing for the entire unified judicial system shall be provided. Adequate and reasonable appropriations shall be made by the legislature for the entire unified judicial system, exclusive of probate courts and municipal courts.[48]

Since the Alabama Supreme Court rejected the use of inherent powers against a county funding authority shortly before state financing came into effect, the Alabama courts have stronger constitutional support for inherent powers now than in the past. The 1973 language did not prevent the newly unified court system from facing a major financial crisis in May and June 1977, but that controversy was resolved in the court's favor without resort to inherent powers.[49]

Recent experience in West Virginia shows most vividly that a state supreme court is prepared to adjudicate the budget decisions of a state legislature. West Virginia is unique in having a constitutional provision that prohibits the state legislature from decreasing any item in the judiciary's budget. This provision aroused little controversy for most of its sixty-year history, because the state legislature funded only limited portions of the state court system. After voters passed a Judicial Reorganization Amendment in 1974, court financing shifted to a state responsibility, and the state judicial budget grew from three million to fourteen million dollars over four years. Legislative interest in and criticism of the judicial budget increased. Finally, the 1978 legislative session decreased five items in the 1978–79 judicial budget.

The West Virginia judiciary chose to defend itself through litigation rather than administrative compromise. Two attorneys petitioned the Supreme Court of Appeals for a writ of mandamus requiring the clerk of the House of Delegates "to record and publish a constitutionally correct and true budget bill" including the five disputed items. Before the supreme court heard the case, four of the five justices of that court (including the chief justice) disqualified themselves. The fifth justice, who declined to disqualify himself, "was thereupon designated to act as Chief Justice of the Court to be composed of himself and four retired judges of the state eligible to be recalled for judicial duties" under the state constitution. Three of the four retired judges had been general trial court judges; the fourth had been both a trial and Supreme Court of Appeals judge. On June 19 the special court filed a *per curiam* opinion unanimously ordering the defendant legislative clerk "to perform his non-discretionary duty."[50]

The West Virginia case was less complex than inherent-powers cases, because the court could base its ruling on specific constitutional language rather than general constitutional principles. Even so, the West Virginia judiciary directly challenged an exercise of legislative budget power. It did not compromise or settle out of court, even though the legislature could have retaliated and begun the process of amending the constitution. Only a few years earlier, in 1972, similar language in the Maryland constitution was eliminated by legislative and voter approval of a state constitutional amendment. The West Virginia case suggests that even the elimination of local financing will not necessarily convert state court strategy to the federal court's consensus approach when questions of resource dependency are at issue.

Wisconsin provides still another example of the effects of judicial activism at the state level. It is perhaps the only state in which inherent powers were invoked in the nineteenth century against a state rather than local funding authority. As a result of that 1874 precedent,[51] the Wisconsin state court budget has for many years been appropriated on a sum sufficient basis. This means that the legislature approves specific dollar amounts at its discretion, but the judicial branch retains the authority to spend state funds beyond the appropriated amount, up to a "sum sufficient" to carry out its constitutional and statutory functions. This form of open-ended appropriation has not been subject to legal challenge in recent years but as in West Virginia is likely to become more controversial if more judicial activities are funded by state rather than local government.

The inherent-powers doctrine is also likely to have important new uses at the local level, as current efforts to reduce local government expenditures, including those mandated by constitutional referenda, generate new conflicts over court expenditures. In Bucks County, Pennsylvania, for example, the trial court administrator is fighting county officials on a number of issues at once. In late summer 1978 the county finance director "expropriated" $99,800 in salary funds from the court's budget; the money was later returned to the court. By January 1979 the county was challenging the court administrator's authority to manage the court's budget, that is, to transfer funds among some thirty-nine budget accounts without obtaining permission of county authorities. In the meantime, the trial court was about to carry forward its second inherent-powers suit in a three-year period.[52] All of this has occurred in a relatively well off suburban county.

In the months following adoption of Proposition 13, California became a laboratory for observing the development of conflict and consensus approaches by state trial courts. California trial courts are almost entirely county financed, making them particular targets for budget cutting. Initially, the trial courts have sought to avoid litigation. Some, as in Alameda County, have let local officials know that courts have a peculiar constitutional status that limits county discretion to trim funds below "necessary" levels.[53] Others, as in Ventura County, have identified themselves as part of the criminal justice process and have been lumped together with law-enforcement agencies, avoiding major cuts. This latter approach of linking the courts to another currently popular institution is potentially dangerous politics. It also ignores the budget realities that are likely to unfold in California counties in the 1980s. Within the decade, county budgets will be trimmed to the point where almost all expenditures will be on mandated items, for example, welfare payments and other benefits set by state statute. The trial courts will find that they will not only have to argue that a given expenditure is "reasonably necessary" under the inherent-powers doctrine, but also that it has a higher priority than other competing items mandated elsewhere in state law. In this setting renewed judicial activism is likely, with its success depending upon the state supreme court establishing firm constitutional support for local inherent-powers mandates.

CONCLUSION

This chapter has argued that state trial and appellate courts are more active than we would conclude from previous research. State courts are not active on a full range of issues, but neither are the federal courts. To find the issues on which a court system is most likely to be active, we must focus on its core values—what the judges understand as their court's essential functions—and the environmental pressures that threaten these essential functions and core values. The analysis that comes out of this perspective has not only required us to refine our views of the passive nature of state trial courts, but also required us to distinguish more sharply between the character of state and federal court systems.

NOTES

1. *See* Jim R. Carrigan, *Inherent Powers of the Courts* (Reno, Nev.: National College of the State Judiciary, 1973), p. 1.

2. Ibid., p. 2.

3. Ibid.

4. Ernest C. Friesen emphasizes this distribution between constitutional and legislative necessity. *See* Ernest C. Friesen, Edward C. Gallas, and Nesta M. Gallas, *Managing the Courts* (Indianapolis: Bobbs-Merrill, 1971), ch. 4.

5. Marian Opala, " 'Inherent' Powers of the Judiciary," unpublished undated paper, p. 2.

6. Ibid.

7. Morgan County Commission v. Powell, 293 So.2d 830 (1974). The chief justice was Howell Heflin, now United States Senator from Alabama.

8. Jim R. Carrigan, "Inherent Powers and Finance," *Trial Magazine* (November-December 1971): 24.

9. Carrigan, *Inherent Powers of the Courts*, p. 19. Data in this paragraph is drawn largely from this booklet, supplemented by post-1973 cases.

10. Smith v. Miller, 384 P.2d 738 (1963).

11. Id. at 741.

12. Carrigan, "Inherent Powers and Finance," p. 24. Carrigan was later appointed to the Colorado Supreme Court and the federal district court.

13. Wayne Circuit Judges v. Wayne County, 190 N.W.2d 228, 233 (1971).

14. Ibid.

15. Judges for the Third Judicial Circuit v. County of Wayne, 172 N.W.2d 436 (1969).

16. Wayne Circuit Judges v. Wayne County, *supra* note 13, at 241 (1971).

17. Judges of the 74th Judicial District v. Bay County, 190 N.W.2d 219 (1971).

18. Commonwealth *ex rel.* Carroll v. Tate, 274 A.2d 193 (1971). Noted in William Scott Ferguson, "Note: Judicial Financial Autonomy and Inherent Power," *Cornell Law Review* 57 (1972): 975.

19. Commonwealth *ex rel.* Carroll v. Tate, *supra* note 18, at 199.

20. *See* Myrna Oliver, "Judge Grillo Still Isn't Talking," *Los Angeles Times,* August 21, 1976; Gene Black, "Needed: Judicial Freedom," *Los Angeles Times,* August 22, 1976. Grillo was censured by the Los Angeles County Bar Association, but in the spring 1977 he won compensation for the plane tickets in San Bernardino Small Claims Court. The county transportation officer went on sick leave in September 1977, later claiming a disability

pension because "the incident caused him stress and strain affecting his nervous system and aggravating a case of gout." *Los Angeles Times,* November 8, 1977, pp. 1, 20.

21. Morgan County Commission v. Powell, *supra* note 7, at 832–33.

22. *In re* Juvenile Director, 552 P.2d 163 (1976). Noted in John C. Taggart, "Note: Judicial Power: The Inherent Power of the Courts to Compel Funding for Their Own Needs," *Washington Law Review* 53 (1978): 331.

23. *In re* Washington State Bar Association, 548 P.2d 310, 312 (1976).

24. O'Coin's v. Treasurer of the County of Worcester, 287 N.E.2d 608 (1972).

25. John M. Connors, "Inherent Power of the Courts—Management Tool or Rhetorical Weapon?" *Justice System Journal* 1 (Winter 1974): 63, 67.

26. Clerk of Court's Compensation v. Lyon County Commissioners, 241 N.W.2d 781 (1976). Noted in Allan Ashman, "What's New in the Law," *ABA Journal* (October 1976): 1338.

27. *Administrative Order No. 1971-6,* 386 Mich. xxix (1971). Exempted from the order were costs due on behalf of indigent felony defendants.

28. Einar Bohlin (court administrator), "Guidelines for Administrative Orders Involving Local Legislative and Funding Bodies," typed memorandum, November 27, 1973.

29. John Mayer, former deputy Michigan State court administrator, brought this example to the author's attention.

30. Avis M. Brown, district court clerk, 67th District Court, Burton, Michigan, brought this case to the author's attention.

31. Connors, "Inherent Powers of the Courts," p. 70.

32. John F. Burke, "The Inherent Powers of the Courts," *Judicature* 57 (January 1974): 247, 250.

33. Connors, "Inherent Powers of the Courts," p. 72.

34. Indiana Legislative Council, "Report of the Interim Study Committee on the Power of Certain Branches of Government to Mandate Funds," typed undated (c. 1976), Exhibit A; Indiana Legislative Council, "Minutes of Powers of Certain Branches of Government to Mandate Funds Interim Study Committee," typed, June 24, 1976, p. 2.

35. "Report of the Interim Study Committee," Exhibit A.

36. Andrew D. Hiduke, former court administrator of the Lake County Superior Court, Crown Point, Indiana, brought this information to the author's attention, as well as providing copies of the Indiana legislative material cited above.

37. "Report of the Interim Study Committee," Exhibit B.

38. Lake County Council v. Arredondo, 363 N.E.2d 218 (1977).

39. *See New York Times,* April 17, 1963, pp. 1, 28; id., June 2, 1963, p. 40.

40. Judges still complained, however. One complaint has become the most noteworthy piece of underground judicial humor in the federal courts: an undated letter from a second circuit judge at the turn of the century, explaining to the comptroller of the treasury why a purchase of water closet paper should not be disallowed. A copy of the letter bears a marginal notation from Learned Hand. The letter was reprinted in *The Second Circuit Newsletter,* September-October 1976.

41. *Ex Parte* Peterson, 253 U.S. 300, 312 (1920).

42. Id. at 314–15.

43. Environmental Defense Fund v. Froehlke, 368 F. Supp. 231 (1973).

44. Geoffrey C. Hazard, Jr., Martin B. McNamara, and Irwin F. Sentilles, III, "Court Finance and Unitary Budgeting," *Yale Law Journal* 81 (1972): 1286.

45. Kenneth M. Holland, "William J. Campbell: Case Study of an Activist U.S. District Judge," *Justice System Journal* 3 (Winter 1977): 143, 152–55.

46. On this topic, *see* Ellen Baar and Carl Baar, "Judges as Middlemen?" *Justice System Journal* 2 (Spring 1977): 210.

47. *See* Friesen, Gallas, and Gallas, *Managing the Courts,* ch. 11, "The Courts as a Social Force."

48. Alabama Constitution, art. VI, sec. 10.

49. The Alabama financial crisis is described in Carl Baar, "The Scope and Limits of Court Reform," *Justice System Journal* 5 (1980): 274, 280–81.

50. State *ex rel.* Bagley v. Blankenship, 246 S.E.2d 99 (1978). Ronald D. Lawson, assistant director of the Administrative Office of the West Virginia Courts, brought this case to the author's attention.

51. *In re* Janitor of Supreme Court, 35 Wis. 410 (1874).

52. H. Paul Kester, court administrator, Seventh Judicial District, Doylestown, Pennsylvania, brought this situation to the author's attention.

53. Allen Hellman, director, Alameda County Office of Court Services, Oakland, Calif., brought this response to the author's attention.

PART III.

STATE-FEDERAL
RELATIONS

7.

G. ALAN TARR

State Supreme Courts and the U.S. Supreme Court: The Problem of Compliance

"Divided loyalties" best characterizes the dilemma confronting state supreme court judges in the American federal system. By virtue of their backgrounds, political experience, and selection, they tend to identify with the state political systems in which they serve.[1] Their primary responsibility as members of these courts, the interpretation and development of state law, promotes a sympathy for state concerns and state perspectives. However, their responsibilities also entail the interpretation of federal law and, more importantly, the consideration of federal constitutional challenges to state law and practices. When operating in this capacity, they are legally subordinate to the U.S. Supreme Court and are obliged to construe federal constitutional provisions in line with relevant Supreme Court precedents, even if this requires the invalidation of state policies.

Recent studies reveal that state supreme courts have responded to this situation by selective noncompliance with Supreme Court mandates.[2] These findings in turn raise four interrelated questions. First, what is the character and extent of state supreme court noncompliance with decisions of the U.S. Supreme Court? Second, what effect does such noncompliance have on the effectiveness of the Supreme Court as a policymaker? Third, what factors account for state supreme court compliance or noncompliance with the Supreme Court's decisions? Fourth, what does the analysis of judicial response indicate regarding how state supreme court judges view their role in the American federal system?

THE EXTENT AND EFFECTS OF NONCOMPLIANCE

Even though state supreme court noncompliance does occur, one may well question the practical importance of the phenomenon. For one thing, the literature documenting judicial noncompliance indicates that it occurs relatively infrequently. Jerry Beatty, using an extremely narrow definition of noncompliance, discovered only eight instances of noncompliance and ten of quasi-noncompliance during the period 1959–69.[3] My survey of the ninety-eight state supreme court establishment decisions from 1947 to 1973 yielded only thirteen noncompliant decisions.[4] Other studies have reported similarly low levels of noncompliance. Thus it appears that state supreme courts rather consistently follow the lead of the Supreme Court on even the most controversial issues. In addition, since the Supreme Court can and does use its discretionary jurisdiction to reverse noncompliant decisions, one might argue that judicial noncompliance typically has little effect on the policies that are actually followed in the various states. However, this contention rests upon an unduly narrow view of the effects of such noncompliance.

It should be noted at the outset that the relative infrequency of judicial noncompliance does not necessarily indicate an unwillingness to challenge the authority of the Supreme Court. First, a state supreme court might have developed a constitutional doctrine—perhaps based on state constitutional provisions—before its adoption by the Supreme Court, and thus mere adherence to its own previous decisions produces compliance. Twenty-two states, for example, had judicially fashioned exclusionary rules before *Mapp* v. *Ohio*, and seven state supreme courts had invalidated Bible reading in public schools before *School District of Abington Township* v. *Schempp.*[5] Second, the Supreme Court might have upheld practices similar to challenged state practices, in which case reaffirmation of state policies would not require noncompliance. In responding to Supreme Court establishment decisions, for example, state supreme court noncompliance occurred only when compliance would have led to the invalidation of state policies. Finally, when the Supreme Court is perceived as insufficiently solicitous of civil liberties, state supreme courts can legitimately rely on state constitutional provisions to provide more extensive protection.[6]

Even more important are effects of state supreme court noncompliance that do not depend upon insulating state policies from Supreme Court invalidation. First, noncompliance necessitates diversion of the Supreme Court's scarce resources of time and energy to regular bureaucratic supervision of the lower courts and inhibits its ability to deal with the multiplicity of other issues demanding its attention. Given the Court's case-load limitations, extensive noncompliance in a particular area or even relatively infrequent noncompliance in a variety of areas would significantly affect the questions the Court addresses.

Second, noncompliance may deter litigants from initiating or continuing attempts to vindicate their rights through the state courts. In some policy areas—for example, the rights of the accused—constitutional issues are considered in the course of litigation initiated by governmental authorities. More frequently, however, vindication of individual rights requires citizen initiative. If litigants expect that state courts will refuse to recognize their claims, they may well acquiesce in constitutional violations rather than undertake costly and drawn-out litigation for an unpopular cause. Furthermore, even litigants who do seek judicial remedy may become discouraged before obtaining their rights when confronted with judicial noncompliance.[7] Of course, should either phenomenon occur, the Supreme Court cannot protect the individual's rights.

Third, even in the interpretation of federal constitutional provisions, the state supreme court retains its superordinate position in the state judicial system. This has important implications for the communication of Supreme Court decisions. As recent commentators have noted, those responsible for the implementation of Supreme Court decisions most frequently receive their information about the decisions indirectly, that is, not from the Court itself but from other sources on whom they rely for faithful transmission of the Court's messages.[8] For them to comply with Supreme Court directives, therefore, they must receive accurate information about the obligations imposed upon them. State supreme courts play a crucial role, both directly and indirectly, in this communications process. They transmit information about constitutional obligations directly to lower state courts in the course of appellate decisions involving federal constitutional challenges to state policies. These decisions may provide the only information lower courts receive concerning Supreme Court decisions, and in any event it is likely to be the most complete and perceived as authoritative.[9] Even if the state supreme court's interpretation appears to conflict with information from alternative sources, the threat of reversal may induce lower court judges to tailor their decisions to the cues provided by their state superior. Bradley Canon's survey of lower court decisions confirms that "a lower state court tends to follow the lead of its state supreme court even when the latter's stance is seemingly at odds with that of the United States Supreme Court."[10] Of course, the fact that the state supreme court is typically protecting state policy against a federally imposed mandate for change provides an additional incentive to adopt its position.

Through their influence on lower court judges, state supreme courts may also have an indirect effect on a much wider audience. Several studies suggest that trial court judges play a crucial role in communicating Supreme Court decisions to nonjudicial actors. In Neal Milner's study of police compliance with the *Miranda* decision, for example, members of all of the police departments surveyed listed local judges as one of their sources of information.[11] A later study of the effects of Burger Court decisions eroding *Miranda* concluded that in assessing their implications for prosecutions, prosecutors consistently took their cues from local courts.[12] Finally, Larry Berkson's study of affected elites in Florida confirms that local judges constitute an important source of information, particularly for attorneys, law officers, and lawmakers.[13] Yet in all instances state supreme courts have most likely provided the cues for these local judges.

Finally, the authority of the Supreme Court's pronouncements derives at least in part from their judicial character, that is, from the perception that they are rooted in law rather than in will. Such a belief allows an individual to disagree with a court decision on policy grounds and yet acknowledge its binding force. This authority, however, may be compromised by criticism emanating from those with similar stature as exponents of the law. As Bradley Canon observed, when "the judiciary's special competence to determine the law . . . is publicly disputed by judges themselves, laymen can be expected to pick up cues and behave accordingly."[14] Indeed, the very infrequency of criticism from this source might be viewed as evidence that it is justified when it does occur. In sum, the effects of state supreme court noncompliance extend far beyond the particular cases in which noncompliance occurs.

STUDIES OF STATE SUPREME COURT RESPONSE

Although research on state supreme court compliance and noncompliance has focused solely on response to the Supreme Court's establishment and criminal justice decisions, it has produced findings of considerable theoretical importance.

COMPLIANCE AND NONCOMPLIANCE

Three alternative understandings of compliance and noncompliance may be found in the impact literature. Some impact studies, focusing on the effectiveness of the Supreme Court as a national policymaker, have been most concerned with the attainment of the Court's purported policy objectives. Action congruent with those objectives has thus been classified as compliance and action counter to those objectives as noncompliance. Other studies have attempted to avoid the difficulties involved in distinguishing compliance and noncompliance by substituting for them the more neutral "responses." Finally, some studies have defined compliance and noncompliance in terms of the fulfillment or nonfulfillment of the legal obligations imposed by Court decisions. For state supreme courts those obligations include decisions of all cases in line with relevant Supreme Court precedents, and thus noncompliance would involve the failure to apply—or to apply properly—the Court's enunciated standards in deciding cases raising similar or related questions.[15] Implicit in this last approach is a recognition that a variety of responses to Supreme Court decisions may nonetheless be "compliant."[16]

This third approach avoids problems that plague the two alternative approaches. One difficulty in defining compliance and noncompliance in terms of the Supreme Court's policy objectives is that the validity of one's analysis then depends upon how accurately one identifies those objectives. In some cases—for example, *Paris Adult Theater I* v. *Slaton*—the Court clearly elucidates its objectives.[17] More frequently, however, the Court's objectives tend to be unclear, or at least open to various interpretations, forcing the researcher to attribute objectives to the Court. Yet the risk of mistake in such attributions is enormous. In assessing the legislative and judicial responses to *Roe* v. *Wade* and *Doe* v. *Bolton*, for example, how does one determine whether restrictions on Medicaid reimbursements for abortions conflict with Court objectives and therefore constitute noncompliance?[18] This in turn raises a related point. The possibility of error exists for the lower court judge as well as for the researcher. Thus even if the researcher correctly identifies the Court's objectives, to categorize a judge's good-faith failure to do so as noncompliance seems merely arbitrary.

Even more important, to define compliance and noncompliance in terms of the Court's policy objectives is to ignore the leeways legitimately available to subordinate courts, for although judges on those courts are legally obliged to decide cases in line with relevant precedents, fidelity to precedent need not advance the Court's objectives. For example, although the Burger Court has circumscribed the rights of defendants, thereby indicating its intention to strengthen the capacity of "law forces" to deal with lawbreakers, some state supreme courts have interpreted state constitutional provisions so as to afford defendants protections not required by the federal Constitution.[19] If one defines noncompliance as action inconsistent with the Court's policy objectives, these decisions presumably qualify. On the other hand, assuming that the interpretations of state constitutional provisions are not disingenuous, they also constitute legitimate judicial behavior. This anomalous result reveals the inadequacy of this approach.

Perhaps because of such difficulties some studies dispense with "compliance" and "noncompliance" in favor of the less problematic "response." This solution, however is unsatisfactory, because it ignores an important and very real distinction. Although the leeways available to lower court judges are broad, they are not unlimited: the judges are required to apply Supreme Court precedents faithfully in deciding cases raising similar or related questions.[20] Lower court judges cannot legitimately fail to follow determinative Supreme Court precedents. They cannot fail to address the constitutional question in a case in order to sustain illegitimate practices. They cannot substitute alternative decisional standards for those the Court has enunciated. They cannot misapply the Court's standards. By analyzing the opinions by which lower court judges justify their decisions, one can obtain the information necessary for distinguishing such behavior from responses within the leeways available to lower court judges.

The importance of distinguishing noncompliance from other responses derives from its illegitimacy, for if noncompliance differs in kind rather than in degree from other responses, one can reasonably expect that the considerations affecting the choice between compliance and noncompliance likewise differ in kind from those affecting judicial choices among alternative legitimate responses. Certainly judicial considerations of costs and benefits must change when noncompliance is contemplated.[21] Noncompliance involves judges in behavior contrary to their acknowledged legal obligations. It involves them as well in behavior contrary to their own expressed views regarding proper judicial behavior.[22] Finally, noncompliant decisions may be reviewed and reversed by the U.S. Supreme Court, a result that not only could be personally and professionally embarrassing but also could serve to frustrate the judges' substantive policy aims.[23] Thus glossing over the differences between noncompliance and other responses forecloses a potentially important field of inquiry.

ESTABLISHMENT OF RELIGION

The book *Judicial Impact and State Supreme Courts* focuses on state supreme court response to U.S. Supreme Court establishment decisions from 1947, when the Court first announced the application of the Establishment Clause to the states, until 1973. The ninety-eight state establishment decisions during the period included thirteen instances of noncompliances. Three hypotheses—each incorporating a particular view of the factors influencing judicial response—were tested to account for the incidence of noncompliance.

The judicial backgrounds hypothesis rests on the assumption that judicial decision making is essentially result oriented, an attempt to maximize personal value preferences formed during a political socialization that for the most part occurred before judicial selection. It further assumes that the background characteristics of judges explain—or at least serve to indicate—their value preferences. Thus the background characteristics of the various judges indicate their individual value preferences, and political system characteristics, which form a part of the background of all court members in a state, indicate shared value preferences. If the hypothesis were valid, one should be able to account for the incidence of noncompliance both within courts and among states on the basis of the background characteristics of individual judges and the characteristics of the political systems in which they operate. To test the hypothesis, I examined the relationships between eight relevant variables and judicial compliance-noncompliance.[24] My analysis indicated that none of these variables was even moderately associated with judicial response. Thus the judicial backgrounds hypothesis could not account for the pattern of judicial response.

A second hypothesis, labelled the Neustadtian hypothesis, rests on the assumption that judicial response depends fundamentally upon the presence or absence of conditions similar to those that Richard Neustadt deemed essential for a self-executing presidential order.[25] More specifically, it maintains that one can account for different levels of compliance with various Supreme Court decisions on the basis of the perceived finality of Supreme Court decisional standards, the clarity of those standards, and the persuasiveness of the Court's justification of its decisions. Since this hypothesis proposes that the decisive consideration influencing state supreme court behavior is the character of the Court's opinions, it coincides with the traditional concern for Supreme Court craftsmanship. To test this hypothesis, I developed a set of variables that operationalized those criteria and calculated rank-order correlations between the performance of the Court's establishment decisions on those criteria and the level of noncompliance following various decisions. My findings indicate that the Neustadtian hypothesis could not account for the pattern of judicial response.

A third hypothesis, the state impact hypothesis, proved to be the most satisfactory in accounting for judicial response. This hypothesis rests on the assumption that state supreme court judges identify themselves with the state political systems in which they serve and thus are unwilling to invalidate important state policies or practices, even if this unwillingness necessitates noncompliance with Supreme Court decisions. Although it thus posits a result-oriented jurisprudence, variation in response derives not from differing values held by various judges, since all presumably want to avoid disrupting state policies, but from variation in the character of the issues under litigation, that is, their status as important state policies. A state supreme court would thus comply with Supreme Court decisions when the challenged practices were reconcilable with them, but when application of the Court's standards would result in invalidation of state practices, the likelihood of noncompliance would be directly related to the disruptive effects that this invalidation would produce. My data tended to confirm these expectations. In no case did state supreme courts fail to comply to invalidate state practices. Furthermore, I found a strong (-0.70) negative correlation between level of disruption and percentage of compliant responses, when the choice was between noncompliance and invalidating practices in the state. Thus the state impact hypothesis proved the most successful in accounting for response in establishment cases. The question remains whether it can also account for response in other policy areas.

CRIMINAL JUSTICE

Given the controversy that the Warren Court's criminal justice decisions provoked, it is not surprising that research on state supreme court response has focused on response to those decisions. The first major study was Bradley Canon's examination of response to *Mapp* v. *Ohio*.[26] In *Mapp* the Supreme Court ruled that evidence seized in violation of the Fourth Amendment could not be admitted in criminal prosecutions in state courts. Canon's study examined nationwide response to this decision in the 60 to 70 percent of all search-and-seizure cases that raised recurring questions not directly addressed by *Mapp*. Using state supreme court decisions to admit or exclude evidence in these cases as his data base, he categorized the courts according to their tendency to construe *Mapp* broadly or narrowly. Tentatively equating compliance with a broad construction and noncompliance with a narrower reading, he found that compliance was not related to the prior adoption or absence of the exclusionary rule in the state. He further noted that regions differed in their response to *Mapp*, with midwestern and southern states less willing to give the decision an expansive reading, a finding he attributed to "regional differences in politico-legal culture."[27]

Neil Romans's study analyzed state supreme court response to *Escobedo* v. *Illinois* and *Miranda* v. *Arizona* before 1968.[28] In *Escobedo* the Court in a rather ambiguous opinion ruled that the right to counsel applied in preindictment interrogations to safeguard suspects' rights against self-incrimination. The *Miranda* decision two years later clarified this earlier ruling, indicating that unless suspects were informed of their rights to counsel and to refuse to respond to police questioning, their confessions would not be admissible in criminal trials. Romans classified courts as liberal or conservative on the basis of their decisions regarding the admissibility of confessions during three periods—pre-*Escobedo*, post-*Escobedo*, and post-*Miranda*—and attempted to account for the variations in "liberalism" he discovered. Three of his findings are particularly noteworthy. First, he found little tendency on the part of courts to modify their decisional patterns as a result of the vague *Escobedo* mandate: only four courts pursued "liberal" courses during the post-*Escobedo* period. Second, the clear decision in *Miranda* led to its acceptance by all courts, but most courts nonetheless refused to accord it a broad reading. Finally, those courts that had liberal policies resisted intrusion in this area, whereas those courts initially classified as conservative were more likely to give a broad reading to *Miranda*. Romans suggested that this surprising finding indicated that innovative (liberal) courts perceived the Court's decisions as interfering with their own policy development, while less innovative (conservative) courts had less institutional loyalty to the policies that *Miranda* invalidated.

John Gruhl analyzed state supreme court response to the Burger Court's apparent undermining of *Miranda*.[29] As noted, in *Miranda* the Court had established stringent requirements governing the admissibility of confessions. However, in a series of cases beginning with *Harris* v. *New York* (1971), the Court began to narrow the scope of that decision.[30] Gruhl's initial hypothesis was that state supreme courts would anticipate the future direction of Court decisions and erode *Miranda* even more than had the Supreme Court. To test this hypothesis, he examined state supreme court decisions from 1971 to 1978 regarding (1) prosecutorial use of illegally obtained statements to impeach credibility, (2) prosecutorial use of defendants' silence to impeach their credibility, (3) admissibility of inculpatory statements following incorrect police warnings, and (4) admissibility of statements following police refusal to cease questioning or police resumption of discontinued questioning. The decisions in these cases failed to confirm his original hypothesis; for despite some regional differences, state supreme courts generally did not seek to undermine *Miranda* more than had the Burger Court.

It is difficult to determine whether Gruhl's findings support any of the three hypotheses. Although Gruhl suggested that state supreme courts generally were complying with *Miranda*, he did not categorize state supreme court decisions as compliant or noncompliant, nor did he provide definitions of these terms. However, if one accepts "erosion" of *Miranda* as noncompliance—a somewhat questionable proposition, given the Supreme Court's decisions in *Harris* and subsequent cases—Gruhl suggested several conclusions regarding state supreme court compliance-noncompliance:

1. "Presumably, the courts enforced *Miranda* where they perceived serious violations, but they eroded it where they did not." Or alternatively: "Perhaps the courts enforced *Miranda* where they perceived obvious violations, but they eroded it where they did not. This explanation is supported by previous research concerning the warnings which suggests that greater clarity leads to greater compliance."[31]
2. "The southern and midwestern courts were most prone to erode *Miranda*, while the western and eastern courts were least. Presumably, the greater conservatism of the South and Midwest extended to judicial interpretation of Miranda."[32]
3. The state supreme courts failed generally to erode *Miranda* more than had the Burger Court, because "perhaps they considered the guidelines firmly entrenched, or, if they did not, perhaps they did not desire to weaken them further."[33]

RESPONSE AND THE STATE IMPACT HYPOTHESIS

Table 7.1 summarizes the findings regarding response to the Court's criminal justice decisions in terms of the three hypotheses. It indicates that these findings appear to provide substantial support for the Neustadtian hypothesis. The state impact hypothesis, on the other hand, appears relatively unsuccessful in accounting for response to the Court's criminal justice decisions. However, on closer inspection these studies furnish additional support for the state impact hypothesis.

One may begin by examining those findings that apparently conflict with the state impact hypothesis. Bradley Canon found that prior adoption or rejection of the exclusionary rule did not affect response to *Mapp*, a finding apparently inconsistent with the proposition that state supreme courts refuse to comply only when important state policies are under attack. Even assuming that one may categorize narrow constructions of *Mapp* as noncompliant, Canon's finding is not necessarily inconsistent with the state impact hypothesis. Since Canon has acknowledged that formal adoption or rejection of the exclusionary rule did not dictate practices in the various states, it is impossible to determine whether those states that failed to comply were indeed upholding state policies.

Table 7.1 Accounting for Response in Criminal Justice Cases

Findings Tending to Support the Judicial Background Hypothesis

1. Patterns of response to *Mapp* along regional lines (Canon)
2. Tendency to erode *Miranda* along regional lines (Gruhl)

Findings Tending to Support the Neustadtian Hypothesis

1. Greater tendency to comply with clear than with unclear decisions (Romans)
2. Greater tendency to comply with clear than with unclear decisions (Gruhl)
3. Failure to erode *Miranda* because of perceived finality of guidelines governing admissibility of confessions (Gruhl)

Findings Tending to Support the State Impact Hypothesis

1. General unwillingness to adopt broad interpretations of decisions contrary to prevailing policies in state (Romans)

Findings Inconsistent with the State Impact Hypothesis

1. Prior adoption or rejection of exclusionary rule by state supreme court not related to compliance/noncompliance (Canon)
2. Prior adoption of liberal policies pertaining to admissibility of confessions inversely related to acceptance of liberal Supreme Court policies in area (Romans)

Neil Romans discovered that conservative courts—those with less stringent requirements governing the admissibility of confessions before *Escobedo*—were more likely than liberal courts to give a liberal interpretation to the *Escobedo* and *Miranda* decisions. This finding, if accurate, is completely inconsistent with the state impact hypothesis. Whereas that hypothesis suggests that state supreme courts will refuse to comply when important state policies are threatened, the conservative courts have tended to comply. Moreover, whereas it suggests that they will refuse to comply only when such policies are threatened, the liberal courts have apparently refused to comply. Romans's data, however, do not warrant rejection of the state impact hypothesis.

First, although liberal construction of the Court's decisions would entail greater change for conservative courts, *Escobedo* threatened all states' policies regarding the admissibility of confessions. Romans noted that even New York, which had the most liberal policy before *Escobedo*, nonetheless needed to change its policy to comply with that decision.[34] Thus there is no reason to expect consistent compliance by liberal courts.

Second, one should not assume that all conservative responses are necessarily noncompliant. An examination of the differences among conservative responses to *Escobedo* supports this skepticism. Courts that responded conservatively limited *Escobedo*'s effect either by asserting the continuing vitality of the voluntariness test for the admissibility of confessions or by distinguishing *Escobedo* on factual grounds. Although the former approach obviously constitutes noncompliance, since it involves substitution of alternative standards for those enunciated by the Court, it is not clear that all decisions distinguishing *Escobedo* were noncompliant. Rather, given the ambiguities of the Court's opinion, it is likely that those decisions more frequently fell within the leeways available to lower court judges. But the liberal courts, to the extent they responded conservatively to *Escobedo*, consistently did so on the basis of such factual distinctions. Presumably, then, they tended to be more rather than less compliant. This finding supports the state impact hypothesis.

Reanalysis of Romans's data furnished additional support for the state impact hypothesis. Figure 7.1 indicates that a greater percentage of liberal than conservative courts interpreted *Escobedo* liberally. Similarly, figure 7.2 indicates that those courts that interpreted *Escobedo* liberally were particularly likely to do the same with *Miranda*. Although the limited number of cases does not permit any firm conclusions, these findings are consistent with the state impact hypothesis.

Other findings suggest that the Neustadtian hypothesis better accounts for response. Gruhl asserted that state supreme courts failed to erode *Miranda* more than had the U.S. Supreme Court in part because of the perceived finality of Court guidelines governing the admissibility of confes-

Figure 7.1 Variations in Response to *Escobedo*.

		Response to *Escobedo*[a]	
		Liberal	Conservative
	Liberal	20% (1)	80% (4)
Position Before *Escobedo*			
	Conservative	8% (3)	92% (36)

a. Six courts, including two liberal and four conservative courts, failed to decide cases involving the admissibility of confessions during the period between the *Escobedo* and *Miranda* decisions.

Figure 7.2 Variations in Response to *Miranda*.

		Response to *Miranda*[a]	
		Liberal	Conservative
	Liberal	67% (2)	33% (1)
Response to *Escobedo*			
	Conservative	27% (12)	73% (33)

a. Two courts, one of which had responded conservatively to *Escobedo* and one liberally, failed to decide cases involving the admissibility of confessions during the period between the *Miranda* decision and the conclusion of Romans's study.

sions. Implicit in this assertion is the assumption that had the guidelines been less final, state supreme courts would have been more willing to undermine them. However, since Gruhl maintained that the Court itself was signalling a retreat from those guidelines, one may well question whether state supreme courts perceived them as settled. The state impact hypothesis provides a more satisfactory explanation of state supreme court behavior. According to that hypothesis, noncompliance occurs only when compliance would jeopardize important state policies. But by the time the Court had decided *Harris* v. *New York,* state supreme courts had—according to Gruhl—accepted the *Miranda* guidelines as authoritative. Since continued adherence to *Miranda* thus did not require abandonment of important state policies, continued compliance with the Court's decisions was to be expected.

Both Romans and Gruhl have maintained that the level of compliance with Supreme Court decisions is directly related to their clarity. If one follows Romans's lead in classifying as compliant only those decisions that advance the Supreme Court's policy objectives, this finding is hardly unexpected. It stands to reason that courts eager to advance the Court's policies will be more successful in doing so once the Court has clarified them. However, if one categorizes as compliant all lower court decisions within permissible leeways, a relationship between the clarity of Court decisions and compliance is more interesting. In clarifying its decisional standards, the Court substantially reduces the leeways available to lower court judges and thus their ability to pursue policies inconsistent with the Court's without engaging in noncompliance. The assertion that the clarity of Court decisions is related to compliance thus means that when faced with the choice between compliance and their policy objectives, judges choose compliance. Gruhl's findings support this assertion, for he found that judges consistently invalidated blatant violations of Court standards, even when (for example, after *Hale* v. *United States*) they had previously allowed such practices. These findings, however, likewise support the state impact hypothesis. That hypothesis suggests that judges will fail to comply only when important state practices are threatened, that is, those that are statewide and have been in operation for a relatively long period. Since Gruhl has indicated that compliance with *Miranda* was not a problem before the Burger Court's decisions, the practices the courts invalidated could not have been well-established state practices. Consequently, failure to sustain these practices through noncompliance is consistent with the state impact hypothesis.

In sum, the state impact hypothesis best accounts for the pattern of response to the Supreme Court's establishment decisions. In addition, it can also account for the major findings reported by Canon, Romans, and Gruhl.[35] But why do state supreme courts behave in this way? What does this indicate about how their members view their role in the American federal system?

EXPLAINING RESPONSE PATTERNS

Utility theory provides a convenient framework for examining the implications of the state impact hypothesis's relative success in accounting for response. The basic assumption of utility theory is that all actors, including judges, behave according to a cost-benefit calculus, seeking through their actions to maximize perceived benefits and minimize perceived costs. Applying this assumption to judicial response, one would expect noncompliance to occur when the expected costs of compliance and benefits of noncompliance exceed the expected benefits of compliance and costs of noncompliance.[36] Therefore, by noting the various factors imposing costs and dispensing benefits for compliance and noncompliance in situations in which each occurs, one can ascertain the relative valuation judges place on these various factors and thus determine which factors influence judicial behavior.[37]

The primary benefit of noncompliance is presumably the maintenance of a favored policy against constitutional invalidation. However, noncompliance can achieve this result only if the U.S. Supreme Court does not review and reverse the noncompliant decision. Whether reversal is likely to occur depends upon three considerations: the likelihood of a petition for Supreme Court review, the likelihood of the Court deciding to review the lower court decision, and the likelihood of the Court reaffirming or extending previous decisions. When a state supreme court fails to comply in a similar case, it is almost certain that the disappointed litigant will seek Supreme Court review, since acceptance of the petition would be tantamount to reversal. In this regard one may note that state supreme courts invalidated important state policies on establishment grounds (that is, acted inconsistently with the state impact hypothesis) only when the challenged practices were similar to practices previously invalidated by the Supreme Court. Although comprehensive data are lacking, one would suspect that noncompliance in related cases also rather consistently generates petitions for review. Data regarding the establishment cases furnishes some support for this supposition: of thirteen noncompliant decisions, ten were appealed to the U.S. Supreme Court. This occurs at least in part, because given the Supreme Court's tendency to accept for review state supreme court decisions with which it disagrees, the prospects for review and reversal are relatively good. Data regarding establishment cases, for example, reveal that the Supreme Court agreed to review eight of the ten noncompliant decisions appealed to it.

This likelihood of review might not impose costs if noncompliance offered an opportunity not only for registering disagreement with the Court but also for inducing the Court to reconsider its decisions. The data, however, suggest that noncompliance does not constitute an effective form of implicit bargaining with the Supreme Court. Instead, judicial review in such circumstances consistently leads to reversal. Even in *Zorach,* the one establishment case in which noncompliance was followed by a Supreme Court retreat, changes in Court personnel and not state court noncompliance appears to have been the decisive factor.[38] Romans's findings support this point: state supreme court resistance did not appreciably affect the thrust of Supreme Court mandates regarding the admissibility of confessions.[39] In sum, the prospect of review provides a strong impetus toward compliance.

A further impetus toward compliance comes from judges' conceptions of their responsibilities. Noncompliance conflicts with both acknowledged legal obligations and the judges' espoused standards for accepted behavior. Henry Glick's interview data, for example, reveal that state supreme court judges rated objectivity in decision making and legal scholarship as the two most desirable judicial characteristics.[40] But since noncompliance involves behavior outside recognized leeways, it is inconsistent with these standards: noncompliance would demonstrate a lack of objectivity, and the opinion justifying the decision would necessarily be subject to telling legal attack. Students of cognitive dissonance have elaborated upon the tensions occasioned by actions that conflict with beliefs regarding correct behavior.[41] To the extent that noncompliance produces such tensions, they would constitute another major cost.

Yet since noncompliance does occur, the benefits of noncompliance must in some instances outweigh its costs. A closer examination of what noncompliance accomplishes reveals why judges fail to comply. Most obviously, noncompliance preserves—at least temporarily—a long-standing statewide program. Yet the possibility of Supreme Court reversal renders its continued preservation uncertain. In addition, however, noncompliance permits state supreme court judges to express their support for challenged programs and to avoid the onus of invalidating programs supported by state public opinion. Despite its irrelevance for judicial continuation in office—judges are characteristically re-elected whatever their decisions—this is a significant consideration. By noncompliance judges identify themselves with the policy majority in the state and the values it espouses, thereby reaffirming their primary allegiance to and solidarity with the regnant political forces (and predominant policy values) in the state. In sum, the choice between compliance and noncompliance is a choice between a purely legal conception of judicial role and one that recognizes that the judge is an official of a particular political system. For a judge whose political and social background has encouraged identification with the predominant values in the state, the choice of noncompliance when important state policies are threatened is hardly surprising.

This conclusion permits several observations. The primary benefit of noncompliance depends not upon success in preserving state programs— their preservation is desirable but at best uncertain—but upon the psychic satisfactions that the judge derives from such noncompliance. The cognitive dissonance literature suggests that a person seeks to harmonize values and behavior. Although noncompliance conflicts with values associated with judicial professionalism, in certain cases compliance conflicts with important state values and also produces dissonance. Resolution of these conflicts by noncompliance reveals the relative valuations placed on these considerations and points to a limited judicial acceptance—despite contrary assertions in the interview data—of a purely legal view of judicial role. At the same time, however, one must emphasize the low absolute level of noncompliance: compliant responses tend to predominate, even when compliance entails invalidation of less widespread or important programs in the state. Thus judicial endorsement of the legal components of judicial role is not a sham: strong countervailing pressures are necessary to divert judges from the behavior dictated by this endorsement. Mere disagreement with the Supreme Court's decisions does not suffice. What is decisive is the status of the practice at issue.

At the same time the values upheld in noncompliant decisions most likely accord with the personal values of the noncompliant judges. In asserting this, one merely recognizes the judges' need to subscribe to dominant social values to achieve prejudicial political success and the tendency, through socialization, to adopt as one's own the long-standing decisions of the political community. If this view is correct, the judicial backgrounds and state impact hypotheses hardly qualify as diametrical alternatives. Nonetheless, the failure of the former and success of the latter in accounting for response have more general implications. The success of the state impact hypothesis indicates that the translation of prejudicial values into outputs is a complex and uncertain process. The political career of the judge and the socialization accompanying it proved more important than social background characteristics in accounting for the values that found expression in judicial noncompliance. Moreover, judicial role conceptions exerted a strong check in most cases on judges' willingness to read personal values into the law. Finally, systematic considerations and not personal values had the decisive impact on judicial willingness to comply.

In sum, state supreme court noncompliance may be viewed as a relatively infrequent but nonetheless important phenomenon that is likely to prove a continuing obstacle to Supreme Court policymaking. It is infrequent, because it occurs only when it is necessary to go beyond available leeways to safeguard a long-standing statewide practice. It is important, both because the practices thereby sustained tend to be important and because of its effects beyond insulation of state practices from constitutional invalidation. Finally, it is likely to prove a continuing obstacle to Supreme Court policymaking, because the Court cannot—without varying the substance of its decisions—influence the decision whether or not to comply. The failure of the Neustadtian hypothesis to account for response indicates that the Court cannot influence response through superior craftsmanship. Since the most effective sanction the Court possesses—review and reversal—did not deter noncompliance, the Court lacks the weapons necessary for imposing its will. As long as state allegiances remain strong among state supreme court judges, the potentiality for conflict will exist whenever cooperation (compliance) is not perceived as beneficial.

NOTES

1. For relevant data, *see* Bradley C. Canon, "The Impact of Formal Selection Processes on the Characteristics of Judges—Reconsidered," *Law & Society Review* 6 (May 1972): 590, table 3; Henry R. Glick and Kenneth N. Vines, *State Court Systems* (Englewood Cliffs, N.J.: Prentice-Hall, 1973), p. 48, tables 3–4, and pp. 49–50.

2. Studies documenting state supreme court noncompliance include G. Alan Tarr, *Judicial Impact and State Supreme Courts* (Lexington, Mass.: Lexington Books, 1977); Jerry K. Beatty, "State Court Evasion of the United States Supreme Court Mandates During the Last Decade of the Warren Court," *Valparaiso University Law Review* 6 (1972): 260–85; Bradley C. Canon, "Reactions of State Supreme Courts to a U.S. Supreme Court Civil Liberties Decision," *Law & Society Review* 8 (1973): 109–34; Neil T. Romans, "The Role of State Supreme Courts in Judicial Policymaking—*Escobedo, Miranda* and the Use of Judicial Impact Analysis," *Western Political Quarterly* 27 (1974): 38–59; John Gruhl, "State Supreme Court Reaction to the U.S. Supreme Court's Post-*Miranda* Rulings" (Paper delivered to the American Political Science Association, Washington, D.C., August 31–September 3, 1978).

3. Beatty classified decisions as noncompliant ("evasive") only when the U.S. Supreme Court twice (1) accepted an appeal, (2) issued a mandate, and (3) overruled the judgment of the state supreme court. Thus noncompliance occurs only when "the state court which resists the initial Supreme Court mandate is overruled for a second time by the Court." He designated decisions as "quasi-evasive" when state supreme courts reaffirmed their previous position following remand and the court failed to grant certiorari, even though some judges on the state supreme court dissented from the reaffirmation. (Beatty, "State Court Evasion," p. 263.)

4. Tarr, *Judicial Impact*, ch. 3.

5. Bradley C. Canon, "Testing the Effectiveness of Civil Liberties Policies at the State and Federal Levels: The Case of the Exclusionary Rule," *American Politics Quarterly* 5 (January 1977): 57; Donald E. Boles, *The Bible, Religion, and the Public Schools* (Ames: Iowa State University Press, 1965), p. 107.

6. *See* Stanley Friedelbaum, "Independent State Grounds: Contemporary Invitations to Judicial Activism," pp. 23–53, this volume.

7. *See* Kenneth N. Dolbeare and Phillip E. Hammond, *The School Prayer Decisions* (Chicago: University of Chicago Press, 1971), pp. 64–69.

8. Stephen L. Wasby, *The Supreme Court in the Federal Judicial System* (New York: Holt, Rinehart and Winston, 1978), ch. 9.

9. *See* Canon, "Testing the Effectiveness," pp. 76–77; Lawrence Baum, "Implementation of Judicial Decisions: An Organizational Analysis," *American Politics Quarterly* 4 (January 1976): 102–3. More generally, *see* Bradley C. Canon and Kenneth Kilson, "Rural Compliance with Gault: Kentucky, a Case Study," *Journal of Family Law* 10 (1971): 300–326.

10. Bradley C. Canon, "Organizational Contumacy in the Transmission of Judicial Policies: The *Mapp, Escobedo, Miranda,* and *Gault* Cases," *Villanova Law Review* 20 (November 1974): 56 n.24.

11. Neal A. Milner, *The Court and Local Law Enforcement* (Beverly Hills, Calif.: Sage, 1971), p. 94, table 5-3; p. 120, table 6-3; p. 144, table 7-3; and p. 173, table 8-3.

12. John Gruhl and Cassia Spohn, "The Supreme Court's Post-*Miranda* Rulings: Impact on Local Prosecutors," *Law and Policy Quarterly* 3 (January 1981): 41–46.

13. Larry C. Berkson, *The Supreme Court and Its Publics* (Lexington, Mass.: Lexington Books, 1978), p. 70, table 6-1.

14. Canon, "Organizational Contumacy," p. 57.

15. Examples of the first approach include Canon, "Reactions of State Supreme Courts," and Romans, "Role of State Supreme Courts." Examples of the second approach include Gruhl, "State Supreme Court Reaction," and Dolbeare and Hammond, *School Prayer Decisions.* Examples of the third approach include Tarr, *Judicial Impact,* and Johannes Feest, "Compliance with Legal Regulations: Observation of Stop Sign Behavior," *Law & Society Review* 2 (May 1968): 447–62.

Cases raise similar questions if they can be placed in the same general category and do not exhibit constitutionally significant factual differences. Cases raise related questions if they exhibit a broader class similarity that invokes application of the same decisional standards.

16. For further development of this point, *see* Daniel C. Kramer and Robert Riga, "The New York Court of Appeals and the U.S. Supreme Court, 1960–1976," pp. 175–99, this volume.

17. Paris Adult Theater I v. Slaton, 413 U.S. 49 (1973).

18. Roe v. Wade, 410 U.S. 113 (1973); Doe v. Bolton, 410 U.S. 179 (1973).

19. *See* the series of articles by Donald E. Wilkes, Jr.: "The New Federalism in Criminal Procedure: State Court Evasion of the Burger Court," *Kentucky Law Journal* 62 (1974): 421–59; "More on the New Federalism in Criminal Procedure," *Kentucky Law Journal* 63 (1975): 874–94; "The New Federalism in Criminal Procedure Revisited," *Kentucky Law Journal* 64 (1976): 729–52.

20. For a discussion of the leeways available to judges and of the criteria for identifying judicial noncompliance, *see* Tarr, *Judicial Impact,* pp. 38–40.

21. Utility theory provides the framework here for examining judicial response. For a detailed discussion of its usefulness for impact research, *see* Robert V. Stover and Don W. Brown, "Understanding Compliance and Noncompliance with Law: The Contribution of Utility Theory," *Social Science Quarterly* 56 (December 1975): 363–75.

22. For supporting data, *see* Henry R. Glick, *Supreme Courts in State Politics: An Investigation of the Judicial Role* (New York: Basic Books, 1971), p. 41, tables 2–3; John T. Wold, "Political Orientations, Social Backgrounds, and the Role Perceptions of State Supreme Court Judges," *Western Political Quarterly* 27 (1974): 239–48.

23. Walter F. Murphy, *Elements of Judicial Strategy* (Chicago: University of Chicago Press, 1964), ch. 4.

24. The variables used in this study included three systemic variables (political culture, region, and public opinion) and five individual characteristics variables (party affiliation, tenure on the court, size of birthplace, mode of selection, and religious affiliation); Tarr, *Judicial Impact.*

25. Richard E. Neustadt, *Presidential Power* (New York: John Wiley & Sons, 1960), pp. 30–36.

26. Canon, "Reactions of State Supreme Courts."

27. Ibid., p. 132.

28. Romans, "Role of State Supreme Courts."

29. Gruhl, "State Supreme Court Reaction."

30. Harris v. New York, 401 U.S. 222 (1971). For a listing of additional Burger Court decisions that appeared to undermine *Miranda, see* Gruhl, "State Supreme Court Reaction," nn. 11–29.

31. Gruhl, "State Supreme Court Reaction," p. 16.

32. Ibid., p. 17.

33. Ibid., p. 16.

34. Romans, "Role of State Supreme Courts," p. 50.

35. No detailed consideration is given here to the findings of regional response patterns reported by Canon and Gruhl, since these findings by themselves do not permit any conclusions. However, Romans did not find similar regional patterns. Instead, liberal responses to

Miranda were most frequent among southern state supreme courts: East, 9.9 percent liberal responses; Midwest, 16.7 percent; South, 58.3 percent; and West, 30.8 percent.

36. For a more schematic formulation of this point, *see* Stover and Brown, "Understanding Compliance," p. 370.

37. For a more detailed consideration of the costs and benefits of compliance and non-compliance, *see* Tarr, *Judicial Impact,* pp. 132–35.

38. Zorach v. Clauson, 343 U.S. 306 (1952). For substantiation of this point, *see* "The 'Released Time' Cases Revisited: A Study of Group Decisionmaking by the Supreme Court," *Yale Law Journal* 83 (May 1974): 1202–36.

39. Romans, "Role of State Supreme Courts," p. 58.

40. Glick, *Supreme Courts,* pp. 39–41.

41. The best general work on cognitive dissonance theory is Jack W. Brehm and Arthur R. Cohen, *Explorations in Cognitive Dissonance* (New York: John Wiley & Sons, 1962). Attempts to apply this theory in judicial impact research include William K. Muir, Jr., *Prayer in the Public Schools: Law and Attitude Change* (Chicago: University of Chicago Press, 1967); Richard Johnson, *The Dynamics of Compliance* (Evanston, Ill.: Northwestern University Press, 1967); Tarr, *Judicial Impact.*

8.

DANIEL C. KRAMER AND ROBERT RIGA

The New York Court of Appeals and the U.S. Supreme Court, 1960–1976

INTRODUCTION

Recent years have seen a growth of interest on the part of political scientists and lawyers in the functioning of the state judiciaries, especially of their high courts. Between 1954 and 1970 the few writers who paid attention to state courts focused largely upon their braking the liberal race-integration and criminal procedure decisions of the Warren Court.[1] However, the personnel changes that converted the Warren Court into the more conservative Burger Court made constitutional scholars more aware that state tribunals can use state law to protect rights that Justices Warren Burger, William Rehnquist, and others are unwilling to admit are shielded by the laws or Constitution of the United States.[2]

This literature on the relationship between the U.S. Supreme Court and state supreme (and other state) courts in the civil rights and liberties arena is excellent, but most of it assumes *sub silentio* that this interaction can be described fully in a scheme of classification that contains only the two categories "state court checking Supreme Court liberalism" and "state court disdaining Supreme Court conservatism." The contact in this area cannot be summarized in a typology this simple. A state court can bridle Supreme Court liberalism or spurn Supreme Court conservatism in various ways; moreover, it is impossible to fit certain types of interaction between the higher and lower tribunals into either of these rubrics. Thus the relationship between the Supreme Court and a state high (or other state) court may in human rights cases take the following forms.

1. The state court "defies" a Supreme Court decision when it refuses to recognize a right for a party that the Supreme Court in that very case has accorded to him, her, or it.

2. The state court "evades" a Supreme Court decision when it refuses to grant a right accorded to a party to that decision to an individual or group in a very similar fact situation. To take a little known but interesting example, although the Supreme Court in *Buchanan* v. *Warley*[3] invalidated residential segregation imposed by law, in *Tyler* v. *Harmon*[4] the Louisiana Supreme Court soon afterward upheld a Louisiana statute allowing cities to forbid persons of one race to move into neighborhoods where the other race was predominant except with the written consent of the homeowners of the majority race.

3. The state court "limits" a Supreme Court decision when it refuses to grant a right accorded to a party to that decision to an individual or group in an analogous, albeit hardly identical, situation. Thus *Mapp* v. *Ohio*[5] made it clear that evidence obtained as a result of most warrantless searches of private residences could not be used in a criminal case in a state court. As Bradley Canon indicated,[6] in *People* v. *Edwards*[7] the California Supreme Court held that *Mapp*'s exclusionary rule did not apply to the product of a warrantless *backyard* search. *Edwards* thus limits *Mapp*.

4. The state court "qualifies" a Supreme Court decision granting a right where it carves out an exception to the rule enunciating the right. For example, a decision that evidence illegally seized may be introduced at a grand jury hearing qualifies *Mapp,* because it creates an exception to the general rule (that *Mapp* can be read as having promulgated) that illegally seized evidence may not be used against a criminal defendant. "Qualification" differs from "limitation" in that it refuses to apply a right in a situation that is literally covered by that right, and "limitation," as noted above, refuses to extend the right in a circumstance not explicitly covered by the right but analogous to the situations to which the right is expressly applicable. "Qualification" differs from "evasion" in that it specifies the circumstances theoretically subsumed under the right to which the right will be held inapplicable, but makes it clear that in a situation other than these circumstances the right will be operative. "Evasion," on the other hand, involves refusing (in practice although perhaps not verbally) to give effect to a right without any concomitant express or implied assertion that it will be disregarded in certain situations only. Finally, "defiance," "evasion," "limitation," and "qualification" of a right are all subcategories of what the editors of this book call "restrictive policymaking."[8]

5. The state court "complies" with a Supreme Court decision when it grants a right accorded to a party to that decision to an individual or group in a very similar fact situation. Thus in *Jackson* v. *State*[9] the Maryland Court of Appeals complied with *Buchanan* v. *Warley* when it overturned a Baltimore ordinance forbidding occupancy of premises by a member of one race on a block where members of the other were the only residents.

6. The state court "expands" a Supreme Court decision when it grants a right accorded to a party to that decision to an individual or group in an analogous situation. In other words, it "expands" a Supreme Court decision when it significantly increases the population the decision protects. For example, *Duncan* v. *Louisiana*[10] held that state courts must accord criminal defendants jury trials in cases where they have been accused of serious offenses. However, in *Baker* v. *City of Fairbanks*,[11] the Alaska Supreme Court held that the state constitution required jury trial for all cases where imprisonment was possible or the loss of a valuable license was likely. *Baker* is, accordingly, an "expansion" of *Duncan*. (The editors of this book would call it an "elaboration" of *Duncan*.[12] We prefer to use the term *expansion,* since *elaboration* means "to fill in the details," and this can be done in a manner that circumscribes rather than augments the right.)

7. The state court may accord to an individual or group a right, the Supreme Court's attitude to which is still uncertain. Mary Cornelia Porter noted[13] that the California Supreme Court in *People* v. *Anderson*[14] declared unconstitutional California's death penalty law before the U.S. Supreme Court in *Furman* v. *Georgia*[15] overturned most capital punishment statutes then on the books as violative of the Eighth Amendment.

8. Certain Supreme Court rulings permit but do not require a state to deny a right. When this happens, the state court may accord its citizens this right anyway. Thus the New Jersey Supreme Court in *Robinson* v. *Cahill*[16] declared that it violated the state constitution to rely primarily on property taxes to fund public education, even though the U.S. Supreme Court in *San Antonio Independent School District* v. *Rodriguez*[17] had asserted a couple of weeks earlier that this sort of funding did not deprive persons living in poor areas of their U.S. constitutional right to the equal protection of the laws.

9. On the other hand, a U.S. Supreme Court decision that allows but does not command a state to spurn a civil rights or liberties claim may be used by the state court to let state or local governments deny that right. When this happens, the state court will be said to permit the state to take advantage of a Supreme Court decision increasing the state's police power. Thus *Plessy* v. *Ferguson*,[18] permitting but not requiring the state to impose racial segregation in public facilities, was one of the cases used by the Florida Supreme Court in *Patterson* v. *Taylor*[19] to uphold a Jacksonville ordinance forcing blacks to sit in the rear section of trolley cars.

10. When taking one of steps 1 through 9, the state court may also be:

a. Presenting the Supreme Court with an opportunity to overrule or significantly modify a decision with which it has become disenchanted[20]

b. Influencing the Supreme Court's jurisprudence by developing a rule that the Court will expressly adopt[21]

c. Issuing an opinion that anticipates a Supreme Court decision without being accorded the honor of citation in the latter.

Thus a, b, and c should be included in any catalog of the possible linkages between state court and U.S. Supreme Court.

This chapter analyzes the decisions of the New York Court of Appeals in certain areas of civil liberties during the period 1960–76 to determine which of these relationships prevailed between the nation's highest court and this topmost New York state tribunal. (These areas are obscenity, search and seizure, the assignment of counsel to indigent defendants, and the warnings given to someone taken into police custody.) The analysis shows that, in practice as well as in theory, the relationship between a state court and the U.S. Supreme Court cannot adequately be described simply by using a dichotomy that views the state court either as a rein upon Supreme Court liberalism or as one that scoffs at Supreme Court conservatism. It also suggests that it is utopian for liberals to view even a high court in a populous, urbanized state as a potential knight in shining armor riding out persistently to battle for human liberty while a U.S. Supreme Court shirks the fray, and that it is likewise unrealistic for conservatives to place their hopes in such a court as an enduring impediment to a Supreme Court recklessly bent on pandering to pornographers and criminals. Yet it also indicates that a major state court may have a genuine impact on the Supreme Court, and that the lower court at times bestirs the higher court as well as vice versa.

During the period under consideration, the New York Court of Appeals had seven members elected for fourteen-year terms. In case of death, resignation, or attainment of the mandatory retirement age of seventy, the governor made an interim appointment. (Thanks to a constitutional amendment approved in 1977, the governor now selects all Court of Appeals judges from a list drawn up by a nominating commission.) Earlier in this century, when Benjamin Cardozo was a member of the Court, it was second in prestige only to the U.S. Supreme Court. In recent decades, although universally admitted to be workmanlike and competent, its reputation for creativity and statesmanship slipped, and its former mantle was assumed by the California Supreme Court.[22] Nonetheless, some think that it is again "#1,"[23] since during the past few years it has issued some seminal decisions while internecine squabbles have tarnished the image of its West Coast rival.[24]

THE OBSCENITY AREA

In 1957 the U.S. Supreme Court began to derive a standard by which obscenity can be ascertained. *Roth* v. *United States/Alberts* v. *California*[25] held constitutional a federal law forbidding the transportation through the mails of "obscene, lewd, lascivious, indecent, filthy or vile" material and a state act outlawing the sale or advertisement of "obscene or indecent" matter. The Court's decision produced a test based on the "prurient interest" concept: whether the average person, applying contemporary community standards, finds that the material, taken as a whole, appeals to prurient interest.

Even as late as *Roth/Alberts,* New York seemed to adhere to the *"Hicklin"* rule for determining obscenity. *People* v. *Doubleday*[26] upheld in a short, *per curiam* opinion an obscenity conviction where the trial court used this strict standard that declares something obscene if it tends to deprave and corrupt those whose minds are open to immoral influences and who might come into contact with it. The defendants contended without success that, contrary to the way the *Hicklin* criterion usually was applied, the court should look to the work's potential effect on mature members of the community and not only to the impression it might make upon the childish and the depraved. *Roth/Alberts* specifically declared that the *Hicklin* rule was not consistent with the First Amendment, and the New York Court of Appeals soon expanded *Roth/Alberts* by establishing a standard for New York State more liberal, from the speaker's point of view, than the "prurient interest" guideline of *Roth/Alberts*. In *People* v. *Richmond County News*[27] the defendant had been convicted on Staten Island for selling an obscene magazine *(Gent)* in violation of Section 1141 of the New York State Penal Law, making it a misdemeanor to sell an obscene book. In a four to three opinion by Judge Stanley Fuld, the Court of Appeals held for the defendant, ruling *Gent* not obscene. Fuld first asserted that the *Roth/Alberts* formula destroyed the old *Hicklin* rule, and that "obscene" now referred to material that dealt with sex in a manner appealing to prurient interest only after the "average person," applying contemporary community standards, could honestly report that the dominant theme of the material taken as a whole appealed to such interest. He went on to hold that *Roth* was intended only to outline the broad boundaries of "obscenity" under the Constitution[28] and that it did not pretend to, and could not, give specificity to the meanings of "obscene" under Section 1141. Fuld then continued that Section 1141 should apply only to hardcore pornography, since only the "slightest crack necessary"[29] of state intrusion into this area should be permitted. *Roth* declared "sex" and "obscenity" not synonymous, and therefore although *Gent* remained tasteless and "unaesthetic," it could not be considered "pornographic." *"Gent,"* concluded Fuld, does not smack of "sick and blatantly perverse sexuality"[30] and accordingly could not be punished as "obscene" under Section 1141.

The U.S. Supreme Court for the fifteen years after *Roth/Alberts* was to furnish state and local authorities with more confusion than clarification in connection with their attempts to bar sexually oriented material without violating the First Amendment. A majority could not be found for any particular amplification of the *Roth/Alberts* rule, although in 1964 Justice William Brennan said for himself and Justice Arthur Goldberg in *Jacobellis* v. *Ohio*[31] that only works utterly without redeeming social value could be branded obscene; and Justice Potter Stewart maintained in a concurring opinion citing *Richmond County News* that the First Amendment protects all sexually oriented matter except "hardcore-pornography." Relying on and complying with procedurally unsatisfactory cases such as *Jacobellis,* the New York Court of Appeals found John Cleland's *Memoirs of a Woman of Pleasure* (more commonly known as *Fanny Hill*) constitutionally protected in *Larkin* v. *Putnam's Sons.*[32] The state had attempted to restrain the sale and distribution of the book under Section 22-a of the Code of Criminal Procedure, which provided for barring the sale of any book that was "obscene, lewd, lascivious, filthy, indecent or disgusting." Justice Francis Bergan, however, accepted the arguments of defense counsel that the book, although erotic, was not obscene, because it had some redeeming social value thanks to the insight it afforded into the life and manners of eighteenth-century London; because it would have no adverse effect on sophisticated twentieth-century values;[33] and because it was not patently offensive to established community standards of decency and morality. *Larkin,* of course, anticipated the Supreme Court's *A Book Named John Cleland's Memoirs of a Woman of Pleasure* v. *A. G. Mass.,*[34] also giving constitutional protection to Cleland's novel about the peregrinations of an eighteenth-century English girl of easy virtue. William Brennan's plurality opinion declared that no book could be held obscene unless:

(a) the dominant theme of the material taken as a whole appeals to a prurient interest in sex; (b) the material is patently offensive because it affronts contemporary community standards relating to the description or representation of sexual matters; and (c) the material is utterly without redeeming social value.[35]

The plurality opinion did not mention *Larkin,* but Justice William O. Douglas's concurring opinion did.[36]

The fact that *Larkin* was a four-to-three case indicated that the Court of Appeals, reflecting the mood of much of the country, was dissatisfied with the permissive standards for determining obscenity enunciated in *Roth/ Alberts* and *Jacobellis.* One of the major worries about the Supreme Court's grant of protection to material dealing with sex was that this matter could fall into the hands of children and adversely affect their psyches and behavior. The New York legislature thus enacted Section 484-h of the New York Penal Law, which in essence declared that certain material not obscene for persons seventeen or older was obscene for minors and consequently banned the sale of this material to minors. In *Bookcase, Inc.* v. *Broderick*[37] the Court of Appeals upheld the legislature's approach on the theory that the state has an interest in the well-being of its youth and in promoting health, welfare, safety, and morality generally. This is a qualification of *Roth/Alberts* and *Jacobellis:* a promulgation of an exception to the rule that something is obscene only where the dominant theme of the material appeals to the prurient interest of the average person for the situation where the sale is to a minor and the work appeals to the prurient interest of minors although not to that of the normal adult. The U.S. Supreme Court smiled upon this "variable" obscenity approach in *Ginsberg* v. *New York,*[38] where it upheld Section 484-h as applied to a luncheonette owner in Long Island who sold a sixteen-year old boy two "girlie" magazines. Justice Brennan's opinion relied heavily upon *Bookcase, Inc.* v. *Broderick,* as the following language demonstrates.

> We conclude that we cannot say that the statute invades the area of freedom of expression constitutionally secured to minors. . . . Rather Sec. 484-h simply adjusts the definition of obscenity to social realities by permitting the appeal of this type of material to be assessed in terms of the sexual interests of such minors . . . *Bookcase, Inc.* v. *Broderick.*[39]
> The state also has an independent interest in the well-being of its youth. The New York Court of Appeals squarely bottomed its decision on that interest in *Bookcase, Inc.* v. *Broderick. . . .*[40]

Justice Brennan's statement that the state has an interest in the well-being of its young people was also buttressed by a lengthy quote from Judge Fuld's concurring opinion in *People* v. *Kahan.*[41] Although Fuld declared there that the state can exercise more control over children's reading matter than over adults', he also insisted, in full compliance with the Supreme Court case of *Winters* v. *New York*[42] and in basic agreement with *Kahan's per curiam* majority opinion, that a predecessor of the law sustained in *Ginsberg* was invalid because its provisions were too vague, thereby making it impossible to differentiate between the children's and the adults' standards. *Kahan,* in turn, was cited in *Interstate Circuit* v. *Dallas,*[43] where the Supreme Court overthrew as too vague a Dallas ordinance prohibiting admission of minors to certain films unless accompanied by a guardian or spouse. *Bookcase, Inc.* v. *Broderick, Kahan, Ginsberg,* and *Interstate Circuit* thus form a quadrumvirate illustrating the Court of Appeals qualifying, complying with, and influencing U.S. Supreme Court decisions.

Miller v. *California*[44] was an effort by the Burger Court to clarify what could be declared obscene under the First Amendment while tightening up the permissive standards of *Jacobellis* and *Fanny Hill.* The major changes from the rules embodied in the plurality opinion of *Fanny Hill* are that the "community standards" in the light of which "appeal to prurient interest" and "patent offensiveness" are to be tested are local rather than national; and that a work with some social value still may be banned if it "taken as a whole, lacks serious literary, artistic, political or scientific value."[45] The New York Court of Appeals was quick to assure the appropriate governmental units of the state that they could take advantage of the additional tools to fight pornography that *Miller* accords them. *People* v. *Heller*[46] held that the distribution of the film *Blue Movie* and the magazine *Screw* could constitutionally be punished. It referred to the fact that it had in a decision appearing even before *Miller* found *Blue Movie* pornographic,[47] declaring in the post-*Miller Heller* that

we found *Blue Movie* obscene even though the pornographic activities depicted were interspersed with some political and social dialogue. We cut through the form, as it were, to the substance and the substance of the film was and remains hard core pornography.[48]

Quoting Judge Henry Friendly's aphorism, "truly pornographic material cannot be rescued by the inclusion of a few verses of the Psalms," the court disposed of *Blue Movie* and *Screw* as hardcore pornography obscene by any standard.

SEARCH AND SEIZURE

In *Mapp* v. *Ohio*,[49] one of its most important decisions of the last decades, the U.S. Supreme Court applied the "exclusionary rule" to the states: that is, it held that evidence obtained in violation of the Fourth Amendment's guarantee against unreasonable searches and seizures could not be introduced in state criminal trials. Previously, the Court had mandated the exclusion of such evidence in federal trials only[50] and had declared in *Wolf* v. *Colorado*[51] that the states, if they wished, could continue to introduce it as long as it were reliable and not obtained by torture. Until *Mapp*, New York was one of those states that did permit the introduction of illegally seized evidence. In fact, Judge Cardozo's famous decision in *People* v. *Defore*,[52] questioning why the "criminal should go free because the constable has blundered," was one of the props upon which *Wolf* explicitly was rested.

The scope of the "exclusionary rule" cannot be understood without some understanding of the basic law of search and seizure as developed by the Supreme Court. Although the initial rule is that searches are "unreasonable" (and thus violative of the Fourth Amendment in itself and as applied to the states by the Fourteenth Amendment) if carried out without a warrant issued upon probable cause, describing the place to be searched and the persons or things to be seized, the Court will permit *warrantless* searches when "incidental to a valid arrest." Since perhaps a majority of searches are justified as "incidental to a valid arrest," it obviously is important to know when an arrest is valid and when a search or seizure can be said to be incidental thereto. Simplifying considerably, the fundamental rule about the lawfulness of warrantless arrests is that "a police officer may arrest a suspect when the officer has probable cause to believe the suspect has committed a felony, or when he himself observes a minor crime being committed in his presence."[53] *Chimel* v. *California*[54] seemed to settle the question of when a search is "incidental" to an arrest. The majority asserted that the police could, when arresting, search without a warrant the suspect's person and the areas within his immediate reach and control. However, they could not search the entire house or, for that matter, every spot in the room in which the arrest took place. Finally, the one other traditional major exception to the rule that searches require warrants is that a car "in transit" may be searched without a warrant when there is probable cause to believe that it contains contraband or the instrumentalities or fruits of a crime.[55]

The Court of Appeals complied with *Mapp* and adopted the exclusionary rule for the courts of New York State. *People* v. *O'Neill*[56] is one of several cases decided on April 5, 1962, in which the court overturned convictions on the ground that they had been based upon illegally seized evidence. In *O'Neill,* four Nassau County detectives, without possessing an arrest or search warrant, drove to Lynne O'Neill's home in March 1960 pursuant to a tip given them by postal inspector James Kenny. The latter, in response to a magazine ad, had begun a correspondence with O'Neill, culminating in his mailing her a ten dollar check and receiving in return four black-and-white photographs of her in the nude. After knocking on the door of her home, they confronted her, asked her if they could enter "to talk," and were admitted. They asked her if she had mailed the pictures; she stated she had. One of them then inquired if any more such photographs were in the house and was told that it was "none of his business." At that, she asked the officers to leave the premises and ran upstairs to the second floor. They followed her, spotting as they went some more pictures on a table in a room off the hallway. Seizing them, one of the officers began picking out additional pictures from a box located in one of the rooms in spite of her persistent pleas not to search "her stuff." Two of the policemen continued their foraging while the others departed for the district attorney's office. Upon their return with an arrest warrant, the defendant was placed in custody, and another room, which she had refused to open earlier, was searched. In it was found most of the evidence upon which she was convicted. In a strong, clear affirmation of *Mapp,* the Court of Appeals reversed her conviction, citing the complete lack of legality of the officers' actions. "As the foregoing recital of the relevant evidence clearly demonstrates, the search of defendant's home was plainly illegal, and the evidence thereby obtained would be inadmissible under *Mapp* v. *Ohio*."[57]

Mapp did not make it clear whether the application of the exclusionary rule was to be retroactive. The retroactivity of a Supreme Court decision involving criminal procedure can be treated in several ways. It can be applied to all convicted persons regardless of when their cases were closed. It can be declared to cover all defendants whose trials commenced and ended before it was issued if and only if their appeals were still pending on that date. It can be made to cover defendants whose trials had begun before it was issued, but only if the trials were still in progress at the time of its promulgation. It can be ruled to apply only to trials begun after it was handed down. In the case of *Mapp*, it can be made to apply only to trials begun after *Mapp* in which the search occurred after *Mapp*. It is reasonable to maintain that the choice of one of the first three alternatives would expand *Mapp*. Although a Supreme Court decision is in legal theory retroactive, in practice one would not naturally read a decision upsetting a long-established aspect of criminal procedure explicitly to protect defendants in trials begun before it was issued. Thus *People* v. *Loria*[58] expanded *Mapp*, since it asserted that for New York State *Mapp* covered trials initiated before it was handed down if appeals from them "in ordinary course" were still alive on that date, assuming that an objection to the introduction of the evidence had been made at trial. However, in *People* v. *Muller*[59] the Court of Appeals limited *Loria* when it held that *Mapp* could not be used for trials begun before *Mapp* where the normal appellate process had been concluded before *Mapp*. *Muller* had been convicted in 1953 on a drug charge. His application for "regular" (that is, normal postconviction) application for leave to appeal had been denied in 1954. Justice Charles Froessel's opinion in *Muller* held that the ordinary appellate process had ended for the defendant in 1954 and that he could not now obtain his freedom merely because illegally seized evidence had been introduced at his trial. *Loria* was declared applicable to cases whose appeal was pending as of June 19, 1961, the date of *Mapp*, and not to appeals that had finally been determined by that date. Muller itself was one of the state decisions cited in *Linklater* v. *Walter*,[60] where the Supreme Court itself declared that *Mapp* did not apply to state convictions that had become final before its appearance. Thus so far the interaction between the Court of Appeals and the Supreme Court in the search-and-seizure realm shows compliance, expansion, and some influence from lower to higher.

Mapp was (and is) viewed as an impediment to the struggle against crime. Consequently, there was (and is) great unhappiness with it, a discontent that soon began to manifest itself in a line of Court of Appeals decisions such as *People* v. *Rivera*.[61] *Rivera* arose when, at 1 A.M. near

Avenue C and 7th Street in Manhattan, police watched two men walk up in front of a bar and grille, stop, peer in the window, walk away, turn around, come back, and look through the window again. Suspicious, the officers ordered the two men to stop and identify themselves, whereupon the duo walked away rapidly. After overtaking them, the police conducted a "patting down" or "frisk" of the two for their (the officers') protection. Their testimony pointed out that the neighborhood was known for its high incidence of street crime and that they had reasonable fear for their own security in approaching the suspects. During the course of the "frisk," one of the officers felt a "hard object" in the back pocket of defendant Rivera and removed a .22 caliber, fully loaded revolver. Rivera was then arrested and convicted of possession of illegal and dangerous firearms.

One could argue that *Mapp* and the Supreme Court's basic rules of search and seizure would prevent the introduction of the revolver. The search was conducted without a warrant and was not incidental to a valid arrest. (The search *preceded* the arrest and provided the "probable cause" that was its necessary legal foundation.) Yet a six to one opinion by Judge Francis Bergan qualified *Mapp* and the prohibition against warrantless searches except incident to a valid arrest by declaring that the frisk (including the search following the patting down) was less an invasion of privacy than was a full search. Therefore, the police ought to be entitled, for their own safety, to "stop and frisk" persons behaving suspiciously albeit not in such a way as to give rise to the "probable cause" needed for arrest. According to the new theory:

> . . . [A]s the right to stop and inquire is to be justified for a cause less conclusive than that which would sustain an arrest, so the right to frisk may be justified as an incident to inquiry upon grounds of elemental safety and precaution which might not initially sustain a search.[62]

The Court of Appeals' creation of the stop and frisk exception to *Mapp* and the no-warrantless-search-except-incident-to-a-valid-arrest rule had, in *Terry* v. *Ohio*,[63] a substantial impact upon the Supreme Court's own jurisprudence. Although Justice Earl Warren's opinion refused to accept *Rivera*'s theory that a stop and frisk is merely a minor inconvenience, it declared (which is the essence of *Rivera*) that when a policeman sees persons behaving suspiciously and has reason to believe them armed, he may, to protect himself and others, "conduct a carefully limited search of the outer clothing of such persons in an attempt to discover weapons which might be used to assault him";[64] and, furthermore, that these weapons may be introduced at the defendants' trials. Footnote 5 of *Terry*[65] noted that the theory behind stop and frisk upon suspicion is "well laid out in the *Rivera* opinion"; no other case is singled out for this approbation.

Chimel v. *California*[66] held that the police could without a warrant search only the area within the suspect's immediate control when an arrest was made. They could not look in other rooms or rummage through desk drawers or closets even in the room where the arrest took place. *Chimel* has not until recently proven popular with the New York Court of Appeals. In *Williams* v. *United States*[67] the Supreme Court itself declared *Chimel* nonretroactive. The Court of Appeals took advantage of this increase in the permissible scope of the state's police power and held unanimously in a *per curiam* decision, *People* v. *Buia*,[68] that *Chimel* would be applied only to searches occurring after June 23, 1969, the date of *Chimel*. More importantly, in several cases the New York Court evaded the requirements of *Chimel*'s contributions to the Supreme Court's basic search-and-seizure jurisprudence. *People* v. *Clements*[69] is the clearest example. The police arrested the defendant in a room of his house other than the bedroom. Acting on a tip provided by a reliable informant that marijuana was hidden in a closed drawer in a dresser in the bedroom, the police searched the drawer and found sixteen bricks of that drug. The majority (four to three) opinion of Judge Hugh Jones legitimated the search and allowed the sixteen bricks to be used as evidence. It claimed that *Chimel* was not violated, since the police, if they had gone to a judge to obtain a warrant, would have had to place a guard at the apartment to prevent the removal of incriminating evidence. The fact that it was, for better or worse, *Chimel*'s purpose to compel the police to get a warrant in this situation was not adequately dealt with.

As noted, the U.S. Supreme Court has long recognized as part of its basic search-and-seizure jurisprudence special rules for the search of a motor vehicle "in transit," that is, actually moving or parked temporarily during the course of a journey. *Carroll* v. *United States*[70] permits the warrantless search of such a vehicle, albeit not incidental to an arrest, only when the police have probable cause to believe that it contains contraband or the fruits or instrumentalities of a crime. *Chambers* v. *Maroney*[71] extended *Carroll* to allow the search to take place later, at the police station or garage, rather than on the road. The New York Court of Appeals has let the state take advantage of the leeway permitted by *Chambers*. In *People* v. *Fustanio*[72] one Hadden was identified as a burglar by a police officer who had surprised him at the scene of the crime. He was later arrested for burglary, and the defendant's automobile, in which Hadden had been a passenger, was seized. (Upon his arrest for speeding earlier that night, the police had obtained the defendant's consent to search the trunk of the car and had seen there a three-foot silver bar with a hook at the end.) The automobile was towed to the sheriff's parking lot; several hours later the trunk was searched again and a police radio and other items were found. This evidence was used against the defendant at his burglary trial. The Court of Appeals decided that the search was legal, albeit warrantless. The initial seizure of the automobile was proper, as there existed probable cause for this taking. Once the police lawfully come into possession of an arrested person's property, they have, the court said, the right to examine it within a reasonable time and at a reasonably convenient place for contraband or other evidence of crime. *Chambers* was cited.

The Court of Appeals allows a legion of sufferings to be inflicted upon the poor chap who parks illegally in a tow-away zone. Not only may the car be towed to a police pound in the boondocks, but a warrantless inventory of its contents may be made there. If the police find guns or drugs when making the inventory, the driver will be arrested, and the guns or drugs will be used against him at his trial. *Chambers* of its own terms does not justify the warrantless seizure of this evidence: parking on Fifth Avenue at rush hour is no indication that the offending vehicle contains contraband. *People* v. *Sullivan*[73] was the decision legitimating warrantless searches of cars towed for parking violations, the Court of Appeals reasoning that such searches protect both owner and police. *Sullivan* qualifies the basic search-and-seizure rule that a car in transit may be searched without a warrant only when probable cause exists. Nonetheless, it cannot now be considered inconsistent with Supreme Court jurisprudence, since that Court accepted its thesis in *South Dakota* v. *Opperman*.[74] *Sullivan* itself was one of the state cases relied upon there.

RIGHT TO ASSIGNED COUNSEL

The well-known U.S. Supreme Court case of *Gideon* v. *Wainwright*[75] holds that a criminal defendant who cannot afford to pay for an attorney has the right to have the state assign him one free of charge, at least when the offense of which he is accused is serious. Justice Hugo Black's opinion emphasized the obvious: that the indigent person charged with crime cannot in most circumstances get a fair trial without counsel to represent his interests. In a sense New York did not need *Gideon;* it had for many years assigned counsel to indigent defendants.[76] Nor was there any departure from this practice following *Gideon*. The only question was whether the Court of Appeals would expand *Gideon* to require the assignment of counsel to indigent parties in cases not involving felonies and serious misdemeanors.

People v. *Witenski*[77] provided such expansion two years later. Here appellants, three teenagers, were caught trespassing in an upstate apple orchard and stealing two dollars' worth of produce. None of the boys had any prior police record. All were removed to the local special sessions court presided over by a justice of the peace, and each was instructed that he was:

entitled to aid of counsel in every stage of these proceedings. You are entitled to an adjournment for that purpose, and upon your request I will send a message to any counsel you name within this jurisdiction. Do you desire counsel? Defendants answered, "no."[78]

The Court of Appeals divided four to three in favor of the defendants, issuing in the process a strong defense of the principles enunciated in *Gideon*. Chief Judge Charles Desmond's majority opinion pointed out that the practice of assigning counsel for poor persons had prevailed in the state since colonial times. It is true, the chief judge said, that no prior case (including *Gideon*, we must note) had ever required that counsel be provided free of charge for persons tried in special sessions court before a justice of the peace. Nonetheless, *Witenski* was emphatic that an indigent defendant must be granted a free attorney in that court, and that this right had to be communicated to the defendant before trial. With regard to the case before the court, Judge Desmond believed that no intelligent, effective waiver of the right to counsel had been demonstrated by the three defendants. The bare statement to ignorant teenagers that they were "entitled to the aid of counsel in every stage" could hardly have been understood by them in its fullest sense, that is, as including their right to free legal aid.

Yet the same year, Chief Judge Desmond and Judge Fuld dissenting, the court in *People* v. *Letterio*[79] limited *Gideon* by declaring that defendants in traffic court did not have to be assigned counsel. In this case one defendant had pleaded guilty to seven speeding and three other moving violations and had been sentenced to a fine of $1,030, forty-two days imprisonment, and an additional prison sentence if he failed to pay the fine. Neither the state legislature nor the state courts had ever required assignment here: "There are, historically, certain minor transgressions which admit of summary disposition."[80] Furthermore, the result of forcing the state to assign counsel in such cases would be monumental chaos— and unnecessary, in light of the fact that traffic court judges, routinely functioning as prosecutors, defense lawyers, as well as judges,[81] already sufficiently insured the existence of fair forums within their courtrooms.

Gideon does not literally apply to certain quasi-criminal proceedings. One is a child-neglect action in family court. If the parent brought up before the court loses in this proceeding, he may be faced with the loss of the child's society as well as later criminal charges. Given these possibilities, the Court of Appeals unanimously expanded *Gideon* and decided in *In re Ella B*[82] that an indigent parent involved in a child-neglect proceeding is entitled to assignment of counsel and to be advised that he has this right. One could argue, furthermore, that it is as important for an indigent to be given free legal assistance in a civil as in a criminal proceeding. A poor person may have a justifiable claim against another for injury to his personal property or for breach of contract; without a lawyer, he will, for practical purposes, be unable to enforce this claim. *Boddie* v. *Connecticut,*[83] although not a right to counsel case, recognized that the expenses involved in civil proceedings may well prevent the poor from making use of certain of their legal rights. *Boddie* provided that in some way or another, the state must relieve an indigent party suing for divorce of the necessity to pay court fees and costs, which at the time in Connecticut averaged about sixty dollars. Complying with *Boddie,* the Court of Appeals required in *Deason* v. *Deason*[84] that Albany County be required to pay for an indigent the costs of service by publication required in a divorce action. The court has, however, limited *Boddie* on two occasions. In a much-publicized decision, *In re Smiley,*[85] it refused to interpret the Supreme Court case as demanding that the state furnish free lawyers for poor defendants and plaintiffs in divorce actions. Chief Judge Charles Breitel's opinion asserted that impoverished matrimonial litigants were not without practical recourse. They perhaps could obtain free legal assistance from the Legal Aid Society or other legal services agencies or could enter into contingent-fee agreements with private attorneys. The same year, *Brown* v. *Lavine*[86] declared that a recipient of public assistance was not entitled to assignment of counsel at an administrative hearing to determine whether such aid should be discontinued. The court felt that even without a lawyer, the hearing itself satisfied the demands of due process. The proceeding was conducted by an impartial officer; the right to testify and produce witnesses was assured; technical rules of evidence did not apply; and the right to judicial review was preserved.

THE *MIRANDA* WARNINGS

According to the still-controversial *Miranda* v. *Arizona,*[87] when a person is taken into custody, police are required to give him the following warnings and rights:

1. He must be informed that he has the right to remain silent.
2. This information must be accompanied with the explanation that anything he says can be used against him in court.
3. He must be told that he has the right to consult with a lawyer and to have the lawyer present with him during the interrogation.
4. He must be informed that if he cannot afford a lawyer, one will be appointed to represent him.
5. He must be in fact permitted to consult a lawyer, to have one assigned to him if he is poor, and to have that attorney present during the interrogation.
6. If he indicates before or during questioning that he wishes to be silent, the questioning must cease.

Aware that *Miranda* was going to prove unpopular with the public and law-enforcement officials, the Supreme Court also held in *Johnson* v. *New Jersey*[88] that *Miranda* "should only apply to trials begun after the decision was announced . . . even though the cases may still be on direct appeal."[89] In New York the Court of Appeals complies with *Miranda,* since it disallows confessions gained in violation of the *Miranda* rules in situations where they clearly should have been applied. Thus in *People* v. *Shivers*[90] the defendant was interrogated by a policeman at gunpoint on a Far Rockaway, New York, street corner about his knowledge of an attempted liquor store holdup. The officer had called the defendant over to the police cruiser, because he seemed to match a description given by an eyewitness. At the trial the officer testified that the defendant was not free to leave during the questioning, and that if he had attempted to do so the officer would have restrained him. After answering the officer's questions, the man was told that he fitted the robbery description and was under arrest. Later the defendant moved for the suppression of one of the statements he had made to the officer before being arrested on the ground that it had been obtained after he had been taken into custody without having been read his *Miranda* rights. The court found for the defendant, ruling that he, in effect, had been placed in custody and deprived of his freedom in a significant way once the officer had drawn his revolver. For *Miranda* purposes, the "custodial interrogation" had then commenced, and therefore, the fruits of this questioning could not be considered admissible as the warnings had not been given.

At the same time that it accepted the stringent limitation on state police powers imposed by *Miranda,* the court greeted with joy the slight modification of that limitation embodied in *Johnson* v. *New Jersey.* In *People* v. *McQueen*[91] the defendant had been implicated in a Hempstead, Long Island, homicide and was eventually removed to a police station for questioning. Within five to ten minutes she confessed to the entire crime, even volunteering to bring the police to her apartment where she showed them the murder weapon and to the scene of the crime where she re-enacted the entire episode for a grateful police audience. Three hours after the defendant had been first taken in for questioning (approximately 6:30 A.M.), she signed a complete confession and later on the same day was formally arraigned on the charge of first-degree murder. At no time whatever was the defendant instructed of her rights by the police, nor did she request the aid of counsel. Her trial began on November 9, 1964, and resulted in a conviction on November 24. The court held her confession admissible on the grounds that *Miranda* had no retroactive application in the state of New York. It relied on *Johnson* and added that there was no reason in going beyond what the Supreme Court required in applying the new rules to prior convictions: "The past can seldom be reformed in the image of the present, and it is manifest that not every type of conviction can be set aside where the wisdom of the present does not coincide with that of the past."[92] It is interesting to compare *McQueen* with *People* v. *Loria,* which applied *Mapp* to a trial commenced before *Mapp* if an appeal from that trial was still pending. Moreover, *Sayers* v. *New York*[93] further limited *Miranda* by declaring that it did not apply to a post-*Miranda* retrial of an individual whose first trial had begun before *Miranda*. The Supreme Court legitimated this practice in *Jenkins* v. *Delaware,*[94] and one of the cases cited to buttress the outcome there was *Sayers*. Once again, we note an instance in which the court of appeals had influence upon the higher court.

   Miranda stressed, as seen, that

once warnings have been given, the subsequent procedure is clear. If the individual indicates in any manner, at any time prior to or *during questioning, that he wishes to remain silent, the interrogation must cease. . . . [A]ny statement taken after the person invokes his privilege cannot be other than the product of compulsion, subtle or otherwise.*[95] (Emphasis ours.)

People v. *Gary*[96] is an evasion of this aspect of *Miranda*. Here the defendant had approached a police officer on the street to tell him that he had just stabbed a man to death. Placed under arrest, he was advised of his *Miranda* rights; he then replied that he wanted to remain silent from that point on. All interrogation would have ceased completely from this point on were *Miranda* to have been observed. However, the defendant was then taken to another police station where, after again being advised of his rights, he was offered a second opportunity to make a statement. Thereupon, he confessed to the crime.

   The question before the Court of Appeals was whether the statement made at the police station could be deemed admissible evidence against the defendant. The unanimous opinion written by Judge James Gibson drew a distinction between the continuation of an interrogation during which the individual has expressed his desire to remain silent and "a subsequent request, upon reiteration of the requisite warnings, for reconsideration of an earlier decision to make no statement."[97] Confessions obtained during questioning of the latter sort were, in the eyes of the court, valid. It is difficult, however, to perceive why police questioning recommencing after a mere hour's break is not part and parcel of the initial interrogation. Nonetheless, although *Gary* constituted an evasion of a portion of *Miranda* when it was decided, it cannot be considered such today. Again, the Court of Appeals demonstrated that it could influence a decision of the Supreme Court—here, *Michigan* v. *Mosely*.[98] In the latter case, a majority of the court held that it was permissible for the police to begin questioning a suspect about a murder two hours after they had stopped asking him about a robbery, because he had invoked his

Miranda right to silence. (The *Miranda* warnings were given before the murder questioning as well as the robbery queries, the questions involving the murder produced some incriminating statements.) In issuing its holding, the Supreme Court cited *Gary* as one of the many state and federal cases that concluded that *Miranda* does not create a per se proscription of further questioning once the suspect has indicated a desire to remain silent.

In 1964, two years before *Miranda,* the case of *Escobedo* v. *Illinois,*[99] a Sixth Amendment right-to-counsel and not a Fifth Amendment privilege against self-incrimination case, was a major progenitor of *Miranda.*[100] It held that when one who has been taken into custody by the police asks to consult with his lawyer and the police refuse the request, any admissions made during his interrogation will later be considered inadmissible evidence. In a *per curiam* opinion, *People* v. *Kulis,*[101] the Court of Appeals qualified *Escobedo* (a decision no more popular than *Miranda* proved to be) by allowing the confession elicited after the denial of the request to contact the attorney to be used on cross-examination to destroy the defendant's credibility as a witness. *Kulis,* in turn, was the precedent for *People* v. *Harris,*[102] in which the court held that a statement gathered in violation of the *Miranda* rules could be used on cross-examination to impeach the defendant where he had taken the witness stand in his own defense. *Harris* was subsequently appealed to the Supreme Court, which, given the opportunity by the New York Court to itself qualify *Miranda* in this fashion, took full advantage of the chance by enunciating the rule propounded by the Court of Appeals in affirming the conviction of the accused.[103]

Strangely, considering the Court of Appeals' antipathy to *Escobedo* and *Miranda* during the years under consideration, both of these cases were influenced by its own prior decisions. *Massiah* v. *U.S.*[104] constituted one of the pillars upon which *Escobedo* rested. *Massiah* held that it was a violation of the Sixth Amendment's right-to-counsel provisions to use an informer, following a defendant's indictment, to elicit from him incriminating statements made in the absence of his counsel. As *Escobedo* noted, *Massiah* cited with approval the Court of Appeals' case of *People* v. *Waterman,*[105] where an opinion by Judge Fuld proclaimed that it was an error to receive in evidence a defendant's statement against himself, made without a lawyer, during questioning that took place between the return of the indictment (defined in the case as the formal commencement of the action) and the arraignment. According to Fuld, this type of questioning infringes upon the defendant's right to counsel, due process, and freedom from testimonial compulsion. Few federal cases were cited for the simple reason that the court was acting in the role of pioneer in this area of right to counsel of a defendant under interrogation.

From *Massiah's* strong assertion of the right to counsel following indictment, it is but a short step to *Escobedo's* declaration that this right belongs to anyone taken into custody, whether before or after the indictment. To take this step, the Supreme Court relied on the leading Court of Appeals case of *People* v. *Donovan*[106] as standing for the position that for the purposes of interrogation in the absence of counsel, no meaningful distinction can be made between the period before and the period following formal indictment. In *Donovan* the defendants had been convicted for murdering a payroll guard in Queens, New York. Both were questioned at the police station and admitted guilt after interrogation. The written confession was obtained from defendant Donovan after a police refusal to let an attorney, retained for him by his family, see him while he was in custody. The court did not weigh the validity, under the federal Constitution, of admitting this evidence, since it thought that allowing it as testimony would violate his state constitutional rights to due process, right to counsel, and self-incrimination. "[H]ere we condemn continued incommunicado interrogation of an accused after he or the lawyer retained by him or his family has requested that they be allowed to confer together."[107] Such interrogation, Judge Fuld wrote, violated principles of fundamental fairness.

Since *Massiah* gave birth to *Escobedo,* and both relied upon decisions of the Court of Appeals, and *Escobedo* begat *Miranda,* the latter is at least partly this court's offspring, however much it may, until recently, have regretted its emergence from the womb. In one other way *Miranda* rests upon doctrines developed by the New York Court. Among the information to be given to the detainee is that, if indigent, the court will assign him an attorney if he so desires. "The warning of a right to counsel would be hollow if not couched in terms which convey to the indigent, the person most often subjected to interrogation, the knowledge that he too has the right to have counsel present."[108] Two cases are cited as authority: one federal, the other, *People* v. *Witenski,*[109] where, as seen earlier, the Court of Appeals held that two boys tried in special sessions court before a justice of the peace had to be informed of their right to assigned counsel.

SUMMARY OF DATA AND CONCLUSIONS

The preceding sections have revealed compliance by the New York Court of Appeals with the major decisions of the U.S. Supreme Court, such as *Mapp, Gideon,* and *Miranda.* Moreover, no example of outright defiance can be found. We did see, though, a couple of evasions of the decisions of the higher tribunal. The most blatant occurred in *People* v. *Clements,*[110] which allowed police to rummage through the desk drawers located in a room other than that in which the defendant was arrested— not withstanding the *Chimel* rule that searches incident to a valid arrest can cover the area only within the suspect's immediate control.

On numerous occasions the court limited or qualified the decisions of the Supreme Court. For example, *People* v. *Rivera*[111] carved out the stop-and-frisk exception to the rule that warrantless searches are invalid unless incidental to a lawful arrest. In *Bookcase, Inc.* v. *Broderick*[112] the court exempted from the *Roth/Alberts* doctrine (that works not appealing to the prurient interest of the average adult cannot be declared obscene) the situation in which the work is sold to a child and appeals to the prurient interest of the average child, although not that of the average adult. *In re Smiley*[113] the court limited *Boddie* v. *Connecticut*[114] by refusing to require the appointment of free lawyers for indigent spouses engaged in divorce proceedings.

When the Supreme Court allowed the state discretion to expand its police powers, the Court of Appeals usually gave its own green light to the relevant state authorities. *People* v. *Heller*[115] employed the tightened obscenity guidelines of *Miller* v. *California*[116] to reaffirm the Court of Appeals' earlier position that the film *Blue Movie* was pornographic; *People* v. *McQueen*[117] made avid use of the permission granted in *Johnson* v. *New Jersey* to deny any retroactivity to *Miranda;* and *People* v. *Fustanio*[118] took advantage of the holding in *Chambers* v. *Maroney*[119] that the "probable cause" search of a vehicle in transit may take place not only on the road, but also after the car has been towed away to the police station.

On a few occasions the court expanded a "liberal" decision of the Supreme Court. *People* v. *Loria*[120] made *Mapp* retroactive to trials beginning before *Mapp* where the appeal was pending as of the date of that decision, and *Gideon* was expanded in *People* v. *Witenski*[121] into a special sessions court presided over by a justice of the peace and, in *In re Ella B,*[122] into a child-neglect hearing. *People* v. *Richmond County News,*[123] with its hard-core pornography test, increased the protection accorded sellers of sexually oriented material under the "primary appeal to prurient interest" standard of *Roth* v. *United States/Alberts* v. *California.*[124]

The Court of Appeals exerted a significant influence upon the Supreme Court in both a "liberal" and "conservative" direction even amid a period of years in which it was no longer considered the leading state court in the nation. *Ginsberg* v. *New York,*[125] in which the Supreme Court accepted the view that something nonpornographic for adults could be considered obscene for children, rested to a considerable extent upon *Bookcase, Inc.* v. *Broderick* and cited with approval *People* v. *Kahan*[126]—a case mentioned in the more "libertarian" decision of *Interstate Circuit* v. *Dallas.*[127] *People* v. *Muller*[128] was noted in *Linkletter* v. *Walker,*[129] which denied full retroactivity to *Mapp.* Furthermore, the Supreme Court had *People* v. *Rivera* very much in mind when it legitimated "stop and frisk" in *Terry* v. *Ohio*[130] and cited *People* v. *Sullivan*[131] in *South Dakota* v. *Opperman,*[132] adding police-garage searching to towing as one of the mishaps that may befall the illegally parked. *People* v. *Gary*[133] was among the decisions mentioned in *Michigan* v. *Mosely,*[134] where the Supreme Court allowed an additional interrogation (prefaced with *Miranda* warnings) to begin a couple of hours after the first interrogation had ended with the suspect asserting his right to silence. We saw, too, that *Escobedo,* the progenitor of *Miranda,* rested upon *People* v. *Donovan*[135] and, more indirectly, upon *People* v. *Waterman*[136]—and that *Miranda's* proposition that an indigent suspect must be told of his right to assigned counsel cited *People* v. *Witenski* as the only state case in point. *People* v. *Richmond County News* was mentioned in Justice Potter Stewart's exposition of his famous and highly libertarian ''hard-core'' pornography doctrine in *Jacobellis* v. *Ohio.*[137] *Larkin* v. *Putnam's Sons,*[138] declaring *Fanny Hill* nonpornographic, was noted in Justice Douglas's concurring opinion in the Supreme Court's own *Fanny Hill* case.[139] (On the other hand, *People* v. *Kulis*[140] led to *People* v. *Harris,*[141] which in turn gave the Supreme Court the opportunity to declare in *Harris* v. *New York*[142] that confessions obtained in violation of the *Miranda* rules may be used on cross-examination to impeach any protestations of innocence the defendant might have made when he took the witness stand on direct examination.) *People* v. *Donovan,* finally, is the one case where the Court of Appeals did more than simply expand a right recognized by the Supreme Court. In its decision to grant defendants the right to obtain a lawyer as soon as they are taken into custody, the court went far beyond prior Supreme Court guarantees and thus created a new right.

In conclusion, it is perfectly legitimate for scholars to focus upon the role played by state courts in frustrating liberal decisions of the Supreme Court or in protecting individual and group rights beyond the point at which that Court is at the moment prepared to go. Henceforth, however, they should be more precise in describing the relationship between the Supreme Court and the state court in a human rights case and realize that this relationship may fall outside the dichotomy: ''frustrate liberal Supreme Court decisions—expand human rights when the Supreme Court won't.'' For example, our discussion of the New York Court of Appeals has demonstrated that Supreme Court liberalism may be combatted by limitation or qualification rather than by the legally less justifiable techniques of evasion and defiance. The state court may comply with libertarian decisions it also limits or qualifies (for example, *Miranda, Mapp*). It may actually expand such decisions (for example, *Mapp, Gideon*), but it also may well allow the state to take advantage of Supreme Court decisions extending state police powers.

It is, moreover, a reasonable assumption that the New York Court of Appeals is a typical high court in a populous, urbanized state. Accordingly, our detailed explication of the relations between the Court of Appeals and the Supreme Court gives the reader a realistic notion of what might be expected from such a court in the future in the way of developing a law of human rights. A tribunal of this sort is likely to defeat the expectations of those who view it as a potential monkey wrench thwarting the efforts of the Supreme Court to mollycoddle criminals and minority groups and likewise to disappoint those who visualize it as a Galahad tenaciously fighting on behalf of the individual whenever the philosophy of the Supreme Court veers in a conservative direction. It will comply with or at most limit or qualify liberal Supreme Court decisions much more than it will evade them; as indicated above, it actually may expand a few of them. On the other hand, we saw only one situation (allowing suspects taken into custody to contact a lawyer) where the court granted a right not yet accorded by the Supreme Court, but several instances in which it permitted the state to take advantage of increased powers that the U.S. Court is willing to grant it. Moreover, the expansion of a liberal decision is likely to be carried only so far and no further. The Court of Appeals refused to expand *Mapp* to cover cases where the appeals process had been completed before *Mapp* or to interpret *Boddie* v. *Connecticut*[143] to require that indigent parties to a divorce case be granted free lawyers or that a similar benefit be given welfare recipients at administrative hearings held to determine their eligibility.

But it would be unfair to conclude simply that the Supreme Court is the commanding officer and that a major state's highest tribunal is a usually obedient but occasionally recalcitrant private. Our discussion of the interaction between the Court and the New York Court of Appeals has made the crucial point that the state supreme tribunal can and has exerted an important influence on the federal. Considered as a whole, the relationship between the two is more analogous to that prevailing between the coach of a professional football team and its quarterback. The quarterback will in most cases follow the coach's game plan. However, this may well be in part the fruit of the quarterback's suggestions. Moreover, he may, on the odd occasion, call for a plunge when the coach has ordered a pass, a sweep when the coach would have preferred an off-tackle slant—or even try a play that he has thought up on the spot. His departures and innovations will be based on his assessment in the huddle or at the start of scrimmage of his team's (and his own) position, problems, and needs: their wisdom will, of course, be determined only through experience.

NOTES

1. *See, e.g.,* "Virgil Hawkins Goes to Law," in *Courts, Judges and Politics,* ed. Walter Murphy and C. Herman Pritchett (New York: Random House, 1961), p. 606.

2. *See, e.g.,* "Comment, Protecting Fundamental Rights in State Courts," *Harvard Civil Right-Civil Liberties Law Review* 12 (1977): 63–111. *See also* Project Report, "Toward an

Activist Role for State Bills of Rights," *Harvard Civil Rights-Civil Liberties Law Review* 8 (1973): 271–350; A. E. Dick Howard, "State Courts and Constitutional Rights in the Day of the Burger Court," *Virginia Law Review* 62 (1976): 873–944; Mary Cornelia Porter, "State Supreme Courts and the Legacy of the Warren Court: Some Old Inquiries for a New Situation," pp. 3–21, this volume.

3. Buchanan v. Warley, 245 U.S. 60 (1917).

4. Tyler v. Harmon, 104 So. 200 (1925).

5. Mapp v. Ohio, 367 U.S. 643 (1961).

6. "Reactions of State Supreme Courts to a U.S. Supreme Court Civil Liberties Decision," *Law & Society Review* 8 (1977): 109, 131 n. 11.

7. People v. Edwards, 458 P.2d 713 (1969).

8. Mary Cornelia Porter and G. Alan Tarr, "Introduction," pp. xi–xvii, this volume.

9. Jackson v. State, 103 A. 910 (1918).

10. Duncan v. Louisiana, 391 U.S. 145 (1968).

11. Baker v. City of Fairbanks, 471 P.2d 386 (Alaska 1970).

12. Porter and Tarr, "Introduction," p. xviii.

13. Porter, "State Supreme Courts." p. 11.

14. People v. Anderson, 493 P.2d 880 (1972).

15. Furman v. Georgia, 408 U.S. 238 (1972).

16. Robinson v. Cahill, 303 A.2d 273 (1973).

17. San Antonio Independent School District v. Rodriguez, 411 U.S. 1 (1973).

18. Plessy v. Ferguson, 163 U.S. 537 (1896).

19. Patterson v. Taylor, 40 So. 493 (1906).

20. Porter and Tarr, "Introduction," pp. xix–xx.

21. Ibid.

22. *New York Times,* November 24, 1969, p. 1.

23. *See New York Times,* February 13, 1977, sec. 4, p. 6, for a contention that the court of appeals has regained its former primacy.

24. *See New York Times,* June 18, 1979, p. B9.

25. Roth v. United States/Alberts v. California, 354 U.S. 476 (1957).

26. People v. Doubleday, 77 N.E.2d 6 (1947).

27. People v. Richmond County News, 175 N.E.2d 681 (1961).

28. Id. at 685.

29. Id. at 685.

30. Id. at 686.

31. Jacobellis v. Ohio, 378 U.S. 184 (1964).

32. Larkin v. Putnam's Sons, 200 N.E.2d 760 (1964).

33. Id. at 763.

34. A Book Named John Cleland's Memoirs of a Woman of Pleasure v. A. G. Mass., 383 U.S. 413 (1966).

35. Id. at 418.

36. Id. at 427.

37. Bookcase, Inc. v. Broderick, 218 N.E.2d 668 (1966).

38. Ginsberg v. New York, 390 U.S. 629 (1968).

39. Id. at 637–38.

40. Id. at 640.

41. People v. Kahan, 206 N.E.2d 333 (1965). The Supreme Court's quote from Judge Fuld's opinion can be found at 390 U.S. 640.

42. Winters v. New York, 333 U.S. 507 (1948).

43. Interstate Circuit v. Dallas, 390 U.S. 676, 683 n. 10 (1968).

44. Miller v. California, 413 U.S. 15 (1973).

45. Id. at 24.

46. People v. Heller, 307 N.E.2d 805 (1973).
47. This prior decision is People v. Heller, 277 N.E.2d 651 (1971).
48. People v. Heller, *supra* note 46, at 816.
49. Mapp v. Ohio, *supra* note 5.
50. Weeks v. U.S., 232 U.S. 383 (1914).
51. Wolf v. Colorado, 338 U.S. 25 (1949).
52. People v. Defore, 150 N.E. 585 (1926).
53. Louis Schwartz and Stephen Goldstein, *Law Enforcement Handbook for Police* (St. Paul, Minn.: West, 1970), p. 122.
54. Chimel v. California, 395 U.S. 752 (1969).
55. Carroll v. U.S., 267 U.S. 132 (1975).
56. People v. O'Neill, 182 N.E.2d 95 (1962).
57. Id. at 97.
58. People v. Loria, 179 N.E.2d 478 (1961).
59. People v. Muller, 182 N.E.2d 99 (1962).
60. Linklater v. Walter, 381 U.S. 618 (1965).
61. People v. Rivera, 201 N.E.2d 32 (1964).
62. Id. at 35.
63. Terry v. Ohio, 392 U.S. 1 (1968).
64. Id. at 30.
65. Id. at 11.
66. Chimel v. California, *supra* note 54.
67. Williams v. United States, 401 U.S. 646 (1971).
68. People v. Buia, 309 N.E.2d 869 (1974).
69. People v. Clements, 339 N.E.2d 170 (1975).
70. Carroll v. United States, 267 U.S. 132 (1925).
71. Chambers v. Maroney, 399 U.S. 42 (1970).
72. People v. Fustanio, 318 N.E.2d 466 (1974).
73. People v. Sullivan, 272 N.E.2d 464 (1971).
74. South Dakota v. Opperman, 428 U.S. 364 (1976).
75. Gideon v. Wainwright, 372 U.S. 335 (1963).
76. *See, e.g.,* People v. Hinsch, 3 A.D. 915; 162 N.Y.S.2d 602 (2d Judicial Dept., 1957).
77. People v. Witenski, 207 N.E.2d 358 (1965).
78. Id. at 359.
79. People v. Letterio, 213 N.E.2d 670, *cert. denied,* 384 U.S. 911 (1965).
80. Id. at 672.
81. Id. at 672.
82. *In re* Ella B, 285 N.E.2d 288 (1972).
83. Boddie v. Connecticut, 401 U.S. 371 (1971).
84. Deason v. Deason, 296 N.E.2d 229 (1973).
85. *In re* Smiley, 330 N.E.2d 53 (1975).
86. Brown v. Lavine, 333 N.E.2d 374 (1975).
87. Miranda v. Arizona, 384 U.S. 436 (1966).
88. Johnson v. New Jersey, 384 U.S. 719 (1966).
89. Id. at 732–33.
90. People v. Shivers, 233 N.E.2d 836 (1967).
91. People v. McQueen, 221 N.E.2d 550 (1966).
92. Id. at 552.
93. Sayers v. New York, 240 N.E.2d 540 (1968), *cert. denied,* 395 U.S. 970 (1969).
94. Jenkins v. Delaware, 395 U.S. 213 (1969).
95. Miranda v. Arizona, *supra* note 87, at 473–74.
96. People v. Gary, 286 N.E.2d 263 (1972).

97. Id. at 264.

98. Michigan v. Mosely, 423 U.S. 96 (1975).

99. Escobedo v. Illinois, 378 U.S. 478 (1964).

100. *See* the first several paragraphs of Chief Justice Warren's *Miranda* opinion.

101. People v. Kulis, 221 N.E.2d 541 (1966).

102. People v. Harris, 250 N.E.2d 349 (1969).

103. Harris v. New York, 401 U.S. 222 (1971).

104. Massiah v. United States, 377 U.S. 201 (1964).

105. People v. Waterman, 175 N.E.2d 445 (1961). Footnote 5 of *Massiah* cited several other New York Court of Appeals cases. *Waterman* was cited at 377 U.S. 205.

106. People v. Donovan, 193 N.E.2d 628 (1963), cited in Escobedo v. Illinois, *supra* note 99, at 486–87.

107. People v. Donovan, *supra* note 106, at 630.

108. Miranda v. Arizona, *supra* note 87, at 473.

109. People v. Witenski, *supra* note 77.

110. People v. Clements, *supra* note 69.

111. People v. Rivera, *supra* note 61.

112. Bookcase, Inc. v. Broderick, *supra* note 37.

113. *In re* Smiley, *supra* note 85.

114. Boddie v. Connecticut, *supra* note 83.

115. People v. Heller, *supra* note 46.

116. Miller v. California, *supra* note 44.

117. People v. McQueen, *supra* note 91.

118. People v. Fustanio, *supra* note 72.

119. Chambers v. Maroney, *supra* note 71.

120. People v. Loria, *supra* note 58.

121. People v. Witenski, *supra* note 77.

122. *In re* Ella B, *supra* note 82.

123. People v. Richmond County News, *supra* note 27.

124. Roth v. United States/Alberts v. California, *supra* note 25.

125. Ginsberg v. New York, 390 U.S. 629 (1968).

126. People v. Kahan, *supra* note 41.

127. Interstate Circuit v. Dallas, *supra* note 43.

128. People v. Muller, *supra* note 59.

129. Linklater v. Walter, *supra* note 60.

130. Terry v. Ohio, *supra* note 63.

131. People v. Sullivan, *supra* note 73.

132. South Dakota v. Opperman, *supra* note 74.

133. People v. Gary, *supra* note 91.

134. Michigan v. Mosley, *supra* note 98.

135. People v. Donovan, *supra* note 106.

136. People v. Waterman, *supra* note 105.

137. Jacobellis v. Ohio, 378 U.S. 184 (1964).

138. Larkin v. Putnam's Sons, *supra* note 32.

139. A Book Named John Cleland's Memoirs of a Woman of Pleasure v. A. G. Mass., *supra* note 34.

140. People v. Kulis, *supra* note 101.

141. People v. Harris, *supra* note 102.

142. Harris v. New York, *supra* note 103.

143. Boddie v. Connecticut, *supra* note 83.

G. ALAN TARR

Bibliographical Essay

Before the 1970s scholarly interest in state supreme court policymaking was almost nonexistent. Political scientists, when they focused on state supreme courts at all, were primarily interested in analyzing the effects of judicial background characteristics—either separately or in combination with institutional and environmental factors—on judicial voting behavior or court outputs. Legal scholars, although interested in decisions as they affected legal practice, did not examine broader policymaking patterns. However, during the 1970s and 1980s several highly publicized decisions and the development of the "new judicial federalism" reawakened interest in state supreme court policymaking. The listings below provide a topical overview of recent research concerning state supreme courts and their policymaking.

THE POLICYMAKING CONTEXT

STATE COURT ORGANIZATION AND ITS IMPLICATIONS

Two aspects of state court organization have considerable influence on state supreme court policymaking. The level of court unification affects the range of administrative control exercised by the chief justice of the state supreme court. Court reformers have argued that unification also promotes greater efficiency and a more uniform administration of justice, but some recent research has cast considerable doubt on these claims. The establishment of an intermediate court of appeals reduces the state supreme court's case load and enables it to concentrate its attention on more important cases.

Court Unification

Baar, Carl. "The Scope and Limits of Court Reform," *Justice System Journal* 5 (1980): 274–90.
_____. *Separate But Subservient: Court Budgeting in the American States.* Lexington, Mass.: Lexington Books, 1975.

The author gratefully acknowledges the assistance of Robert F. Williams, who supplied materials that assisted in the compilation of this bibliography.

Berkson, Larry, and Susan Carbon. *Court Unification: History, Politics, and Implementation*. Washington, D.C.: U.S. Government Printing Office, 1978.

Carbon, Susan, and Larry Berkson. *Literature on Court Unification: An Annotated Bibliography*. Washington D.C.:U.S. Government Printing Office, 1978.

Gallas, Geoff. "The Conventional Wisdom of State Court Administration: A Critical Assessment and an Alternative Approach." *Justice System Journal* 2 (1976): 35–55.

––––––. "Court Reform: Has It Been Built on an Adequate Foundation?" *Judicature* 63 (1979): 28–38.

Hays, Stephen W. *Court Reform: Ideal or Illusion?* Lexington, Mass.: Lexington Books, 1978.

Saari, David. "Modern Court Management: Trends in Court Organization Concepts—1976." *Justice System Journal* 2 (1976): 19–34.

Tarr, G. Alan. "Court Unification and Court Performance: A Preliminary Assessment," *Judicature* 64 (1981): 356–68.

Intermediate Courts of Appeals

Fair, Daryl. "State Intermediate Appellate Courts: An Introduction," *Western Political Quarterly* 24 (1971): 415–24.

Flango, Victor Eugene, and Nora F. Blair. "Creating an Intermediate Appellate Court: Does It Reduce the Caseload of a State's Highest Court?" *Judicature 64* (1980): 74–84.

Groot, Roger D. "The Effects of an Intermediate Appellate Court on the Supreme Court Work Product: The North Carolina Experience," *Wake Forest Law Review* 7 (1971): 548–72.

Hopkins, James D. "The Role of an Intermediate Appellate Court," *Brooklyn Law Review* 41 (1975): 459–78.

STATE SUPREME COURT JUSTICES

The literature on state supreme court justices has generally focused on three issues. First, some studies have documented the social and political backgrounds of the justices, often as a preliminary to analysis of how these backgrounds characteristics influence judicial decision making. Second, other studies have focused on judicial selection either to reveal the politics underlying the process or to analyze how mode of selection affects the sorts of justices selected and the character of their decisions. Finally, a third set of studies have examined the views that state supreme court justices hold of how they should exercise their responsibilities.

Social and Political Backgrounds

Beatty, Jerry K. "Decision-Making on the Iowa Supreme Court—1965–1969," *Drake Review* 19 (1970): 342–67.

Borowiec, Walter A. "Pathways to the Top: The Political Careers of State Supreme Court Justices," *North Carolina Central Law Review* 7 (1976): 280–85.

Canon, Bradley C. "Characteristics and Career Patterns of State Supreme Court Justices," *State Government* 45 (1972): 34–41.

Feeley, Malcolm M. "Another Look at the 'Party Variable' in Judicial Decision-Making: An Analysis of the Michigan Supreme Court," *Polity* 4 (1971): 91–104.

Heiberg, Robert A. "Social Backgrounds of the Minnesota Supreme Court Justices: 1858–1968," *Minnesota Law Review* 53 (1969): 901–37.

Heller, Francis H. "The Justices of the Kansas Supreme Court, 1861–1975: A Collective Portrait," *University of Kansas Law Review* 24 (1975–76): 521–35.

Jaros, Dean, and Bradley C. Canon, "Dissent on State Supreme Courts: The Differential Significance of Characteristics of Judges," *Midwest Journal of Political Science* 15 (1971): 322–46.

Julian, Stephen W. "The Utah Supreme Court and Its Justices, 1896–1976," *Utah Historical Quarterly* 44 (1976): 267–85.

Lee, Francis Graham. "Party Representation on State Supreme Courts: 'Unequal Representation' Revisited," *State and Local Government Review* 11 (1979): 48–52.

Nagel, Stuart, "Ethnic Affiliations and Judicial Propensities," *Journal of Politics* 24 (1962): 92–110.

———. "Political Party Affiliation and Judges' Decisions," *American Political Science Review* 55 (1961): 843–50.

Patterson, John W., and Gregory J. Rathjen. "Background Diversity and State Supreme Court Dissent Behavior," *Polity* 9 (1976): 610–22.

Stecher, Jamie B. W. "Democratic and Republican Justice: Judicial Decision-Making on Five State Supreme Courts," *Columbia Journal of Law and Social Problems* 13 (1977): 137–81.

Ulmer, S. Sidney, "The Political Party Variable in the Michigan Supreme Court," *Journal of Public Law* 11 (1962): 352–62.

Judicial Selection

Atkins, Burton M., and Henry R. Glick. "Formal Judicial Recruitment and State Supreme Court Decisions," *American Politics Quarterly* 2 (1974): 427–49.

Canon, Bradley C. "The Impact of Formal Selection Processes on the Characteristics of Judges—Reconsidered," *Law & Society Review* 6 (1972): 579–93.

Dubois, Philip L. *From Ballot to Bench, Judicial Elections and the Quest for Accountability.* Austin: University of Texas Press, 1980.

Flango, Victor Eugene, and Craig R. Ducat. "What Difference Does Method of Judicial Selection Make: Selection Procedures in State Courts of Last Resort," *Justice System Journal* 5 (1979): 25–44.

Glick, Henry R. "The Promise and Performance of the Missouri Plan: Judicial
    Selection in the Fifty States," *University of Miami Law Review* 32 (1978):
    509–41.
Herndon, James. "Appointment as a Means of Initial Accession to Elective
    State Courts of Last Resort," *North Dakota Law Review* 38 (1962):
    60–73.
Jacob, Herbert. "The Effect of Institutional Differences in the Recruitment
    Process: The Case of State Judges," *Journal of Public Law* 13 (1964):
    104–19.
Landinsky, Jack, and Allan Silver. "Popular Democracy and Judicial
    Independence: Electorate and Elite Reactions to Two Wisconsin Supreme
    Court Elections," *Wisconsin Law Review* (1976): 128–69.
Watson, Richard A., and Rondal G. Downing. *The Politics of Bench and Bar:
    Judicial Selection Under the Missouri Nonpartisan Plan*. New York:
    John Wiley & Sons, 1969.

Judicial Role Conceptions

Becker, Theodore. "A Survey of Hawaiian Judges: The Effect on Decisions of
    Judicial Role Variations," *American Political Science Review* 60 (1966):
    677–80.
Beiser, Edward N. "The Rhode Island Supreme Court: A Well-Integrated
    Political System," *Law & Society Review* 8 (1974): 167–86.
Brennan, William J., Jr. "State Supreme Court Judge Versus United States
    Supreme Court Justice: A Change in Function and Perspective,"
    University of Florida Law Review 19 (1966): 225–37.
Ducat, Craig R., and Vincent Eugene Flango. *Leadership in State Supreme
    Courts: Roles of the Chief Justice*. Beverly Hills, Calif.: Sage, 1976.
Glick, Henry R. *Supreme Courts in State Politics: An Investigation of the
    Judicial Role*. New York: Basic Books, 1971.
———, and Kenneth N. Vines. "Law-Making in the State Judiciary: A
    Comparative Study of the Judicial Role in Four States," *Polity* 2 (1969):
    142–59.
Vines, Kenneth N. "The Judicial Role in the American States." In *Frontiers of
    Judicial Research*. Edited by Joel B. Grossmen and Joseph Tannenhaus.
    New York: John Wiley & Sons, 1969.
Wold, John T. "Political Orientations, Social Backgrounds, and the Role
    Perceptions of State Supreme Court Judges," *Western Political Quarterly*
    27 (1974): 239–48.

THE PROCESS OF DECISION

As judicial scholars have long recognized, the processes by which decisions are made often affect their substance. Therefore, researchers in recent years have begun to analyze at the state level the same aspects of internal operations that have fascinated students of the United States Supreme Court. They include the process of case selection, interpersonal relations among the justices, the role of state chief justices in marshalling their courts, and the process of opinion assignment.

Although many of these studies have focused on individual courts, they have laid the groundwork for comparative analysis of intercourt dynamics.

In addition to this scholarly research, the reports of the National Center for State Courts, designed to assist state courts in remedying administrative problems, also furnish valuable background on internal operations of state supreme courts.

Baum, Lawrence. "Judicial Demand-Screening and Decisions on the Merits: A Second Look," *American Politics Quarterly* 7 (1979): 109–19.

_____. "Policy Goals in Judicial Gatekeeping: A Proximity Model of Discretionary Jurisdiction," *American Journal of Political Science* 21 (1977): 13–36.

McConkie, Stanford S. "Decision-Making in State Supreme Courts: A Look Inside the Conference Room," *Judicature* 59 (1976): 337–43.

Sickels, Robert J. "The Illusion of Judicial Consensus: Zoning Decisions in the Maryland Court of Appeals," *American Political Science Review* 59 (1965): 100–104.

Slotnick, Elliot E. "Who Speaks for the Court? The View from the States," *Emory Law Journal* 26 (1977): 107–47.

OVERVIEWS OF STATE SUPREME COURT POLICYMAKING

Atkins, Burton M., and Henry R. Glick. "Environmental and Structural Variables as Determinants of Issues in State Courts of Last Resort," *American Journal of Political Science* 20 (1976): 97–115.

Glick, Henry R., and Kenneth N. Vines. *State Court Systems*. Englewood Cliffs, N.J.: Prentice-Hall, 1973.

Kagan, Robert A., et al. "The Business of State Supreme Courts, 1870–1970," *Stanford Law Review* 30 (1977): 121–56.

_____. "The Evolution of State Supreme Courts," *Michigan Law Review* 76 (1978): 961–1001.

"Note: Courting Reversal: The Supervisory Role of State Supreme Courts," *Yale Law Journal* 87 (1978): 1191–218.

THE IMPACT OF STATE SUPREME COURT DECISIONS

Aside from analysis of specific decisions and their immediate effects, little research has been undertaken until recently on the effects of state supreme court decisions. Among the few studies of this sort are:

Frank, Stephen I. "The Oversight of Administrative Agencies by State Supreme Courts—Some Macro Findings," *Administrative Law Review* 32 (1980): 477–500.

_____. "State Supreme Courts and Administrative Agencies," *State Government* 51 (1978): 119–23.

Johnson, Charles A. "Judicial Decisions and Organizational Change—Some Theoretical and Empirical Notes on State Court Decisions and State Administrative Agencies," *Law & Society Review* 14 (1979): 27–56.

Lehne, Richard, and John Reynolds, "Impact of Judicial Activism on Public Opinion," *American Journal of Political Science* 22 (1978): 896–904.

CONSTITUTIONAL POLICYMAKING

Before the incorporation of provisions of the federal Bill of Rights, a process accelerated during the Warren Court era, state bills of rights provided the primary protection for individual liberties. The advent of the Burger Court has produced a renewed attention to, and increased reliance on, state constitutional guarantees. It has also spawned a voluminous literature on constitutional policymaking by state supreme courts focusing on this "new judicial federalism." Some of these studies have advocated greater use of state constitutional protections either to avoid reversal by the U.S. Supreme Court or to permit the independent development of state constitutional law. Other studies have addressed the jurisprudential concerns that arise in interpreting state constitutional guarantees. Finally, another set of studies has analyzed by what extent state supreme courts have availed themselves of the opportunities provided by the new judicial federalism.

As this summary suggests, the literature on constitutional policymaking has focused almost exclusively on civil liberties issues. Little research on other important aspects of state constitutional law have been undertaken, a gap in research that future studies should seek to remedy.

CONSTITUTIONAL POLICYMAKING: PRE-1970

Force, Robert. "State 'Bills of Rights': A Case of Neglect and the Need for a
    Renaissance," *Valparaiso University Law Review* 3 (1969): 125–82.
Graves, W. Brooke. "State Constitutional Law: A Twenty-Five Year
    Summary," *William and Mary Law Review* 8 (1966): 1–36.
Hetherington, John A. C. "State Economic Regulation and Substantive Due
    Process of Law," *Northwestern University Law Review* 53 (1958):
    226–51.
"Note: Counterrevolution in State Constitutional Law," *Stanford Law Review* 15
    (1963): 309–30.
Paulsen, Monrad G. "The Persistence of Substantive Due Process in the
    States," *Minnesota Law Review* 34 (1950): 91–118.
————. "State Constitutions, State Courts and First Amendment Freedoms,"
    Vanderbilt Law Review 4 (1951): 620–42.
Swindler, William F. "State Constitutional Law: Some Representative
    Decisions," *William and Mary Law Review* 9 (1967): 166–76.

THE NEW JUDICIAL FEDERALISM

Bice, Scott H. "Anderson and the Adequate State Ground," *Southern
    California Law Review* 45 (1972): 750–66.
Brennan, William J., Jr. "State Constitutions and the Protection of Individual
    Rights," *Harvard Law Review* 90 (1977): 489–504.
Burger, Warren E. "The Interdependence of Our Freedoms," *Akron Law
    Review* 9 (1976): 403–10.
Collins, Ronald K. L. "Reliance on State Constitutions—Away from a
    Reactionary Approach," *Hastings Constitutional Law Quarterly* 9 (1981):
    201–19.

"Comment: The Independent Application of State Constitutional Provisions to Questions of Criminal Procedure," *Marquette Law Review* 62 (1979): 596–621.

Countryman, Vern. "Why a State Bill of Rights?" *Washington Law Review* 45 (1970): 454–73.

Douglas, Charles G., III. "State Judicial Activism—The New Role for State Bills of Rights," *Suffolk University Law Review* 12 (1977): 1123–50.

Driscoll, Dawn-Marie, and Barbara J. Rouse. "Through a Glass Darkly: A Look at State Equal Rights Amendments," *Suffolk University Law Review* 12 (1977): 1282–311.

Falk, Jerome B., Jr. "Foreword: The State Constitution—A More Than Adequate Non-federal Ground," *California Law Review* 61 (1973): 273–86.

Galie, Peter J. "Pennsylvania's Constitution and the Protection of Defendants' Rights, 1969–1980: A Survey," *University of Pittsburgh Law Review* 42 (1981): 269–311.

_____. "State Constitutional Guarantees and the Protection of Defendants' Rights: The Case of New York, 1960–1978," *Buffalo Law Review* 28 (1979): 157–94.

_____, and Lawrence P. Galie. "State Constitutional Guarantees and Supreme Court Review: Justice Marshall's Proposal in Oregon v. Hass," *Dickinson Law Review* 82 (1978): 273–93.

Howard, A. E. Dick. "State Courts and Constitutional Rights in the Day of the Burger Court," *Virginia Law Review* 62 (1976): 874–944.

_____. "State Constitutions and the Environment," *Virginia Law Review* 58 (1972): 193–229.

Kelman, Maurice. "Foreword: Rediscovering the State Constitutional Bill of Rights," *Wayne Law Review* 27 (1981): 413–33.

Lehne, Richard. *The Quest for Justice: The Politics of School Finance Reform.* New York: Longman, 1978.

Linde, Hans A. "First Things First: Rediscovering the States' Bills of Rights," *University of Baltimore Law Review* 9 (1980): 379–96.

_____. "Without 'Due Process': Unconstitutional Law in Oregon," *Oregon Law Review* 49 (1970): 133–87.

Morris, Arval A. "New Horizons for a State Bill of Rights," *Washington Law Review* 45 (1970): 474–96.

"Note: Camping on Adequate State Grounds: California Ensures the Reality of Constitutional Ideals," *Southwestern University Law Review* 9 (1977): 1157–1210.

"Note: Expanding Criminal Procedural Rights Under State Constitutions," *Washington and Lee Law Review* 33 (1976): 909–33.

"Note: Of Laboratories and Liberties: State Court Protection of Political and Civil Rights," *Georgia Law Review* 10 (1976): 533–64.

"Note: The New Federalism: Toward a Principled Interpretation of the State Constitution," *Stanford Law Review* 29 (1977): 297–321.

"Note: Private Abridgement of Speech and the State Constitutions," *Yale Law Journal* 90 (1980): 165–88.

"Note: Rediscovering the California Declaration of Rights," *Hastings Law Journal* 26 (1974): 481–511.

"Project Report: Toward an Activist Role for State Bills of Rights," *Harvard Civil Rights-Civil Liberties Law Review* 8 (1973): 271–350.

Treadwell, Lujuana W., and Nancy W. Page. "Equal Rights Provisions: The Experience Under State Constitutions," *California Law Review* 65 (1977): 1086–112.

Welsh, Robert, and Ronald K. L. Collins. "Taking State Constitutions Seriously," *The Center Magazine* 14 (September-October 1981): 6–17; with "Discussion": 17–35, 38–43.

Wilkes, Donald E., Jr. "More on the New Federalism in Criminal Procedure," *Kentucky Law Journal* 63 (1975): 873–94.

———. "The New Federalism in Criminal Procedure: State Court Evasion of the Burger Court," *Kentucky Law Journal* 62 (1974): 421–51.

———. "The New Federalism in Criminal Procedure Revisited," *Kentucky Law Journal* 64 (1976): 729–52.

NONCONSTITUTIONAL POLICYMAKING

Despite the recognition that state cases that do not raise constitutional issues may nonetheless have broad effects, research on such state supreme court policymaking has lagged. Social scientists have recently rediscovered common law policymaking, as indicated by the studies of tort law innovation and its effects. Thus far virtually no research has examined other doctrinal and nondoctrinal avenues of state supreme court policymaking.

Canon, Bradley C., and Dean Jaros. "The Impact of Changes in Judicial Doctrine: The Abrogation of Charitable Immunity," *Law and Society Review* 13 (1979): 969–86.

———, and Lawrence Baum. "Patterns of Adoption of Tort Law Innovations: An Application of Diffusion Theory to Judicial Doctrines," *American Political Science Review* 75 (December 1981): pp. 975–87.

Croyle, James L. "The Impact of Judge-Made Policies: An Analysis of Research Strategies and an Application to Products Liability Doctrine," *Law & Society Review* 13 (1979): 949–68.

Keeton, Robert E. *Venturing to Do Justice: Reforming the Private Law.* Cambridge, Mass.: Harvard University Press, 1969.

STATE-FEDERAL RELATIONS

The extensive literature on the new judicial federalism, cited above, deals in depth with the proper relationship between state and federal courts. Other studies—the compliance-noncompliance literature—has focused on conflicts between the U.S. Supreme Court and state supreme courts. A final group of studies have analyzed patterns of interaction and mutual influence involving state supreme courts and the U.S. Supreme Court.

COMPLIANCE-NONCOMPLIANCE

Baum, Lawrence. "Lower Court Response to Supreme Court Decisions: Reconsidering a Negative Picture," *Justice System Journal* 3 (1978): 208–19.

Beatty, Jerry K. "State Court Evasion of the United States Supreme Court Mandates During the Last Decade of the Warren Court," *Valparaiso University Law Review* 6 (1972): 260–85.

Canon, Bradley C. "Reactions of State Supreme Courts to a U.S. Supreme Court Civil Liberties Decision," *Law & Society Review* 8 (1973): 109–34.

Murphy, Walter F. "Lower Court Checks on Supreme Court Power," *American Political Science Review* 53 (1959): 1017–31.

Romans, Neal T. "The Role of State Supreme Courts in Judicial Policymaking—Escobedo, Miranda and the Use of Judicial Impact Analysis," *Western Political Quarterly* 27 (1974): 38–59.

Tarr, G. Alan. *Judicial Impact and State Supreme Courts,* Lexington, Mass.: Lexington Books, 1977.

Vines, Kenneth N. "Southern State Supreme Courts and Race Relations," *Western Political Quarterly* 18 (1965): 5–18.

INTERACTIONS AND INFLUENCE

Brennan, William J., Jr. "Some Aspects of Federalism," *New York University Law Review* 39 (1964): 945–61.

Greene, Roland J. "Hybrid State Law in the Federal Courts," *Harvard Law Review* 83 (1969): 289–326.

Karst, Kenneth L. "Serrano V. Priest: A State Court's Responsibilities and Opportunities in the Development of Federal Constitutional Law," *California Law Review* 60 (1972): 720–56.

Mosk, Stanley. "Contemporary Federalism," *Pacific Law Journal* 9 (1978): 711–21.

Wefing, John B. "Search and Seizure—New Jersey Supreme Court v. United States Supreme Court," *Seton Hall Law Review* 7 (1976): 771–826.

MISCELLANEOUS

Glick, Henry R. "Policy-Making and State Supreme Courts: The Judiciary as an Interest Group," *Law & Society Review* 5 (1970): 271–91.

Hale, Dennis F. "How Reporters and Justices View Coverage of a State Appellate Court," *Journalism Quarterly* 52 (1975): 106–10.

Tarr, G. Alan. "State Supreme Court Policymaking: A Bibliographic Note," *NEWS* 16 (Fall 1981): 1–3.

Index

Age discrimination, 45
Alabama Supreme Court, on inherent-powers doctrine, 131, 146. *See also* State courts; State supreme courts
Alaska Supreme Court: on civil liberties, 32; on doctrine of independent state grounds, 41; and judicial activism, 4, 6, 14–15, 16; on right to privacy, 8, 45; on search and seizure, 35. *See also* State courts; State supreme courts
Arizona Supreme Court, 131. *See also* State courts; State supreme courts
Arkansas Supreme Court, 96, 131. *See also* State courts; State supreme courts
Article III, 24
Ashe v. Swenson, 38

Baker v. Fairbanks, 14–15, 16, 177
Bell, Justice John, 95
Bergen, Justice Francis, 180, 185
Berkson, Larry, 158
Black, Charles, quoted, 5
Black, Justice Eugene, 133
Black, Justice Hugo, 34, 143, 187
Blackmun, Justice Harry, 24, 26, 43
Blue Movie, obscenity ruling on, 182
Boddie v. Connecticut, 189, 194, 196
A Book Named John Cleland's Memoirs of a Woman of Pleasure v. A. G. Mass., 180. *See also Fanny Hill*
Bookcase, Inc. v. Broderick, 181, 194
Brandeis, Justice Louis, 141–42
Breitel, Judge Charles, 189
Brennan, Justice William J., Jr., xi, xix, 35; attitude of, toward "new

federalism," 3, 4, 18; on benign discrimination, 28; on double jeopardy, 38; on obscenity, 180, 181
Brown v. Lavine, 189
Buchanan v. Warley, 176
Builder-vendor implied warranty, 91
Burger, Justice Warren, 18, 31
Burger Court: on death penalty, 11; and federal rights, 6; and "new federalism," 3, 4, 17–18, 47; on rights of defendants, 159

California state courts, financing of, 148
California Supreme Court: on builder-vendor implied warranty, 91; on capital punishment, 6, 7, 11, 39–40; on cruel and unusual punishment, 40; on equal protection, 7, 32; and evasion of federal claims, 7; on exclusionary rule, 34, 136, 137; on individual rights and civil liberties, 32, 33; on inherent-powers doctrine, 131; and judicial activism, 4, 6, 34; on product liability, 88; on racial discrimination, 28; on right to privacy, 45; on search and seizure, 4, 15, 35, 36; on sovereign immunity, 86; on tort law, 88, 97, 98, 99. *See also* State courts; State supreme courts
Campbell, Justice William J., 143
Canon, Bradley, cited, 157, 162, 164
Capital punishment, court rulings on, 6, 7, 11, 14, 39–40
Cardozo, Justice Benjamin, 84
Carrigan, Jim R., 132

About the Contributors

CARL BAAR. Professor Baar is an associate professor in the Department of Politics at Brock University, St. Catherine's, Ontario, Canada. He received the Ph.D. in political science at the University of Chicago, has done postgraduate work at the Institute for Court Management at the University of Denver Law Center, and was a Russell Sage Fellow in Law and Social Sciences at the Yale Law School. He is the author of *Separate But Subservient: Court Budgeting in the American States* (Lexington Books, 1975) and of essays on court administration that have appeared in *Justice System Journal, Judicature,* and in essay collections such as *Managing State Courts* (West Publishing Co., 1977) and *Judicial Administration: Text and Readings* (Prentice-Hall, 1977).

LAWRENCE BAUM. Professor Baum is an associate professor in the Department of Political Science at Ohio State University. He received the M.A. and Ph.D. in political science from the University of Wisconsin. He has published widely in the field of public law, with articles appearing in *American Political Science Review, Western Political Quarterly, Policy Studies Journal, Justice System Journal, British Journal of Political Science, Law & Society Review,* and *American Journal of Political Science,* as well as in essay collections such as *American Court Systems* (W. H. Freeman, 1978), *Public Law and Public Policy* (Praeger Publishers, 1977), and *Economic Regulatory Policies* (Lexington-Heath, 1976). His most recent book is *The Supreme Court* (Congressional Quarterly, 1981).

BRADLEY C. CANON. Professor Canon is a professor in the Department of Political Science at the University of Kentucky. He received the M.S. in political science from Florida State University and the Ph.D. from the University of Wisconsin. He has served on the editorial boards of the *American Journal of Political Science* and the *American Politics Quarterly.* His articles have appeared in *American Journal of Political Science, American Politics Quarterly, American Political Science Review,* and *Western Political Quarterly,* as well as in numerous law reviews and in article collections such as *American Court Systems* (W. H. Freeman, 1978) and *Judicial Administration* (Prentice-Hall, 1977).

STANLEY H. FRIEDELBAUM. Professor Friedelbaum is a professor and chairperson in the Department of Political Science at Rutgers University, New Brunswick, New Jersey. He received the M.A. in political science from Rutgers University and the Ph.D. from Columbia University. He is the author of *Contemporary Constitutional Law* (Houghton Mifflin, 1972) and of several monographs on New Jersey government. His articles on public law have appeared in *The Supreme Court Review, University of Chicago Law Review*, and *Emory Law Journal,* as well as in publications such as *Civil Liberties: Policy and Policy Making* (D. C. Heath, 1976) and *Politics in New Jersey* (Eagleton Institute, 1975).

HENRY R. GLICK. Professor Glick is a professor of political science at Florida State University. He received the Ph.D. in political science from Tulane University. He is the author of *Supreme Courts in State Politics* (Basic Books, 1971) and coauthor of *State Court Systems* (Prentice-Hall, 1973). His articles on state court systems have appeared in *Polity, American Politics Quarterly, State Government,* and various law reviews.

RUSSELL S. HARRISON. Professor Harrison is an associate professor and chairperson in the Department of Political Science at Rutgers University, Camden, New Jersey. He received the Ph.D. in political science at the University of North Carolina at Chapel Hill. He is the author of *Equality in Public School Finance: Validated Policies for Public School Finance Reform* (Lexington Books, 1976) and of articles in *Publius* and *The Rutgers-Camden Law Journal.*

DANIEL C. KRAMER. Professor Kramer is an associate professor in the Department of Politics, Economics and Philosophy at the College of Staten Island, CUNY. He received the LL.B. from Harvard Law School and the Ph.D. in political science from the University of Pennsylvania. He is the author of *Participatory Democracy, Developing Ideals of the Political Left* (Schenkman Publishing Co., 1972) and of articles that have appeared in *Social Science, Journal of Public Law, University of Illinois Law Forum, Temple Law Quarterly, The Urban Lawyer,* and *Publius.*

MARY CORNELIA PORTER. Professor Porter is a professor and chairperson in the Department of Political Science at Barat College, Lake Forest, Illinois. She received the Ph.D. in political science from the University of Chicago. Her articles on public law have appeared in *The Supreme Court Review, Baylor Law Review,* and *Publius.*

ROBERT RIGA. Mr. Riga is management assistant in the Suffolk, New York, Cooperative Library System. He received the M.A. in library science from the Palmer Library School and the M.A. in history from Richmond College, SUNY. He has published in *Publius*.

G. ALAN TARR. Professor Tarr is an assistant professor of political science at Rutgers University, Camden, New Jersey. He received the Ph.D. in political science from the University of Chicago. He is the author of *Judicial Impact and State Supreme Courts* (Lexington Books, 1977) and coauthor of *American Constitutional Law and Interpretation* (St. Martin's Press, forthcoming). A former consultant to the National Center for State Courts, his most recent research on state courts appeared in *Judicature*.